GARLAND STUDIES IN MEDIEVAL LITERATURE
VOL. 10

THE SHORT LYRIC POEMS OF JEAN FROISSART

GARLAND REFERENCE LIBRARY
OF THE HUMANITIES
VOL. 1749

GARLAND STUDIES IN MEDIEVAL LITERATURE

THE SHORT LYRIC POEMS OF JEAN FROISSART

Fixed Forms
and the Expression
of the Courtly Ideal

Kristen Mossler Figg

GARLAND PUBLISHING, Inc.
New York & London / 1994

Library of Congress Cataloging-in-Publication Data

Figg, Kristen Mossler, 1952–
    The short lyric poems of Jean Froissart : fixed forms
and the expression of the courtly ideal / by Kristen
Mossler Figg.
        p.   cm. — (Garland studies in medieval
literature ; vol. 10)(Garland reference library of the
humanities : vol. 1749)
    Includes bibliographical references and index.
    ISBN 0–8153–1351–9
    1. Froissart, Jean, 1338?–1410?—Poetic works.
2. Froissart, Jean, 1338?–1410?—Translations into
English.   3. Dialect poetry, French—France—
Picardy—Translations into English.   4. French
poetry—To 1500—Translations into English.
5. Lyric poetry—History and criticism.   I. Title.
II. Series.   III. Series: Garland studies in medieval
literature ; v. 10.
PQ1461.F8Z66   1994
841'.1—dc20   93–38223
                                                              CIP

Printed on acid-free, 250-year-life paper
Manufactured in the United States of America

Contents

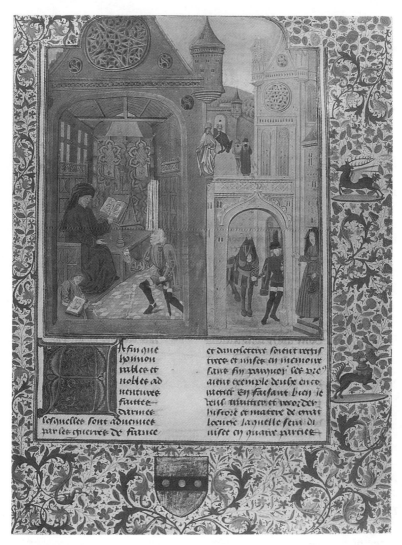

Robert de Nemur reading while receiving king's messenger. Jean Froissart writing (far left corner). Late fifteenth-century manuscript, BL MS Royal 14 D. Reprinted by permission of the British Library.

Series Editors' Foreword

Garland Studies in Medieval Literature (GSML) is a series of interpretative and analytic studies of the Western European literatures of the Middle Ages. It includes both outstanding recent dissertations and book-length studies, giving junior scholars and their senior colleagues the opportunity to publish their research.

The editors welcome submissions representing any of the various schools of criticism and interpretation. Western medieval literature, with its broad historical span, multiplicity and complexity of language and literary tradition, and special problems of textual transmission and preservation as well as varying historical contexts, is both forbidding and inviting to scholars. It continues to offer rich materials for virtually every kind of literary approach that maintains a historical dimension. In establishing a series in an eclectic literature, the editors acknowledge and respect the variety of texts and textual possibilities and the "resisting reality" that confronts medievalists in several forms: on parchment, in mortar, or through icon. It is no mere imitative fallacy to be eclectic, empirical, and pragmatic in the face of this varied literary tradition that has so far defied easy formulation. The cultural landscape of the twentieth century is littered with the debris of broken monomyths predicated on the Middle Ages, the autocratic Church and the Dark Ages, for example, or conversely, the romanticized versions of love and chivalry.

The openness of the series means in turn that scholars, and particularly beginning scholars, need not pass an *a priori* test of "correctness" in their ideology, method, or critical position. The studies published in GSML must be true to their premises, complete within their articulated limits, and accessible to a multiple readership. Each study will advance the knowledge of the literature under discussion, opening it up for further consideration and creating intellectual value. It is also hoped that each volume, while bridging the gap between contemporary perspective and past reality, will make old texts new again. In this way the literature will remain primary, the method secondary.

For the tenth volume of this series, Kristen Figg presents a meticulous reading of the important, but generally neglected short lyric poems of Jean Froissart. She succeeds in situating Froissart within the cultural and literary context of fourteenth-century Europe, and her examination of a representative number of his lyric forms (*pastourelles, chansons royales, ballades, virelais,* and *rondeaux*) demonstrates their richness of theme and poetic virtuosity. For all of the poems discussed, she provides a very readable and faithful English translation and has thus made it possible for English scholars unfamiliar with the original Middle French forms to understand and appreciate the influence Froissart had on Chaucer and other authors of the age. Figg's study focuses on the themes, techniques, meters, and rhythms that Froissart employed in his poetry, on how his poetry fits into the poetic tradition, and on the place of Froissart in literary history. In her Introduction she reviews the life and works of Froissart, as well as the critical literature on his works, clearly defines her own area of investigation (the short lyrics), and cogently argues for their general reevaluation in terms of their thematic, metrical, and rhetorical virtuosity and diversity. In the three major chapters of her book she analyzes the five poetic genres, providing close readings of individual poems and demonstrating her rare critical sensitivity to the poetic techniques and nuances they exhibit. Froissart emerges from this study as a master of the short lyric forms, one who is able to deal effectively with conventional themes and a broad range of historical subjects, as well as with a host of technical, structural and rhetorical concerns.

Christopher Kleinhenz   Paul E. Szarmach
Univ. of Wisconsin-Madison   SUNY-Binghamton

Acknowledgments

I wish to thank my former teachers, Joseph L. Baird and John R. Kane, for their guidance on the dissertation that led to the writing of this book, and Sally K. Slocum, who first introduced me to the joys of medieval literature. I am also most grateful to James R. Cooney for his unfailing confidence and encouragement, Judith Wootten for her help in proofreading, Wallace Aiken for his technical assistance, and John Block Friedman for his perceptive comments and suggestions.

The Kent State University Regional Campus system provided financial support for this project; I am also indebted to Librairie Droz and North Carolina Studies in the Romance Languages and Literatures for permission to reprint poems from their editions. Finally, I must thank my husband, my son, and my daughter, who were patient with my preoccupations and generous with their help.

The Short
Lyric Poems
of Jean Froissart

I
Introduction

To students of fourteenth-century English literature, the name of Jean Froissart has long been familiar. He is recognized not only in connection with his *Chroniques*, the massive and detailed historical work for which he is best known, but also as an influential literary figure whose poetry served as both a direct source and a general model for the works of his younger English contemporary, Geoffrey Chaucer. Still, among critics Froissart's literary contributions remained for many years largely unexamined; overshadowed by a widespread belief in the superiority of his historical writing, his poetry received little direct critical attention in either the French- or the English-speaking world. This situation persisted until the 1970s, when scholars reassessed his importance as a poet and began the important work of publishing modern critical editions and analytical studies.[1] Thus, it is only in the last twenty years that Froissart the poet has emerged as something more than a footnote to Chaucer and has begun to take on the status of an author worthy of being studied and appreciated in his own right.

Such a resurgence of interest is certainly justified in the context of literary history. While the *Chroniques* greatly surpassed the poetry in popularity in the centuries following Froissart's death,[2] there is plenty of evidence that Froissart himself spent much of his lifetime defining himself primarily as a poet.[3] His efforts until the age of thirty-five were in large part dedicated to the development of highly refined poetic techniques that allowed him to produce well-received works in a wide and varied range of genres, including long allegorical narratives, shorter *ditties*, lyric poems in seven *formes fixes*,[4] and even an

3

Arthurian verse romance of over 30,000 lines. While the romance, *Meliador*, was anachronistic in its use of an episodic style more typical of earlier centuries,[5] Froissart's other poems were quite representative of contemporary tastes, following closely in the tradition established by Guillaume de Machaut.[6] Froissart's choice of genres, his themes, and his style placed him firmly in the mainstream of fourteenth-century literary activity, earning him the patronage of such diverse figures as Queen Philippa of England, Duke Wenceslas of Luxembourg, and Count Guy of Blois.[7] Clearly, his mastery of such a wide range of literary genres at a level apparently so pleasing to the aristocratic audiences of his day must establish Froissart as a figure deserving careful consideration by anyone hoping to understand the poetic theory and practice of the age.

And yet, though much has been done to lay the groundwork for such consideration, two major difficulties remain for scholars who are not specialists in Middle French. First, while all the long narratives and some of the shorter *ditties* have received individual critical attention, little has yet been done to explore the lyrics. This substantial body of work comprises one hundred ninety-nine poems that are collected by genre in the manuscripts (thirteen *lays*, twenty *pastourelles*, six *chansons royales*, forty *ballades*, thirteen *virelays*, and one hundred seven *rondeaux*), as well as an additional thirty intercalated poems (including three *complaintes*) that appear only within the context of the long narratives. Second, there does not yet exist any large body of translations of Froissart's poems to assist readers who are unfamiliar with the peculiarities of fourteenth-century Picard-dialect French. Since Froissart's historical role as a poet is at least as important in English literature as in French, a substantial collection of translated poems would be useful both for familiarizing readers with the range of texts and for facilitating close examination of those poems worthy of being pursued in more depth.

This study will address these two needs by providing analysis and translation of selected poems from each of the five short lyric genres. While this approach is regrettably limited by the exclusion of the *lays* and *complaintes*, the focus on short forms will allow a broader sampling of poems, through which the controlling themes and underlying theories that unite all the lyrics will become apparent. At the same time, the process of identifying and illustrating the characteristics that distinguish each short genre from the others will reveal some of the variety and artistic inventiveness that made Froissart such a highly appreciated practitioner of the characteristic poetic forms of his day.

Froissart's Reputation and Influence

That Froissart was a figure of international importance and influence has long been established by both the events of his life and his role in literary history. Born around 1337[8] in Valenciennes, a city near the modern-day border of Belgium, Froissart first achieved prominence when he came to England in 1361 on the recommendation of the count of Hainaut to serve the count's niece, Philippa, who was the wife of Edward III. Froissart, then in his mid-twenties, served as the queen's secretary until 1366 and remained in her service until her death in 1369. From the start, Froissart appears to have functioned more as a poet than a clerk, having apparently obtained his position by virtue of his reputation as an already accomplished writer. In a French-speaking court that was attuned to the "skilled discipline, the polished speech, the elegance and flexibility of Romance metres,"[9] his expertise in the highly developed French literature of the day obviously made him most welcome. Indeed, as late as 1395, when Froissart visited England to present a collection of his poetry to Richard II, his work was still so well regarded that he not only was cordially received but was given a "gilded silver goblet . . . containing more than a hundred pieces of gold."[10] Having come from a French-speaking area that was not subject to the French crown, Froissart had an international perspective that made him a perfect vehicle for expressing the shared vision of a social class that transcended geographical boundaries.[11]

Whatever natural talent Froissart had for his role as a court poet was enhanced early on by the patronage of Queen Philippa. During his eight years under her protection, Froissart not only enjoyed the attentions of a courtly audience, but also enlarged his horizons through frequent travel. In 1365 Froissart journeyed to Scotland, where he met King David Bruce, and then toured eastern England with Edward Despenser. Later travels took him to the home of a future patron, Duke Wenceslas of Brabant, and into areas as far-ranging as Brittany, Aquitaine, Italy, and Germany, where he was present at such major events as the marriage of Lionel, Duke of Clarence, in Milan and the birth of the future Richard II of England in Bordeaux. As historians have noted, these experiences gave him the opportunity to begin gathering materials for his chronicles and to gain credibility among those whose exploits he would later report. But they also may be interpreted as a form of initiation into the life of the court. Though he himself was probably from a bourgeois background, such a wealth of contact would have provided almost unlimited opportunities for him to become familiar with the aristocratic perspective on life. By the time Queen Philippa died in 1369, he could justifiably claim that "elle me fist et crea."[12]

From this favored position in the English court, Froissart was well prepared to move on to a close relationship with Duke Wenceslas of Brabant. Again, though Froissart was certainly at this time working on early versions of his *Chroniques*, the most important direct service that he rendered his patron seems to have been as a poet. It was for Wenceslas that Froissart wrote *La Prison amoureuse*, a work that combines a series of correspondence and an exchange of lyrics between two characters who in many ways resemble the poet and his patron.[13] Among several levels of interpretation, it is possible to see a kind of apprenticeship in the art of the lyric between Froissart and the Duke, who himself, as an accomplished courtier, was interested in the writing of poetry. In fact, Wenceslas later entrusted Froissart with the composition of *Meliador*, a romance which incorporated all of the Duke's own lyric verse. It was only after Wenceslas' death in 1383, when Froissart came under the patronage and protection of Count Guy de Blois, that he seems to have finally given up his role as a poet to dedicate himself completely to the writing of history. All in all, the evidence seems clear that Froissart's reputation in his own day was built not just on his popularity as a chronicler, but on a broad and complex range of skills, within which his understanding of courtly attitudes and tastes--in addition to his obvious technical gifts--played a major role.

The significance of Froissart's role as a representative of aristocratic thought has only recently begun to be fully appreciated. It has, of course, long been understood that the *Chroniques* were intended to record, glorify, and revive the spirit of chivalry that had once characterized the ruling class, as Froissart himself attests in the Prologue to Book I.[14] But, perhaps in part because of modern repugnance to such an elitist set of goals, the possibility of a similarly conscious purpose in the poetry was for many years not considered.

The rigorous adherence to conventions that characterized the poetry of Froissart and his contemporaries made it easy to dismiss their work as mere court entertainment, a pleasant game that involved following formulaic rules in artificially elegant language. This interpretation was not seriously challenged until Daniel Poirion published in 1965 his study on the evolution of the courtly lyric, in which he clarified the connection between the demand for idealized, technically demanding formal art and the ruling class's need for reaffirmation of its identity in changing, turbulent times.[15] As subsequent studies of his narrative poems have shown, Froissart was far from blind to this kind of theoretical relationship, a point proven perhaps most notably by his revival of the long, episodic verse romance to display the values of knighthood in *Meliador*.[16] Indeed, more than any other writer of his day, Froissart combined expert control of all the traditional conventions with purposeful advocacy of the conservative world view that spawned them.

Likewise, recent criticism has revealed that there is a good deal more complexity and self-consciousness in Froissart's stance as an artist than had previously been recognized. In spite of being "old-fashioned" in his social ideas, Froissart was, as Dembowski points out, part of a "'new wave' of late medieval writers who were increasingly conscious of their role as authors."[17] Such consciousness led to the development of a complex concept of the *persona*, which, as Kevin Brownlee explains in his study of Machaut, transcended the simple equation of poet as lover.[18] Combining elements of the "clerkly narrator figure of Old French hagiography and romance, the first-person lyric voice of the *grand chant courtois*, and a new conception of the professional artist,"[19] Machaut introduced a poetic voice that could, in a sense, discuss itself as it shifted from prologue to story, from reality to dream, or from plot to intercalated lyric. This kind of self-examination and self-commentary has likewise been the focus of several recent studies of Froissart, demonstrating the possibility of a highly significant new level of interpretation in which the poet reveals his thoughts on issues of creativity, the relationship between poet and patron, and the art and significance of composition itself.[20]

It is only from this revised historical and critical perspective that it is possible to assess fairly Froissart's role in relation to Chaucer. For it seems to me unlikely that Chaucer would have viewed Froissart as merely an ordinary representative of conventional taste when drawing upon his plots, imagery, and style to create poems of his own. This is the assumption, however, that has frequently been made in considering one of the best known and earliest borrowings, the opening lines of Chaucer's *Book of the Duchess*. As the passages below demonstrate, the beginning of the English poem seems to be almost a direct translation of the opening lines of Froissart's *Le Paradis d'Amour*:[21]

> Je sui de moi en grant mervelle
> Coument tant vifs, car moult je velle
> Et on ne poroit en vellant
> Trouver de moi plus travellant,
> Car bien sachiés que par vellier
> Me viennent souvent travellier
> Pensees et merancolies . . .

> I have gret wonder, be this lyght,
> How that I lyve, for day ne nyght
> I may nat slepe wel nygh noght;
> I have so many an ydel thoght,
> Purely for defaute of slep,
> That, by my trouthe, I take no kep
> Of nothing, how hyt cometh or gooth.

Chaucer scholars have argued in favor of interpreting this borrowing as evidence of continuity between the French and English traditions or, alternatively, because of the nature of the changes that Chaucer made, as evidence of a "decisive break with contemporary French practice."[22] In either case, the tendency has been to see Froissart mostly as a stepping stone on the way to Chaucer, someone whose work Chaucer could simply build upon or react against on the path to his own greatness. In light of Dembowski's recent, more sophisticated analysis of the narrative persona in *Le Paradis*, however, both of these relationships seem overly simplistic. If in this early poem Froissart was, in fact, not simply dealing in "ritualized poetics" that extolled the "received doctrine of courtly love,"[23] but rather, as Dembowski argues, was making an ideological point about his own "poetic self,"[24] then it is likely that Chaucer was inviting his audience to recall not only Froissart as the representative of a pleasing (or worn out) tradition, but also as a maker of new meanings, one who was "thoroughly conscious of his craft."[25] Though the poetic accomplishments of the two authors may not, in the end, have been equal, full understanding of the relationship between them depends upon reading each in his own context with equal attention to ideology and individual thought. That Chaucer himself was reading Froissart carefully is suggested by the variety of other borrowings that have been identified. In another section of the *Book of the Duchess*, for example, one finds a reference to a minor god named "Enclimpostair," a supposed son of Morpheus who, in all of medieval literature appears only in this work and Froissart's *Le Paradis*. The history of the attempts to discover a source or etymology for this name has been traced by Normand Cartier, who concludes that Froissart himself probably concocted it, combining the words "enclin" and "postere" to come up with something meaning "lean-back" or "lazy-bones."[26] Cartier attributes Froissart's inventiveness to his having "learned the game of anagrams" from Machaut, but this invention also fits into a larger pattern of mythological invention that appears frequently in Froissart's work.[27] The fact that the name shows up in the *Book of the Duchess* demonstrates Chaucer's willingness to echo not only Froissart's conventional plot mechanisms and forms, but also the playfulness and flexibility of his story-telling.

Roland M. Smith has noted a less certain but equally interesting group of possible borrowings.[28] As Smith observes, Chaucer's insistence on distinguishing between "Dane" and "Diane" in the *Knight's Tale* (2062-64) is very similar to the distinction emphasized by Froissart in *L'Espinette Amoureuse* (1572-74 and 1717-68). Likewise, Froissart's poems provide the same distinctive details about Actaeon that appear in the *Knight's Tale*, and Froissart's mention of the Indian queen "Candace" (in *L'Espinette* and Ballade 9) provides a precedent for this character's appearance in Chaucer's *Parlement of Fowls*. Chaucer's reference to the "conquerour of Brutes Albyon" in the "Complaint to His Purse" may be traced to Froissart's Ballade 31, which focuses on the fulfillment of Diana's prophecy to Brutus and contains the words "conquerant," "Bructus," and "Albion" within a ten-line span.

Perhaps most striking of all, however, are the parallels between Chaucer's "Absalome ballade" in the *Legend of Good Women* (149-64) and Froissart's Ballade 6 on the excellence of his lady. In this poem, Froissart uses rime-royal stanzas with only three rhymes, returning at the end of each stanza to a refrain that expresses the superiority of "ma dame":[29]

> Ne quier veoir Medee ne Jason,
> Ne trop avant lire ens ou mapemonde,
> Ne le musique Orpheus ne le son,
> Ne Hercules, qui cerqua tout le monde,
> Ne Lucresse, qui tant fu bonne et monde,
> Ne Penelope ossi, car, par Saint Jame,
> *Je voi asses, puisques je voi ma dame.*

> I have no wish to see Medea or Jason,
> To read further in the mysteries of the globe,
> To know the music of Orpheus or its sound,
> Or Hercules, who travelled all the world,
> Or Lucretia, who was so good and pure,
> Or even Penelope, for by Saint James above,
> *I see enough when I see my lady love.*

Using the identical stanza form and a very similar metric pattern, Chaucer likewise creates an image of incomparability:

> Hyd, Absalon, thy gilte tresses clere;
> Ester, ley thou thy meknesse al adoun;
> Hyd, Jonathas, al thy frendly manere;
> Penalopee and Marcia Catoun,
> Make of youre wifhod no comparysoun;
> Hyde ye youre beautes, Ysoude and Eleyne:
> *My lady cometh, that al this may disteyne.*

As Smith points out, Froissart's poem is more like Chaucer's "in both substance and form" than any of the other numerous poems that had previously been cited as possible sources for Chaucer.[30] Froissart's poem is, of course, very much like a pair of poems by Machaut (Ballades 38 and 39), one by Deschamps (Ballade 40), and another of Froissart's own *ballades* (Ballade 38), all of which use an almost identical refrain and share numerous verbal echoes, almost as if each poet were expected to provide his own "version" of this particular exercise in flattery. The existence of so many similar poems makes it impossible to prove that Chaucer did indeed model his *ballade* after Froissart's, but, at the same time, it makes it apparent how influential the school of Machaut remained and how clearly the young Chaucer still looked to French models as a guide to developing this aspect of his poetic vision.

It is perhaps from this broader perspective of the "school of poetry" that Froissart's place in literary history can best be appreciated, for the style of poetry which he helped refine included a variety of devices and characteristics that became fundamental to the generation that followed. As John H. Fisher states, for example, one technique Chaucer certainly learned from the French school was the "practice of embedding lyrics formally or thematically within a romantic narrative."[31] Again, since Chaucer had read works by both Machaut and Froissart, and since both employed this technique extensively, it would be impossible to say for certain which of them influenced him more. But it is perhaps to Froissart that one needs to look more carefully to understand how complex the tradition really was, both because, as Arthur Moore points out, Froissart put intercalated lyrics in "nearly all" his allegorical narratives,[32] and because it is in Froissart's works that Moore finds lyrics to be mere unintegrated ornamentation, a usage which he implies that Chaucer in some sense corrected. Moore's point, of course, is that Chaucer's use of the lyrics is superior because it is more organic, having fuller "dramatic significance" and causing less interruption of the narrative[33]--an interpretation which assumes, apparently according to a Chaucerian model, that the lyric should be in the poem to serve the narrative and not the other way around. But recent readings of Froissart have indicated that his intention--and his achievement--were quite different, with the lyrics themselves serving as a focal point, perhaps the primary means of expressing the theme in a genre which no longer had the allegorical complexity that was characteristic of the narrative of preceding centuries.[34] As later parts of this study will suggest, any understanding of Chaucer's borrowing of lyrics must depend first of all on a full appreciation of how the earlier lyrics functioned as poems, both by themselves and in the contexts in which they appeared.

In addition to the use of the lyric, other conventions shared by Chaucer and Froissart are so pervasive and so subtly differentiated as to require close intertextual reading. This is particularly true in matters of language and imagery, for an important effect of the French influence was, as Peter Dronke notes, to introduce a "deliberately restricted," "stylized" poetical language which depended on a range of conventions for variation.[35] The cult of the daisy, "la marguerite," is, for example, a convention particularly favored by the lyric poets of the French school. References to the perfection of this flower, and thus of the lady who bears the flower's name, turn up in a number of poems by Machaut, Froissart, and Deschamps, as well as in Chaucer's Prologue to the *Legend of Good Women*. Froissart's contribution to this tradition includes the 192-line *Dittié de la flour de la margherite*, a *ballade* from *Le Paradis d'amour*, two *pastourelles*, and the anagrammatic appearance of the name for the object of the poet's love in *L'Espinette*.[36] As James Wimsatt has pointed out, Froissart's elaboration of the lover's habit of watching the flower open and close may be characterized as a link between the simple mention of this act in one of Machaut's poems and an even more expansive treatment in Chaucer.[37] Again, as in the case of the intercalated lyrics, one might be tempted to praise Chaucer at Froissart's expense, since for Chaucer the conventional daisy is only one element in a much more complex poem, while for Froissart it is the very essence of the poem itself. But Bernard Ribemont, in "Froissart, le mythe et la marguerite," has shown how Froissart's use of the marguerite as symbol involves both mythological invention and a process of "auto-citation," a self-conscious manipulation of traditional materials that focuses attention on the very act of composition.[38] This purposeful invention, along with others cited earlier, contradicts the impression of pure conventionality usually associated with Froissart's use of symbol and example. Thus, if Froissart's work has been seen in the past as helpful for the general purpose of providing a context for understanding Chaucer's symbolism, it may be acknowledged now as more important for the way it demonstrates the subtle arts of invention and variation that required the audience to recognize how one poem was playing off a whole set of apparently similar ones.

When one considers Froissart's place in the history of poetry, a final element that seems especially important is his command of rhythm and meter. It has often been argued that Chaucer's introduction of iambic pentameter into English verse grew out of his familiarity with the French decasyllable,[39] a line for which Chaucer had no native models but which was used by Froissart in his *Orloge amoureus*, his *Dittié de la margherite* and *Dit dou bleu chevalier*, all of his *chansons royales*, some *ballades*, and all 107 of his independent *rondeaux*. This last use of the line is especially important, for it was an innovation in the fourteenth century, a move away from the traditional seven-syllable line which Froissart used only in the eight *rondeaux* that are inserted in his narratives.[40] Such extensive use would seem to indicate that

Froissart felt particularly comfortable with the ten-syllable line, and since his command of the technical aspects of poetry has never been questioned even by his greatest detractors, a study of his lyrics would seem likely to reveal a great deal about how the French decasyllable could be used and what qualities might have made it particularly appealing for adaptation into English.

Likewise Froissart's lyrics give us examples of a great variety of stanza forms. Although some of these were too complex and artificial to have made much impact on later generations of poets, others had important applications in both French and English, including the French *ballade* stanza Chaucer chose for his *Monk's Tale* and the rhyme royal of *Troilus and Criseyde*. Froissart's use of different stanza forms in poems that range from the high seriousness of his *lay* on the death of Queen Philippa to the gentle irony of the *rondeaux* provides important information about the relationship between tone, rhetorical purpose, and form as it was conceived in an age very different from our own.

The Lyrics

To a poet with Froissart's technical skill and conservative sympathies, the appeal of the lyric as a primary mode of expression is easy to understand. For the fourteenth-century lyric style was the product of an artistic revival which took the traditional courtly themes and motifs of the preceding centuries and brought them new life through an emphasis on form. The doctrine of idealized love had, of course, been a source of inspiration for troubadours and trouvères in the twelfth century, and had gained complexity in the thirteenth century with the *Roman de la Rose*. Yet it still maintained its appeal for the aristocratic audience of the fourteenth century, which, in an age of declining influence, was struggling to maintain an unchanged perception of its own system of elevated courtly sensibilities. Thus, one finds nothing that is new, in and of itself, in Froissart's depiction of the ideal lover: wounded by the arrow of love, he suffers love-sickness and risks martyrdom because of his lady's lack of Pity, and yet he continues to serve loyally because of Hope and the belief that love-service is the most ennobling of occupations.

But while the main motifs of courtly literature had not changed, the mode of presentation, with its emphasis on fixed lyric forms and virtuosity in rhyme and rhythm, was essentially new. Most of the traditional lyric forms of previous centuries, such as the *chanson de toile*, *chanson d'aube*, *pastourelle*, and love debate, were inadequate for broad interpretations of *fin' amors* because of the limitations of being narrowly defined by the particular dramatic situations in which they were placed. Having apparently developed from a combination of popular song, meridional influences and Latin poetic theory,[41] they had lost much of their vitality by the end of the thirteenth century and offered little opportunity for further development. But the strong rhythms and regularly placed refrains of the still primitive *chansons de danse*, such as the *rondet* and *ballette*, seem to have suggested to court poets a more metrically complex style of poetry that offered a new, dramatically unrestricted context for the expression of the subtleties of refined love. By the time Machaut set down the rules for the *formes fixes*, the aesthetic of the age challenged poets to reinforce the elitism of courtly doctrine by achieving a perfection of structure that was in many ways as idealized as the themes about which they wrote.

One measure of how important the lyrics were to Froissart is the central role they played in the plots and themes of his narrative works, beginning with *Le Paradis d'amour*, his earliest long poem (*ca.* 1361-62). In this very traditional dream narrative, the first-person narrator prays for the gift of sleep to alleviate the melancholy brought on by his lack of success in love. Once asleep, he finds himself in a dream garden, peopled by allegorical characters such as *Plaisance*, *Esperance*, and eventually the god of Love himself. Throughout the poem the narrator expresses his feelings through lyrics--first with a *complainte* renouncing love, and later with two *rondeaux*, a *lay*, a *virelay*, and a *ballade*--comprising a total of 471 lines out of a poem of 1723. The lyrics function in part as a source of refined pleasure, as, for example, when *Plaisance* and *Esperance* require the narrator to recite a *rondeau* and they all join in and sing as they walk along (842-45). But the lyrics also represent a superior and therefore very serious form of expression, as demonstrated when *Plaisance* suggests to the narrator that he present his feelings to the god of Love in the form of a *lay* (1024-35). As Dembowski has pointed out, the *lay* "contributes to the plot development" by showing "psychological evolution in the protagonist."[42] Furthermore, every lyric except one is commented upon "as to its quality or its form" by one of the story's characters--and thus, indirectly, by Froissart himself.[43] Such conscious attention reinforces the audience's sense that the production of lyrics is an important pursuit indeed.

The focus on lyrics is continued in each of the next two major narratives. *L'Espinette amoureuse* (*ca.* 1370?), another poem taking place in a garden with allegorical characters, increases the number of lyrics to fourteen, so that the lyric poems make up almost a third of the 4192-line work. Likewise, in *La Prison amoureuse* (1371-72) the lyrics make up a substantial portion of the total poem, this time playing an even more important role in the plot. In this poem Froissart tells the story of the correspondence between a lover who calls himself "Rose" and the poet-narrator who acts as his advisor under the pen name of "Flos." In twelve long prose letters and 3899 lines of verse (733 lyric) the two protagonists discuss the nature of love. Success in love is linked explicitly to the composition of lyrics as Rose and Flos exchange examples of their poetic efforts. The collecting of lyrics becomes part of the fictional rationale for putting their correspondence together as a book.

Finally, with the *Joli Buisson de Jonece* (begun around 1373), Froissart returns to a more traditional plot. Continuing the story begun in the *Espinette*, he expresses the problems of a thirty-five-year-old poet who suspects that he may have lost his inspiration. Here again, the lyrics play an important role, reinforcing both the light-hearted tone of his dream vision and the more somber mood of reality when he awakens. In surprising counterpoint to the twenty love lyrics interspersed throughout the narration, he ends with a *lay* to the Virgin, making a symbolic break with his career as lover/poet and creating a new use for the highly developed lyric form that had, in earlier narratives, served only to express the sentiments of *fin' amors*.[44]

In addition to writing and incorporating the intercalated lyrics that appear in these *dits* and most of the shorter *ditties*, Froissart also undertook a more unusual task. In *Meliador*, an unfinished work of over 30,000 lines, he created an original Arthurian romance into which he incorporated all the lyrics written by his patron, Wenceslas of Brabant. As Dembowski demonstrates in his book-length study *Jean Froissart and His Meliador*, there is a clear relationship between the inclusion of these *formes fixes* lyrics and the theme of chivalric revival, for which Wenceslas himself seems to have been an idealized model. As a carefully defined set of genres that "emphasize[d] the contrived, arranged, *ordené* character of the art (and of the world that this art wishes to portray)," the lyrics reinforced a view of the world that stressed order and recalled the glories of the past.[45] That Froissart was willing to undergo the difficulties of incorporating 79 short poems into his plot,[46] while at the same time inventing a new mythology of young Arthurian heroes, testifies to his sense of the intrinsic value of lyric form.

This sense of intrinsic value extends, of course, beyond the narrative framework. One need only look at the number of independent lyrics in the manuscripts to get some sense of how much time Froissart must have devoted to their composition. While the 107 independent *rondeaux* are all of the eight-line variety, each one asserting and developing a single image or idea, the thirteen *lays* all exceed two hundred lines in length and involve the creation of multiple moods through complicated variations in rhythm and rhyme. Indeed, when Froissart's narrator in *Le Paradis* is asked to compose a new *lay* for presentation to the god of Love (lines 1023-42), he objects on the grounds that it would take half a year to complete (though luckily, as a worthy lover he has one already finished that will fill the bill). As noted earlier, Froissart chose the *lay* form to express his devotion to the Virgin Mary at the end of the *Joli Buisson*, thus marking the end of his career as lover/poet, and he chose the same form to honor his great benefactor, Queen Philippa, at the time of her death. This latter poem, especially--described by Dembowski as combining "eloquent elegance with simple pathetic and religious expression"[47]--attests to Froissart's care in choosing and adapting the lyric genre that would best support his purpose. The genre's length, formality, and structural capacity for expressing shifting moods allowed him to represent the complex interweaving of grief and adoration that accompanied his mourning of the queen.[48]

More familiar to modern audiences is Froissart's adaptation of the traditional *pastourelle* to create a new perspective on historical events. Using a form that resembles the *chanson royale* (thus creating a link with the *formes fixes*) and a narrative context that recalls the popular *pastourelles* of the previous century, Froissart devised a framework within which he could act as a narrator/witness to scenes in which shepherds and shepherdesses commented upon specific real-life occasions, such as an aristocratic wedding, a battle, or a royal procession. Although only seven of the twenty *pastourelles* are usually classified as historical,[49] the topicality of many of the others--with discussions of fashion, lovemaking, feasting, and so on--suggests as well that Froissart was interested in the genre because of the way it allowed him to portray a contemporary point of view different from (though, of course, compatible with) that of his audience. Unlike the narrative poems, which portray exclusively the interests and sentiments of the upper class, the *pastourelles* suggest an idealized image of a whole society in which the parts are well ordered and social roles effectively defined. It is thus in this lyric genre that the link between Froissart the historian and Froissart the poet is most clearly developed.

While it would be hard to argue that all the lyric poems are as innovative in their conception as either the elegiac *lay* or the historical *pastourelles*, the remaining genres demonstrate a broad range of subjects and rhetorical techniques, all of which must be considered in forming an opinion of Froissart's skill as a poet. Though these genres each deal mainly with expressions of *fin' amors*, it would, in fact, be a mistake to group them all together as if they were equal in quality or inspiration. Froissart himself seems, for example, to have had less interest in the *complainte* than in the *lay*, having left only three examples of this long, difficult form with its melancholic tone and demanding progression of rhymes. None of the *complaintes* appear in the independent collections. Likewise, he wrote few *virelays* aside from those that appear in narrative context, perhaps because this very musical form (judged among the most beautiful by some readers) left little room for intellectual development. A related--though somewhat more serious--objection might be applied to the *chansons royales*, of which there are only six; in these poems, the didactic purpose that dominates the genre seems nearly to predetermine the content. Readers judging only from examples of these three genres would find virtuosity and grace, but also limitations that were probably recognized by the poet himself.

In contrast, however, the *rondeau* and *ballade* seem to have offered Froissart rhetorical structures that could be adapted to many purposes. The pattern of assertion and commentary built into the *rondeau* could be used to develop conventional imagery, present an example, explore doctrinal questions, or apply a maxim to a specific case. With a shift in diction, such a poem could become intensely serious or sharply satirical. Likewise, the three-stanza *ballade* gave form to a kind of progressive logic that was not limited to a single theme or tone. Even the generally unsympathetic scholar B.J. Whiting found "more variety in Froissart's forty-three ballades" than in Machaut's two hundred.[50]

In this comparison to Machaut lies a final point that must be made about the nature and importance of Froissart's lyrics. For whereas Machaut had been both a poet and a musician, blending his talents as a composer with his accomplishment in perfecting the *formes fixes*, Froissart worked solely as a poet, writing lines that, in many cases, were apparently designed to be set to music, but which did not depend upon musical performance for their value. In this sense, Froissart's lyrics lie entirely within the literary tradition, reflecting his sense of how words, structures, and images could be made to represent the most elevated sentiments in the courtly world. As Dembowski put it, it was Froissart who developed all the lyric genres "jusqu'à leur conclusion logique."[51]

Manuscripts and Editions

Froissart's lyrics, along with his long and short narrative poems, are found in two manuscripts housed in the Bibliothèque Nationale de Paris. Both of these manuscripts are very legible and are believed to have been prepared under the direction of Froissart himself.[52] However, there are some important differences that have led modern editors to choose the one usually designated A (B.N. MS fr. 831) for the base manuscript, while consulting B (B.N. MS fr. 830) for additional poems and variants, a practice that will also be followed in this book.

The most important distinction between the two is that the language of A is, in spelling and declension, much closer to Froissart's own Picard dialect than is the language of B. In his introduction to *Le Paradis d'amour; L'Orloge amoureus*, Dembowski explains that A was probably prepared for an English audience, perhaps being the very manuscript that was presented to Richard II. Manuscript B, on the other hand, appears to have been destined for a French readership, since the spelling has been systematically changed to reflect the *francien* dialect.[53] Accordingly, all of Froissart's editors have preferred A, including his earliest editor, Auguste Scheler, who was nonetheless forced to use B because of difficulties caused by the Franco-Prussian War.[54]

If the two manuscripts were indeed destined for different countries, it would also explain the fact that certain poems are missing from manuscript A. Scheler hypothesized in his discussion of the manuscripts that Froissart would have naturally avoided including, in a collection intended for King Richard, any poems seeming to favor the French or Scottish courts, as indeed those that are missing do.[55] The poems that have been omitted include four short narrative *dits* and also, more importantly for our purposes, six *pastourelles*, all of which deal specifically with events or themes identifiably French. Manuscript A, on the other hand, includes two *ballades* missing from B: one discussing the destiny of England (and thus perhaps offensive to the French) and the other (as Dembowski has noted) offering a potentially offensive anti-courtly treatment of the narrator's dining habits.[56] It is thus necessary to follow the standard practice of drawing from both manuscripts to obtain a complete collection of lyrics.

One further distinction between the manuscripts concerns the order of presentation. Using external evidence as well as Froissart's own catalogue in *Le Joli Buisson*, Ernest Hoepffner established that, in B, both the major *dits* and the *pastourelles* were arranged to reflect the chronological order of their composition.[56] Within this arrangement, however, all of the lyrics (which were, of course, written over a number of years) are grouped together between *La Prison amoureuse* and *Le Joli Buisson de jonece* in the order of *Lays, Pastourelles, Chansons royaux et serventois, Ballades, Virelays,* and *Rondeaux.* In the A manuscript, on the other hand, the *Lays* and *Pastourelles* come before *La Prison,* which in turn is followed by the *Chansons, L'Espinette amoureuse* (here apparently out of chronological order), and then the *Ballades, Virelays,* and *Rondeaux.* As Baudouin has demonstrated in her edition of the *Ballades et Rondeaux,* Froissart appears to have followed at least a roughly chronological order in arranging the lyrics within each genre.[58] But what seems to be worth noting in the two manuscripts is that Froissart changed his mind when faced with the problem of having to choose a secondary principle of order for placement of the lyric collections among the longer works. In the A manuscript, it appears that he may have been trying to create lyric interludes between the narratives, while in B he chose to emphasize the collection of his lyrics thematically, as a corpus. In both arrangements the presentation of lyrics is completed before *Le Joli Buisson,* thus avoiding a return to these courtly genres after Froissart as narrator marks the end of his career as lover/poet. In B, however, the arrangement puts stronger thematic emphasis on the change of direction, since Froissart offers such a heavy concentration of lyric poems at a point that, chronologically, must be seen as the culmination of a major stage in his career.

Whatever questions may remain about the principles of arrangement, it may be said that, in general, the manuscripts offer few difficulties. Besides being legible and quite similar to each other in content, they offer, for readers of the lyrics, the advantage of each containing double copies of the many poems that appear both in the context of a narrative and in the independent collection. In some cases the two versions of a lyric are essentially identical, while in others the variations point to the difference in context between the poem intended to stand alone and the one that supports the plot, theme, or tone of a larger work.[59] In the latter case, the contrast between versions offers an opportunity for exploring Froissart's versatility and artistic control as a lyric writer, as well as the principles that guided his use of intercalation.

Still, one problem has not yet been entirely resolved in transcribing the lyrics from the manuscripts. In the fixed forms that have refrains (the *ballades*, *virelays*, and *rondeaux*) the scribes usually did not bother to copy the entire refrain after its first appearance in the poem, using instead the symbol &c after the first few words to suggest the repetition. This practice does not cause any problem in reestablishing the text of the *ballades*, since they follow a clear stanzaic pattern: the same single line (or pair of lines in four of the early poems) reappears at the end of each succeeding stanza. But for the *virelays* and *rondeaux*, the problem is complicated by the fact that the structure is not strictly stanzaic: in each case, the poems begin with a refrain of two or more lines, which then recurs in whole or in part, at intervals that were determined--at least theoretically--by the structural pattern of the music that accompanied them.[60] Thus if one follows a pattern consistent with the musical lines written by Machaut and other composers of the day, it seems that in the type of *rondeau* that Froissart most often wrote, only the first line of the refrain would be repeated in the middle of the poem, while both lines would be repeated at the end, as illustrated here in Rondeau 5:

Je voel morir poursieuans ma querelle
Comme loyaus servans au dieu d'Amours;
Tout pour l'amour de ma dame la belle,
Je voel morir [poursieuans ma querelle].
Quant mors serai, quoi que soit dira elle,
Mes esperis le servira tous jours.
Je voel morir [poursieuans ma querelle
Comme loyaux servans au dieu d'amours].

In contrast, in the *virelay* the music would suggest full repetitions of the refrain (usually four lines) after each set of two non-refrain stanzas, even though the manuscripts show only a few words of the first line followed by *&c.*

It would appear that modern editors could resolve questions about form fairly easily by following the musical patterns, as Baudouin has done in her edition. But the manuscripts themselves sometimes discourage this practice. In *Le Paradis*, for example, a *rondeaux* that should, according to musical theory, have eleven lines (with a repetition of only line one of the refrain in the middle and all three lines of the refrain at the end) is written in Manuscript A with an *&c* in line five that suggests a total line count of at least twelve:

Puis que Plaisance l'accorde
Et Esperance autressi
A moi oster de soussi,
C'est drois que je le recorde,
Puis que Plaisance l'acorde, &c
Car mon coer teire la corde
De joie, onques ne fist si.
Bien me plaist a vivre ensi,
Puis que Plaisance &c.   (851-59)

The decision of Bastin and McGregor to print a twelve-line version could be supported by the fact that Froissart himself was not a musician and that no musical settings exist for any of his work; thus, one could argue that he may have been far enough removed from the musical tradition to have varied the form, as Christine de Pisan did several years later.[61] In a purely literary lyric, such variation would be acceptable and, in the case of the *virelay*, probably preferable to the excessive repetition of the musical form.

Still, this explanation is not wholly satisfactory, in light of Froissart's conservative message. In their narrative contexts the lyrics are a reflection of the courtly entertainment enjoyed by aristocratic audiences, for whom dancing and singing were familiar and highly valued activities.[62] It seems unlikely that Froissart would have his narrator say that he sang his *rondeau* (as he does, for example, at line 864 of *Le Paradis*), if it could not, in the correctly expanded form, be sung.[63] Likewise, it seems more consistent to imagine the *virelays* in a configuration that allows for the possibility of music, even though the shorter form that McGregor prints (with only the first line of the refrain repeated as an ending to the third and fifth "stanzas") seems more coherent to a reader.[64] Since Froissart's audience would have known how to expand refrains without following explicit instructions, it is not unlikely that what appear to us to be variations in form are really just scribal errors in the placement of an *&c*--errors that could, at the time, easily have been overlooked. With this in mind, I will be following Baudouin's practice of assuming that Froissart's lyrics were consistent with musical form.

Critical Approaches

Since the main purpose of my study is to make Froissart's lyrics more accessible to scholars outside the narrow circle of Middle French specialists, it is not my intention to suggest an entirely new critical approach. Rather, in the pages that follow I have tried to apply systematically some of the most fruitful analytical perspectives and methodologies already current in Froissart studies, with the goal of offering a useful set of readings that will bring knowledge of the short lyrics nearer to the level established for the other genres. Such readings depend especially upon the work of those critics who, in the last twenty-five years, have developed a workable theoretical stance that has then allowed more specific investigations into issues of context and artistry as they apply to the fourteenth century and to Froissart as an individual.

Before the 1970s, the most serious problem impeding the study of the lyrics was the largely uncontested assumption that literature could be judged from a single, supposedly universal, set of standards. Although, for example, F.S. Shears recognized the importance of including some consideration of the poetry in his 1930 study entitled *Froissart: Chronicler and Poet,* his brief treatment of the lyrics seems mainly to be an attempt to demonstrate that some of Froissart's poems could appeal to twentieth-century tastes, primarily as a result of their "light-hearted" style, which, he claims, stands "far removed from the mystical longing and abstract analyses of the troubadours."[65] Similarly, in praising only the shortest lyrics for the fact that their "substance and form are admirably balanced," while complaining of the monotony of certain longer works,[66] Shears' analysis demonstrates a narrowly modern point of view that does not take into account the highly developed theory underlying the specific features unique to each of the various lyric genres. Although Shears was more sympathetic to the poetry than some of the other critics of the same era, such an impressionistic approach could do little to establish a sound theoretical basis for analysis of the poetry as serious literature.

Thus it is significant that in the 1970s scholars began insisting upon examining Froissart's poetry in the context of its own critical standards, rejecting the assumption of the earlier school who consciously chose, as Whiting put it, to arrive at judgments "without entering into the difference between fourteenth century tastes and our own."[67] The shift in attitude towards a more informed approach was explained most succinctly by Dembowski in his 1979 study entitled "La position de Froissart-poète dans l'histoire littéraire: bilan provisoire," where he argues for the historical importance of clarifying "la relation entre l'élément conservateur de Froissart, son obéissance à la convention, et ses 'renouvellements'."[68] Rather than attempting to depict Froissart as an innovator--a role that is clearly inconsistent with his choice of genre, tone, and matter--or merely taking a stance that would excuse him for his adherence to conventions, Dembowski insisted upon the value of examining Froissart as the embodiment of an important tradition. Such examination requires the abandonment of a purely evolutionary view of literary history which would, for example, try to place Froissart on a line between earlier French literature and the works of Chaucer. Instead, Froissart becomes the ideal subject for those who hope to understand the poetic movement of which he is the "digne continuateur."[69]

Thus it is important that his whole body of work be examined as a theoretical system, with less regard for the attractiveness of individual poems or passages (the central criterion for choosing poems in early studies) and more concern for patterns of poetic features working together to produce a purposeful, unified effect. As Elizabeth Salter argues in her study of fourteenth-century English poetry, personal reactions to the works of this period are always open to question, since "the foundations upon which such art is based differ radically from those most familiar to us."[70] Not only does the poetry of this age conform to its own set of standards governing the relationship between function and form, but it operates on a "different plane of significance," rejecting "dramatic verisimilitude" in favor of conventional patterns more suitable for expressing the complex system of thought that characterized refined love.[71] It is only through entering into a medieval frame of reference, with both its theories and its copious supply of "instant associations,"[72] that a modern reader has any hope of developing the sensibility that will lead to understanding.

A key example of this kind of "frame of reference" is the medieval concept of "Imagination," which, as Douglas Kelly has explained in two different studies, provides a foundation for understanding Froissart's handling of myth, allegory, and conventional imagery.[73] Kelly defines Imagination as "la faculté de la pensée qui préserve la forme des choses dans l'esprit," and he describes the artist's task as a sort of imitation of the medieval concept of creation, a process through which God assigns an idea or concept to a species and Nature places the essence of the species into individual beings.[74] For the artist, meaning must be "projected . . . into matter," and, therefore, effective use of "Images" involves adapting matter to sense rather than the other way around.[75] Although, as Kelly points out, modern readers have a tendency to see only the similarities among medieval poems, particularly in the repetition of conventional imagery and in traditional comparisons to mythological figures, the originality of the poems resides both in the poet's ability to choose appropriate matter to transmit his vision and in his skill at bringing new, clearer, or more complete meaning to stories and images that the audience has already thought about in a different context but can never fully comprehend.

Kelly's work, along with J.D. Burnley's related book on the language of Chaucer, suggests that any thorough analysis of Froissart's poetry must be informed by the process of "relating language structures to conceptual structures."[76] This approach has particular significance for the study of the lyrics, since they, even more than the narratives, have so often been dismissed for their reliance on familiar patterns. As these studies make clear, even though a list of names, a reference to a flower, or a pattern of behavior may be totally conventional, the context it appears in is always a little different from contexts that have been used before. In particular, "habitually co-occurring groups of words," "repeated verbal strategies," and "finely differentiated semantic patterns" are likely to be associated with important cultural concepts that the poet is invoking through a sort of semantic shorthand.[77] The modern reader, who lacks the particular range of literary experience of medieval audiences, must make an extra effort to recognize subtle nuances.

Similarly, the modern reader must make a focused effort to compensate for a lack of experience in responding to variations in form. While the technical demands of some of the *formes fixes* are so exaggerated as to seem like mere game-playing to modern readers, they were taken very seriously by practitioners of the day who used the term *Seconde Rhétorique* to honor a style that they considered to be the legitimate successor, in a Romance language, to the "First Rhetoric" established by writers of Latin verse.[78] Given this evidence of the poets' own heightened sense of formal significance, any good reading of the short lyrics would certainly have to take into account the inherent potential of each lyric genre, as well as the range of flexibility that the artist exercises within the established framework.

The complexity--and value--of this task is illustrated in Poirion's study on the evolution of the courtly lyric, which provides the most comprehensive and detailed examination available of the theoretical correspondences between the individual fixed forms and specific patterns of thought.[79] By dividing the lyrics into those with primarily circular structures (the *rondeau* and the *virelay*), those with radiating structures (the *chanson royale* and the *ballade*), and those based on a pattern of progressive repetition (the *lay* and the *complainte*), Poirion provides a clear outline of the rhetorical potential of each form, a potential which, of course, was exploited in many different ways--and to varying degrees of effectiveness--by different artists. Thus, for readers of Froissart the framework proposed by Poirion raises the important, and as yet largely unanswered, critical question of how well Froissart's poetry met the challenge of using variations in formal arrangement for the expression of significant and artistically coherent meaning. Such a question can be answered only through careful

examination of numerous poems, and it will be one of my main
contentions throughout this study that, when looked at from this point
of view, Froissart's lyrics show admirable artistic control indeed.

One final area of research that has helped form the groundwork
for an understanding of Froissart's artistry is the examination of his use
of specific rhetorical features. Besides relying frequently on
conventional imagery and mythological example, which have already
been mentioned, Baudouin has pointed out that Froissart often used
such classical tropes as apostrophe, interrogation, enumeration, and
antithesis.[80] Among the most interesting rhetorical habits she mentions,
however, is Froissart's frequent quoting of proverbs, a predilection that
was investigated in some detail by Whiting in 1935. Since Whiting's
main purpose was to contribute to the knowledge of medieval proverbs
rather than to analyze Froissart as a writer, he said little about
rhetorical effectiveness, except to comment that Froissart, unlike
Chaucer, did not use proverbs to "ornament a passage, characterize an
individual or adorn a tale."[81] Nonetheless, his catalogue of sayings,
which labels each proverb according to its source, is useful because it
reveals certain patterns of usage that might otherwise go unnoticed.
One finds, for example, that while there are many proverbs in the
rondeaux, there is none listed as appearing in a *chanson royale*. This
distinct contrast must certainly represent an inherent difference in the
type of theme or development that Froissart considered appropriate for
these two genres; likewise, to varying degrees, the presence or absence
of proverbial sayings in other genres is likely to provide clues to the
nature of each of the lyric types. Supplemented by J. Morawski's more
generalized study of French proverbs before the fifteenth century,
which offers information on the typical style and thematic distribution
of proverbs in the language,[82] Whiting's article provides a sound
starting place for an examination of Froissart's attitudes towards, and
manipulations of, common wisdom. Along with the various studies
discussing Froissart's attitudes towards chivalry and his relationships
with his patrons, this kind of cultural information helps to build a sense
of the context that made Froissart's lyrics meaningful and effective for
his audience.

The chapters which follow are arranged by genre, in an order that
is intended to emphasize the most significant characteristics of the lyric
poems. Chapter 2, for example, will begin with a short discussion of

the *lay* (a long form that cannot be discussed in full) in order to prepare for analysis of the shorter, but equally formal *chansons royales*. This chapter will focus most strongly on Froissart's methods of handling conventions and technical demands. Next, Chapter 3 will treat the *pastourelles*, which are distinctive for their historical subjects and dramatic perspective. Finally, Chapter 4 will examine the *ballades*, *virelays*, and *rondeaux*, forms which illustrate Froissart's strong sense of structure and rhetoric. As these chapters will show, the lyrics display an impressive range of techniques, tones, and patterns of thought, making them well worth the effort of close analytical reading.

Notes: Chapter I

1. Anthime Fourrier has completed modern editions of the following *dits*: *L'Espinette amoureuse*, (1963; Paris: Klincksieck, 1972); *La Prison amoureuse* (Paris: Klincksieck, 1974); *Le Joli Buisson de Jonece* (Geneva: Droz, 1975). Other modern editions include Peter Dembowski, *Le Paradis d'amour; L'Orloge amoureus* (Geneva: Droz, 1986); and a collection of the shorter narratives in Anthime Fourrier, *Dits et Debats* (Geneva: Droz, 1979). All of the lyrics except the *complaintes* appear in Rob Roy McGregor, Jr., *The Lyric Poems of Jehan Froissart: A Critical Edition* (Chapel Hill: U of North Carolina, 1975). Two of the lyric genres were also edited in Rae S. Baudouin, *Ballades et Rondeaux* (Paris & Geneva: Droz, 1978). The French texts of Froissart's *ballades* and *rondeaux* are reprinted from Baudouin with permission of Librairie Droz; texts of Froissart's other lyrics (Lay 3, *chansons*, *ballades*, *virelays*, and *rondeaux*) are reprinted from McGregor with permission of North Carolina Studies in Romance Languages and Literatures.

2. The history of popular response to the *Chroniques* is discussed in detail by J.J.N. Palmer in his introduction to *Froissart: Historian* (Suffolk: Boydell, 1981), 1-5.

3. This point is made by Richard Barber in his discussion of Froissart's early contacts with the aristocracy in England ("Jean Froissart and Edward the Back Prince" in J.J.N. Palmer, *Froissart: Historian*, 25-35), where he argues that Froissart probably did not have a historical purpose in mind when he travelled with members of the English court. The importance of poetry in Froissart's early career is also emphasized in Peter F. Dembowski's *Froissart and His Meliador: Context, Craft, and Sense* (Lexington KY: French Forum, 1983), 25-59.

4. The number of fixed forms as prescribed by Machaut was six: The *lay*, the *complainte*, the *chanson royale*, the *ballade*, the *virelay*, and the *rondeau*. Froissart may be said to have added a seventh by writing his *pastourelles* in a form that was a close variation upon the *chanson royale*. For a discussion of this similarity in form, see F.J.A. Davidson, "Froissart's Pastourelles," *Modern Language Notes* 8 (1898): 229-31.

5. For an early discussion of the dating of *Meliador*, see George L. Kittredge, "Chaucer and Froissart," *Englische Studien* 26 (1899): 322-35. The most thorough study of this poem is Dembowski's *Froissart and His Meliador*, which explains Froissart's purpose and method in reviving a form of the romance genre which recalled the traditions of the previous century. *Meliador* was the last Arthurian verse romance to be written in French; lacking the careful plot structure of a contemporary work such as *Sir Gawain and the Green Knight* or the cohesiveness of Malory's later reworking of the Arthurian cycle, it was designed to be read aloud in installments, as Froissart did when he visited the court of Gaston de Foix in 1388-89.

6. See, for example, the similarities listed by William Calin, *A Poet at the Fountain: Essays on the Narrative Verse of Guillaume de Machaut* (Lexington: UP of Kentucky, 1974), 246.

7. Froissart's own list of benefactors in the *Joli Buisson* includes thirty names (lines 230-373). Recent studies of the influence of patronage on his writings include Nigel Wilkins, "A Pattern of Patronage: Machaut, Froissart and the Houses of Luxembourg and Bohemia in the Fourteenth Century," *French Studies* 37 (1983):257-81;

George T. Diller, *Attitudes Chevaleresques et Réalités Politiques Chez Froissart* (Geneva: Droz, 1984); Douglas Kelly, "The Genius of the Patron: The Prince, the Poet, and Fourteenth-Century Invention," *Studies in the Literary Imagination* 20 (1987): 77-97; and M. T. de Medeiros, "Le Pacte encomiastique: Froissart, ses *Chroniques* et ses Mécènes," *Le Moyen Age: Revue Historique* 94 (1988): 237-255.

8. Discussions of Froissart's date of birth and other biographical information can be found in McGregor, 11-16, and Dembowski, *Jean Froissart and His Meliador*, 25-59. Early biographical research on Froissart was undertaken by Jean-Baptiste de La Curne de Sainte-Palaye, whose *Memoirs of the Life of Froissart* (London: Nicholson) was published in 1801. For other early studies with a biographical approach, see Maurice Leleu, "Les Poésies de Froissart," *Mémoires de l'Académie des Sciences, de Lettres et des Arts d'Amiens* 36 (1889): 31-131; M. Kervyn de Lettenhove, *Froissart: Etude littéraire sur le XIVme siècle* (Paris: Durand, 1857) and Mary Darmesteter, *Froissart* (Paris: Hachette, 1894).

9. Wolfgang Clemen, *Chaucer's Early Poetry*, trans. C.A.M. Sym (London: Methuen, 1963), 8.

10. McGregor, 16, translating from the *Chroniques*.

11. Gustave Cohen, in *Anthologie de la littérature française du Moyen-âge* (Paris: Delagrave, 1946), 146, describes Froissart as being "hennuyer et picard de langue" more than French. For a discussion of bilingualism in the English court, see Rossell Hope Robbins, "*Geoffroi Chaucier, poète français*, Father of English Poetry," *Chaucer Review* 13 (1978): 93-115. For further evidence of the international nature of fourteenth-century literature, as well as of Froissart's knowledge of English poetry, see James I. Wimsatt, "The *Dit dou Bleu Chevalier*: Froissart's Imitation of Chaucer," *Medieval Studies* 34 (1972): 388-400.

12. *Joli Buisson*, l. 236.

13. Wenceslas himself suffered literal imprisonment for over a year following his defeat at the Battle of Bastweiler. For a detailed analysis

of the parallels between his historical experiences and the allegorical references in the poem, see Claude Thiry, "Allégoire et histoire dans la *Prison amoureuse* de Froissart," *Studi Francesi* (1977): 15-29. William S. Kibler, "Poet and Patron: Froissart's *Prison amoureuse*," *L'Esprit Créateur* 18 (1978): 32-46, suggests that the *Prison* may be a collaborative work that includes actual letters from Wenceslas, in response to which Froissart offers his patron lessons in poetry and interpretation.

14. The Prologue to Book I begins with this statement of purpose: "Afin que les grans merveilles et li biau fait d'armes . . . soient notablement registré, et ou tamps present et à venir, veu et congneu, je . . . me voel ensonniier de l'ordonner et mettre en prose selonch le vraie information que j'ay eu des vaillans honmes, chevaliers et escuiers qui les ont aidiés à acroistre . . ." Froissart's intention becomes clearer as he goes on to explain his desire to discuss "le pourpos de proece" without which "ne poet li gentilz homs venir à parfaite honneur ne à glor dou monde." He then demonstrates his dedication to the chivalric values of the past by advising that every young man who wishes to advance must "regarder et considerer comment leur predicesseur, dont il tiennent leurs hyretages et portent espoir les armes, sont honnouré et recommendé par leurs biens fais. . . . Li noms de preu est si haus et si nobles et la vertu si clère et si belle que elle resplendist en ces sales . . ." (I, 1-4). All passages from Books I-3 are quoted from *Chroniques de J. Froissart,* 13 vols. (Paris: Société de l'Histoire de France, 1869-1957) and will be identified as SHF. Passages from Book 4 will be quoted from *Œuvres de Froissart*, ed. Kervyn de Lettenhove (Brussels: Devaux, 1871), and will be referred to as Lettenhove.

15. Daniel Poirion, *Le Poète et le Prince: L'Evolution du lyrisme courtois de Guillaume de Machaut à Charles d'Orléans* (1965; rpt. Slatkine, 1978). For a more specific study of the relationship between Froissart's poetry and chivalric values, see Peter F. Dembowski, "Chivalry, Ideal and Real, in the Narrative Poetry of Jean Froissart," *Medievalia et Humanistica* n.s. 14 (1986): 1-15.

16. Froissart's attempt to revive episodic verse romance for illustrating the chivalric virtue of *ordenance* might be compared, for

English readers, to Edmund Spenser's plan to illustrate Magnificence through the allegorical Arthurian epic of *The Faerie Queen*. In both cases there was a conscious attempt to draw on traditional language and example to inspire idealized behavior, and in both cases the authors were committed to public service. Neither of these ambitious works was finished.

17. Dembowski, *Jean Froissart and His Meliador*, 26.

18. Kevin Brownlee, *Poetic Identity in Guillaume de Machaut* (Madison: U of Wisconsin P, 1984).

19. Brownlee, 3.

20. See, for example, Philip E. Bennett, "The Mirage of Fiction: Narration, Narrator, and Narratee in Froissart's Lyrico-Narrative *Dits*," *Modern Language Review* 86 (1991): 285-97, which discusses Froissart's questioning of the writing experience in *Le Paradis*, *L'Espinette* and *Le Joli Buisson*; Peter F. Dembowski, "Tradition, Dream Literature, and Poetic Craft in *Le Paradis d'Amour* of Jean Froissart," *Studies in the Literary Imagination* 20 (1987): 99-109, which discusses Froissart's consciousness of his role as a lyric poet; Claire Nouvet, "Pour une Economie de la Délimitation: La *Prison Amoureuse* de Jean Froissart," *Neophilologus* (1986): 341-56, which discusses the subversion of the notion of reality in the text; and Rosemary Morris, "Machaut, Froissart, and the Fictionalization of the Self," *The Modern Language Review* 83 (1988): 545-55, which discusses the self-conscious search for matter to replace the Arthurian romance and the subsequent return to lyric stasis.

21. This likeness is discussed by Kittredge in "Chaucer and Froissart," 156. Froissart's poem is quoted from Dembowski (lines 1-7); Chaucer's is quoted from *The Riverside Chaucer*, ed. Larry D. Benson (Boston: Houghton Mifflin, 1987), 1-7.

22. The earlier view of continuity is espoused, for example, by James I. Wimsatt in *Chaucer and the French Love Poets* (Chapel Hill: (U of North Carolina Press, 1968) and "Chaucer and French Poetry," *Writers and Their Backgrounds: Geoffrey Chaucer*, ed. Derek Brewer

(Athens OH: Ohio University Press, 1975). The quoted passage is from Barbara Nolan, "The Art of Expropriation: Chaucer's Narrator in *The Book of the Duchess,*" *New Perspectives in Chaucer Criticism,* ed. Donald M. Rose (Norman OK: Pilgrim Books, 1981): 203.

23. Nolan, 207.

24. Dembowski, "Tradition," 108.

25. Dembowski, "Tradition," 108.

26. Normand Cartier, "Froissart, Chaucer, and Enclimpostair," *Revue de Littérature Comparée* 38 (1964): 34.

27. Cartier, 28. For discussions of Froissart's pattern of mythological invention, see Audrey Graham, "Froissart's Use of Classical Allusion in His Poems," *Medium Ævum* 32 (1963): 24-33; Jean-Louis Picherit, "Le Rôle des éléments mythologique dans le *Joli Buisson de Jonece* de Jean Froissart,*" *Neophilologus* 63 (1979): 498-508; and Nancy Bradley-Cromey, "Mythological Typology in Froissart's *Espinette amoureuse,*" *Res Publica Litterarum* 3 (1980): 207-221. The broader issues of typology are also discussed in the same issue by Mary Ann Burke, "A Medieval Experiment in Adaptation: Typology and Courtly Love. Poetry in the Second Rhetoric," 165-75.

28. Roland M. Smith, "Five Notes on Chaucer and Froissart," *Modern Language Notes* 46 (1951): 27-32.

29. The complete text and English translation of this *ballade,* as well as Ballades 9 and 31, appear in Appendix A. All translations are my own. The Chaucer poem which follows is from Benson, Text F, 11. 249-255.

30. Smith, 30.

31. John H. Fisher, *John Gower* (London: Methuen, 1965), 75.

32. Arthur K. Moore, "Chaucer's Use of Lyric as an Ornament of Style," *Comparative Literature* 3 (1951): 38-39.

33. Moore, 32.

34. Wimsatt, *Chaucer and the French Love Poets*, 57.

35. Peter Dronke, *The Medieval Lyric* (London: Hutchinson University Library, 1968), 147.

36. The "Dittié de la Flour de la Margherite" appears in Anthime Fourrier, *Dits et Debats*. The lyrics referred to are Ballade 7, Pastourelle 17, and Pastourelle 19. Although most critics agree that the lady's name in the *Espinette* (l. 3389) should be interpreted as "Margerite," William W. Kibler argues in his article "Self-Delusion in Froissart's *Espinette Amoureuse*," *Romania* 97 (1976): 80-81, that the other name mentioned, "Violette," is more appropriate and more likely to be correct.

37. James I. Wimsatt, *The Marguerite Poetry of Guillaume de Machaut* (Chapel Hill: U of North Carolina Press, 1970), 33.

38. Bernard Ribemont, "Froissart, le mythe et la marguerite," *Revue des Langues Romanes* 94 (1990): 129-37. For a discussion of the daisy as a developing symbol of Froissart's poetic identity, see Sylvia Huot, "The Daisy and the Laurel: Myths of Desire and Creativity in the Poetry of Jean Froissart," *Yale French Studies* (1991): 240-51.

39. See, for example, Paull L. Baum, *Chaucer's Verse* (Durham: Duke UP, 1961); and John H. Fisher, "Chaucer and the French Influence," in Donald M. Rose, ed., *New Perspectives in Chaucer Criticism* (Norman OK: Pilgrim Books, 1981), 188.

40. Dembowski, "La Position de Froissart-poète dans l'histoire littéraire: bilan provisoire," *Travaux de linguistique et de littérature* 16 (1979): 140. Dembowski has analyzed the metrical features of the decasyllabic line in some detail in "Metrics and Textual Criticism," *L'Esprit Créateur* 27 (1987), 90-100, where he points out that the decasyllable was a line that Machaut also used frequently in his lyrics.

41. For an overview of the history of these forms, see Robert Bossuat, *Le Moyen Age* (Paris: Gigord, 1931), 79-94, 235-36.

42. Dembowski, "Tradition," 106.

43. Dembowski, "Tradition," 102.

44. For a discussion of the significance of this poem in Froissart's career, see Michelle A. Freeman, "Froissart's *Le Joli Buisson de Jeunesse*: A Farewell to Poetry?" in *Machaut's World*, ed. M. P. Cosman and B. Chandler, Annals of the New York Academy of Sciences 314 (New York, 1978), 235-48.

45. Dembowski, *Jean Froissart and His Meliador*, 125.

46. The theoretical considerations that guided lyric insertion in the *Meliador* are discussed in Jane H.M. Taylor, "The Lyric Insertion: Towards a Functional Model," *Courtly Literature: Culture and Context*, ed. Keith Busby and Erik Kooper (Amsterdam: Benjamins, 1990). Taylor's work builds upon the theory proposed by Jacqueline Cerquiglini in *"Un Engin Si Soutil": Guillaume de Machaut et L'Ecriture au XIVe Siècle* (Geneva & Paris: Slatkine, 1985).

47. Dembowski, *Jean Froissart and His Meliador*, 45.

48. For a translation and short discussion of this poem, see my "Jean Froissart's *Lay de la mort la Royne D'Engleterre*," *Allegorica* 14 (1993): 61-76.

49. For a discussion of this classification of poems, see McGregor, 38-45.

50. B.J. Whiting, "Froissart as Poet," *Medieval Studies* 8 (1946): 189-216.

51. Dembowski, "La Position," 147.

52. Froissart says in his *Chroniques* that he "had a manuscript prepared" for Richard II ("J'avoie . . . fait escripre, grosser, et enluminer . . ." Lettenhove, ed., 15: 141); scholars agree that Manuscript A may be the same one that was presented to the king. For a description of the two manuscripts and a list of their contents, see

McGregor, 17-20, and Dembowski, *Le Paradis*, 6-12. Though Sylvia Huot appears to be in error when she notes that the collected lyrics are placed in the same position in both manuscripts (238), she offers a useful discussion of Froissart's role as a compiler in *From Song to Book: The Poetics of Writing in Old French Lyric and Lyrical Narrative Poetry* (Ithaca: Cornell U Press, 1987), 238-41, 302-327.

53. Dembowski, *Le Paradis*, 4.

54. Auguste Scheler, ed., *Œuvres de Froissart: Poésies*, vol. 3 (Brussels: Devaux, 1870-72), lxxi.

55. Scheler, 3.xi.

56. Dembowski, *Le Paradis*, 9.

57. Ernest Hoepffner, "La Chronologie des *pastourelles* de Froissart," *Mélanges offerts à M. Emile Picot*, 2 (Paris, 1913), 27-42.

58. Baudouin, xiv-xvii.

59. The most notable difference is in Ballade 8, which has an entirely different third stanza in the *Paradis d'Amour* than in the collected lyrics. This poem is discussed in detail in Chapter 4.

60. For a thorough discussion of the metrical requirements imposed by musical form, see Nigel Wilkins, "The Structure of Ballades, Rondeaux and Virelais in Froissart and Christine de Pisan," *French Studies* 23 (1969): 337-47. Wilkins resolves the problem of how to expand refrains of unspecified length by demonstrating the relationship between musical form and text. He explains that in a *rondeau*, for example, the musical pattern will always be I-II-I-I-II-I-II (each numeral representing a musical phrase), so that the total number of lines of text can be determined according to whether the repeated musical sections correspond to single lines (A-B-a-A-a-b-A-B) or to multiple lines (AB-B-ab-AB-ab-b-ab-b).

61. Wilkins, "Structure," 343-45.

62. The various forms of dance in the fourteenth century are discussed by Robert Mullally, "Dance Terminology in the Works of Machaut and Froissart," *Medium Ævum* 59 (1990): 248-59.

63. In the *Joli Buisson*, for example, lyrics are said to be "recited," "read," or "sung"; instances of singing occur at lines 2532-33, where a *virelay* is "chantés," and at 2670-72: "Et de chanter tous pourveus / Un rondelet bel et plaisant."

64. McGregor does not discuss his principle of expanding refrains in his edition. Since he does not list Wilkins' article in his bibliography, it is possible that he was unaware of the information it provides.

65. F.S. Shears, *Froissart: Chronicler and Poet* (London: George Rutledge & Sons, 1930): 196-98. A similar approach to the poetry is taken by Julia Bastin in *Froissart: Chroniqueur, Romancier et Poète*, 2nd ed. (Brussels: Office de Publicité, 1948), which offers a sympathetic overview of all the poetic works. Maurice Wilmotte, on the other hand, in *Froissart* (Brussels: Renaissance du Livre, 1942) describes Froissart's poetry as monotonous and "inférieure" (40).

66. Shears, 217, 210.

67. Whiting, "Froissart," 189.

68. Dembowski, "La position," 141.

69. Dembowski, "La position," 146-47.

70. Elizabeth Salter, *Fourteenth-Century Poetry: Contexts and Readings* (Oxford: Clarendon Press, 1983), 6-7.

71. Salter, 14.

72. Salter, 5.

73. Douglas Kelly, *Medieval Imagination: Rhetoric and the Poetry of Courtly Love* (Madison: U of Wisconsin Press, 1978); and "Les Inventions ovidiennes de Froissart," *Littérature* 41 (1981): 82-92.

74. Kelly, "Les Inventions," 82.

75. Kelly, *Medieval Imagination*, xii.

76. J. D. Burnley, *Chaucer's Language and the Philosophers' Tradition* (Cambridge: Brewer, 1979), 1.

77. Burnley, 2

78. Bossuat, 84.

79. Poirion, 311-422.

80. Baudouin, xlii-xlvi.

81. B.J. Whiting, "Proverbs in the Writings of Jean Froissart," *Speculum* 10 (1935): 293.

82. J. Morawski, ed., *Proverbes français antérieure au XVe siècle* (Paris: Champion, 1925). Other useful sources for researching the meaning of proverbs include Randle Cotgrave, *A Dictionarie of the French and English Tongues* (London, 1611; rpt. Columbia: U of South Carolina Press, 1950); and James Woodrow Hassell, Jr., *Middle French Proverbs, Sentences, and Proverbial Sayings* (Toronto: Pontifical Institute of Medieval Studies, 1982).

II
Lays and *Chansons Royales*:
Creating Meaning Through Form

In choosing a starting place for a close examination of Froissart's short lyrics, one must admit from the outset that some genres provide an easier--that is to say, less frustrating--point of entrance for the contemporary reader than do others. There would be little difficulty, for example, in finding a way to write an appreciative analysis of the compact eight-line *rondeau*, since it usually meets modern standards for density of meaning, often provides a well-focused perspective on a familiar individual motif, and sometimes even surprises the reader with a subtle rhetorical twist. Likewise, the skilled reader could enjoy the *pastourelle* both for its vivid story-telling and for Froissart's inventive adaptation of existing formal restraints to suit a new and very specific purpose--one that can arguably be said to represent a unique and personal poetic vision. In each of these cases, the genre provides material for analysis that falls within the guidelines of modern poetics, where technical skill in the fulfillment of a predetermined form is expected to be coupled with such qualities as variety in theme, freshness of imagery, inventiveness of thought, and economy of expression.

The problem, of course, is that such contemporary modes of analysis tend to obscure rather than clarify the issues that are most problematic in Froissart. While some genres do introduce "new" themes and images, the fact remains that his most typical lyrics show a predictable and narrow concern for the sufferings of the unfulfilled lover, expressed through familiar conventional motifs and rhetorical devices. Moreover, while some poems, especially in the shorter genres, are tightly organized and rhetorically purposeful, others seem diffuse or even static, likely still to give twentieth-century readers the impression, expressed decades ago by Julia Bastin, that "la contrainte de la forme paralyse la pensée."[1] Indeed, one of the most striking qualities of Froissart's lyrics is the fact that, while all of the genres are clearly designed to convey the same relatively limited number of themes and motifs, the poems vary significantly in style from one fixed form to another, displaying a sometimes puzzling "unevenness" in tone, logic, and texture.

In searching for a way to characterize Froissart's work, early critics tended merely to offer faint praise with the simple observation that such virtuosity is impressive in itself. But there is danger in dismissing these stylistic variations so easily, for such a conscious pursuit of purely formal variation suggests an underlying system of thought that is more theoretically complex than is reliance on a single set of aesthetic standards. Such a system seems to value not just the individual poetic effects that are created--though those may be considerable--or even the ideas conveyed, but rather the very process involved in the continual reexamination of certain fundamental social ideals whose true wealth of meaning can be revealed only through systematic and purposeful shifts in style, context, and perspective.

Given, then, this difference in emphasis between the poet's theoretical stance and our own, it is probably most fruitful to begin an examination of the lyrics with those genres that conform least to modern expectations, thus forcing attention onto the conventions and structures themselves. Among the shorter lyrics that comprise the focus of this book, it is the five-stanza *chanson royale* which fits this description best, since this genre presents what might be described as a rather wordy treatment of conventional themes using both conventional imagery and a conventional rhetorical arrangement. In contrast to the structurally similar *pastourelle*, which offers both narrative interest and a distinctive point of view, the *chanson* relies mainly on its sounds, rhythms, and careful adherence to doctrine for its success. As the first of the short lyrics to be examined, it will serve as a suitable frame of reference for further discussions of technique in other short lyrics. But in order to establish a clearer idea of the complexity of the variations between genres, it will be helpful to look first at an example of the *lay*, a much longer lyric form that illustrates within itself the combination of psychological sophistication and technical subtlety underlying Froissart's lyric system as a whole.

Probably more than any other genre, the lyric *lay* demonstrates the degree to which technical skill and the concept of formal perfection dominated fourteenth-century French poetry. The rules of the genre require that the poem be made up of twelve stanzas, each of which "must differ from its neighbor in measure, rhyme, and number of lines," except that the last stanza must have exactly the same form as the first.[2] In addition, each stanza must employ only two different rhymes, and the stanzas generally must be divisible into two or four equal parts which, if the poem were set to music, would correspond to repetitions of specific melodic sequences. As these complex rules would suggest, the *lay* was not one of the simple dance forms that gained acceptance at court in the thirteenth century, but rather, as explained by Jean Maillard, a metrically complex genre with a long history reaching back to the Celtic societies of the fourth to seventh centuries.[3] Although the most famous of its various manifestations was the narrative type made popular by Marie de France in the twelfth century, the composition of the *lay* as a lyric form often involved an emphasis on rhythm and melody that largely overshadowed the importance of content.[4] Combining the appeal of courtly tradition with great rhythmic variety and a potential for unlimited virtuosity, the *lay* was thus ideally suited for inclusion in the art of the Second Rhetoric. Largely through the influence of the poet-musician Machaut, it came to be regarded as the highest of the fixed lyric forms.

One thing that soon becomes clear from studying the *lays* is that these long, complicated poems are composed according to standards of theme and unity that are not only different from our own, but quite distinct from those that govern the shorter lyric genres. As Daniel Poirion suggests, the various stanzas, with their individual rhythmic patterns, seem to correspond to the varying moods and emotions of the poem's speaker, expressing "la durée et la diversité dans la vie psychologique, sans nécessairement verser dans l'analyse discursive."[5] According to Poirion, the stanzas are united less by a particular idea than by the presence of a persona, the "moi" whose personal life is revealed in its many different dimensions with much less concern for causality than for dynamics. Indeed, the internal logic of these poems is primarily associative rather than inferential. The resulting potential for shifts in tone is illustrated in Lay 3, in which even the first stanza displays the fluid movement and complex interconnections between positive and negative emotions:

Lay 3

Pour resjoïr mon martire
Voel je mon coer mettre en voie
            D'avoir joie.
            Che m'envoie
Uns douls espoirs, Diex li mire,   5
Qui me vient compter et dire
Que de riens il ne m'anoie
            Ne larmoie
            Ne gramoie.
            Bien poroie   10
Avoir che que je desire;
Et puis qu'en confort me tire,
C'est bien raisons que le croie
            Et que soie
            Ou que voie,   15
            Ne que voie
Liés et joieus et sans ire;
Car mieuls ne poroie eslire,
Se par souhet advenoie
            Ne venoie   20
            Ou voloie,
            Qu'en la quoie
Ma dame amer, c'est sans dire.

            [In order to lighten my suffering
            I wish to put my heart on the path
                        Towards joy.
                        Sweet hope sends me
            This comfort, may God reward it,
            Which comes to me to say
            That it will not bring me worry
                        Or cause me to weep
                        Or make me sorrowful.
                        I might indeed
            Have that which I desire;
            And since hope leads me into comfort,

It is certainly reasonable that I
        believe it
And that I be,
      Wherever I am,
      Wherever I go,
Happy and joyous and without anger;
For I could not choose anything better—
If things turn out as I wish
      Or end up
      Where I desire—
Than to love my serene lady;
But that, of course, goes without saying.]

Car tant est et belle et gente,
      Par me foi,   25
Que Nature li deubt rente,
      Je le croi,
De donner fourme excellente.
      Car pour quoi?
Attemprance represente   30
      Son arroi.

   [For she is both so beautiful and so noble,
        By my faith,
   That Nature is obliged to her,
        I believe,
   For serving as an excellent model.
        And why is this?
   Her bearing is the epitome
        Of moderation.]

      Ce m'esjoïst
      Et resjoïst
En confort et en leece,
      Et adoucist   35
      Et esclarcist
Moult grandement ma tristece.
      Amours me mist,
      Quant il me prist,
Hors d'ignorance et de rudece.   40
      Point ne mesprist
      Quant il m'aprist
A amer en ma jonece.

[This gladdens me
And cheers me
Into comfort and rejoicing,
And it greatly
Softens
And brightens my sadness.
When Love claimed me,
He put me
Beyond all crude and ignorant behavior.
He did not lead me astray
When he taught me
To love in my youth.]

Ignorant   45
Et non sachant
Que j'estoie, et jone enfant,
Me monstra sans ensegnier
Le plaisant
Et le poissant
Fet d'amours; j'en sçai bien tant,   50
Car pris fui sans manecier
D'un samblant
Douls et riant
De ma dame en regardant;
Ne le quier més oubliier.   55
Son servant
Lui servant
Me rendi par couvenant,
Que tous sui en son dangier,

[Ignorant
And unknowing
As I was, just a young boy,
He showed me without teaching
The pleasing
And powerful
Effects of love; I know it well
Because I was taken by surprise
As I looked at
The sweet and smiling
Countenance of my lady;
I will never seek to forget it.

I swore
To be
Her liege servant,
So that now I am completely in her power,]

    Et serai   60
    Tant com vivrai:
Ma dame adiés servirai;
Je li doi d'obeïssance.
    Quant li jurai,
    Ce fu en mai,   65
Que flours, roses, lis et glai
Prendent cruçon et substance.
    Pour ce l'ai
    Mis en mon lai
Qu'Amours, qui m'en fist l'assai   70
Par sa trés douce ordenance,
    Me dist: "Fai
    Sans nul delai
De ceste ta dame." Et j'ai
Obeï a sa plaisance.   75
    Dont espoir ai
    Qu'encor arai,
Quant mieuls desservi l'arai,
De tous mes mauls aligance,

    [And I will remain so
    For as long as I live:
I will serve my lady from this day forward;
I owe her my obedience.
    When I took my oath to her,
    It was in May,
When flowers, roses, lilies and glads
Grow and flourish.
    I have put this
    Into my poem because
Love, who suggested this to me
In his sweet command,
    Told me: "Make a poem
    About this lady of yours
Without delay." And I
Obeyed his wish.
    Therefore I hope

That I will still have
Relief from all my sufferings,
When I have deserved it more,]

Se Fortune, li perverse   80
    Et diverse,
Qui maint homme au besoing faut,
    Ne m'assaut.
Mais je le sench si cuverse,
    Le traverse,   85
Qu'elle met un homme en haut,
    Ne l'en chaut
Comment voist, puis le reverse
    Et le berse
A un trop villain bersaut.   90
    Tout tressaut
Mon coer, qui le sent si verse
M'anoit j'en aroie faut.[6]
    Petit vault
Li lieus ou elle converse.   95

[If Fortune, the perverse
    And inconstant one,
Who fails many a man in his need,
    Does not assail me.
But I sense that she is so vile,
    That contrary creature,
That she sets a man on high,
    Without caring
What happens, then sends him reversals
    And shoots at him
As at a common target.
    All atremble
Is my heart, which must be troubled
    By such hostility.
The place where she dwells
    Is of little value.]

La fausse ypocrite
Sodacre et traïte,
Elle est si despite
Qu'elle ne fait cure
De riens ou habite.   100

N'a si saint hermite
De chi en Egypte,
S'au diffamer cure,
Que mal n'en recite,
Ne tout son merite   105
Noient ne pourfite,
Qui qu'elle asseüre
Tantost est desdite;
Ne poet estre escripte,
Comptee ne dite   110
Sa fausse nature.

    [This deceitful hypocrite is
    Evil and treacherous,
    And she is so scornful
    That she has no concern
    For anything anywhere.
    There is no hermit so holy
    From here to Egypt,
    That people would not speak evil of him
    If she chose to dishonor him,
    Nor would all his merit
    Protect him at all,
    For whoever she supports
    Is promptly abandoned;
    No one can fully write,
    Recount or tell
    Her deceitful nature.]

Trop felon
Sont si don;
Oquison
N'i a nulle desraison;   115
Che dient le anchiien.
Absalon,
Priamon
Ne Noiron,
Ne le roi Laomedon,   120
Ne Grieu ne li Troiien,
Salemon
Ne Caton
Ne Platon,
Ne sceurent comparison   125

Faire de son fol maintien.
    Il n'est hom,
    Tant soit bon
    Ne preudon,
Qu'elle prise un seul bouton;   130
De tant le congnois je bien.

    [Her gifts are
    Too treacherous;
    Chance is
Not reasonable at all;
Thus say the ancients.
    Neither Absalom,
    Nor Priam
    Nor Nero,
Nor King Laomedon,
Neither Greek nor Trojan,
    Solomon
    Nor Cato
    Nor Plato
Knew how to make any sense
Of her insane behavior.
    There is no man,
    As good or as valiant
    As he may be,
That she values as much as a button;
That much I know very well.]

Et pour ce s'effree
Soir et matinee
Mon coer grandement,
    Qui le sent   135
Si mal avisee;
Plus tost est tournee
Que kocés au vent.
    Mais briefment
Ja la foursenee   140
Pour sa grant posnee
N'ara nullement
    Sentement,
Pooir ne entree
Dessus ma pensee.   145
Car elle se rent

Liegement,
Et est ja donnee
Dou tout et voee,
Au commandement   150
    Plainnement
Ma dame honnouree,
Qui de moi amee
Est si loyaument,
    Vraiement,   155
Qu'onques fame nee
Ne fu si doubtee
Ne si liement,
    Humlement
Servie et loee.   160
Toute asseüree
Qu'il n'ert aultrement,
Sans delaiement
    Tiengne s'ent.

[And for this reason
Night and day
My heart greatly fears,
    And it feels
Weak in its resolve;
It is more easily turned
Than the weathercock in the wind.
    But soon now
This raging one
Despite all her great arrogance
Will have absolutely
    No effect,
No power or access
To my thoughts.
For my mind surrenders
    Totally to its sovereign,
And is now completely
Given over and dedicated,
Fully,
    To every command
Of my honored lady,
Whom I love
So loyally,
    Truly,

That no woman ever born
Was ever so respected
Or so joyously,
        Humbly
Served and praised.
Completely assured
That it will never be otherwise,
        She expects this
Without hesitation.]

Et s'ensi il avenoit   165
Que ja ne voie avenir,
        Mieuls morir
Ameroie, et a bon droit,
Que Fortune, qui bien voit,
        Sans desir   170
Me vosist, ne retolir
La grasce qui me pourvoit
        D'esjoïr
Et de joïr. Quanque soit,
S'ai je voloir dou souffrir   175
        Et moi tenir
En fermeté si a droit
Que servir et obeïr
        Sans partir
A ma dame; et ce seroit   180
Pour le Fortune asservir,
        Qui languir
Et priés perir me feroit;
Mes espoirs bien me poroit
Tout ce faire soustenir,   185
        Et servir
Que de ce m'esjoïroit
        Que desir.

[And if it would happen
That I should not see a happy outcome,
        I would prefer
To die, and rightly so,
Rather than have Fortune, who sees well,
        See me
Without desire, or take away
The reprieve that is provided to me

In delighting
And rejoicing. Whatever happens,
I have the will to be patient
    And to remain
Steadfast so truly
That I will serve and obey
    My lady
Without end; and the result would be
For me to enslave Fortune,
    Who would hope to make me
Languish and almost die;
My hope could certainly
Make me endure all this,
    And would serve
To make my desire
Gladden me.]

Si ne m'ai que faire
De l'espoenter,   190
Més la debonnaire,
Ma dame honnourer,
Servir sans retraire,
Cremir et amer;
Et son douls viaire,   195
Simple, gent et cler,
Que Diex volt pourtraire
Et Nature ouvrer
Par droit exemplaire,
La me voel mirer.   200
Il me doit bien plaire
Tel vie a mener,
Je ne m'en doi taire
Mais toutdis parler;
Ce m'est necessaire   205
Pour reconforter
Et pour mon contraire
Arriere bouter.

    [Thus it is not my business
    To be afraid,
    But rather to honor my lady,
    The gracious one,
    To serve her without ceasing,

To venerate and love her;
And her sweet face,
Modest, noble and bright,
Which God chose to fashion
And Nature to create
According to a perfect example,
Upon *that* I wish to reflect.
It must indeed please me
To lead such a life,
I must not remain silent
But instead speak of it always;
This is necessary
To bring me comfort
And to put my difficulties
Behind me.]

Més tant voel je contredire
Le Fortune, qui guerroie   210
  Et desvoie
  Et fourvoie
Tamaint coer et le martire,
Que ja pour tout son mestire
Ne sera, quoi qu'estre en doie,   215
  Ne m'esjoie
  N'esbanoie
  Et que n'oie
Volontiers jeuer et rire,
Car espoirs li rent estire,   220
Et a lui il se raloie.
  Il le loie
  Et desloie
  Et le ploie
Et le fait a ses piés gire.   225
En son bon confort me mire
Et ossi, s'el en faisoie,
  Je seroie
  En le voie
Et ou point dou desconfire.   230

[But I so wish to resist
Fortune, which attacks
  And misleads
  And deceives

And tortures so many hearts,
That never, for all her superiority,
Will it happen, no matter what,
    That I do not rejoice
    And make merry
    Or that I do not gladly
Hear playing and laughing,
For Hope opposes Fortune,
And against her he contends.
    He binds her
    And releases her
    And bends her down
And makes her lie at his feet.
I think only of the comfort Hope provides
For if I did otherwise,
    I would be
    On the path towards defeat
And upon the point of perishing.]

The opening statement of the poem introduces what will be a
consistent pattern of conventional, mostly abstract language. Although
references to "coer" and "voie" might technically be called
metaphorical, the image that they create is clearly not intended to draw
upon the power of the senses. The purpose instead seems mainly to be
to provide verbal cues that identify the stance of the persona and that
place this poem, along with all others that follow the conventions of the
fixed forms, within the tradition of proper amorous speech. More
important for a thorough understanding of this genre, however, is the
way that the first line juxtaposes the near-rhyming words "resjoïr" and
"martire," setting up an immediate tension between pleasure and pain.
It is through this tension that the poem expresses formally the emotional
struggle that is central to the lover's experience, and to the extent that
this tension is recreated and explored, the poem becomes an artistic
performance that is both proof of the lover's worthiness and a
reflection of his spiritual journey.

The importance of conventional vocabulary in this poetic
exploration can be seen in the opening stanza. After the initial
introduction of the opposing terms that will govern the poem, the stanza
begins a pattern of alternation between the positive and the negative,
starting with the idea that the persona is pursuing the path towards
"joie." The possibility of a satisfying outcome is reinforced in line 5

with the phrase "douls espoirs," but within the same sentence the concept is linked to a reminder of love's propensity for bringing on worry, weeping, and sorrow, expressed through the dense series of rhyming verbs "anoie," "larmoie," and "gramoie" (7-9). The next statement asserts the lover's confidence in being able to achieve that which he desires, with the idea of "confort" set forth as an apparently achievable goal. But again the tension is reinforced as the persona suggests the need to urge himself to be happy, saying first that it is right or reasonable for him to believe in the possibility of success ("bien raisons que le croie") and then revealing that he will make a conscious choice to remain "liés," "joyeus," and "sans ire" (13-17). In this case the short rhymed lines seem calculated to emphasize the intensity of the persona's resolution ("Et que soie / Ou que voie, / Ne que voie"), which, of course, would not be necessary unless there were some difficulty involved. Likewise, the choice of the phrase "sans ire" balances the positive adjectives "liés" and "joyeus" by suggesting within the resolution for calm the possibility of anger. Thus, the meaning of the stanza lies much less in the overt sentiment of the persona or the details of his particular story than in the manipulation of conventional elements to create an accurate portrayal of a spiritual and emotional condition. When the poet ends the stanza with the apparently simple idea that loving his lady is the best of all possible outcomes, there is perhaps some authorial irony in the assertion that this, of course, goes without saying.

For it is the poem as formal experience rather than the poem as message that is the ideal lover's primary concern. As the stanzas go forward, the persona who hopes to place himself within the realm of *fin' amors* is restricted to the idealized language and thought patterns that are appropriate to the shared experience of the few who have risen above the particularity of ordinary life. Yet at the same time, the poet faces the challenge of choosing from among the conventional elements those that will create a meaningful sequence in which the sounds, rhythms, rhetorical devices, and images blend into a convincing representation of the alternating anxieties and comforts of desire. Thus, in stanza two, having finally arrived at a moment of calm with his focus on the "serene lady" ("la quoie" 22), it seems psychologically appropriate for the poet to be able to leave his introspection and introduce the more analytical concept of a woman who serves as a model for Nature. This conventional compliment, in the tradition of the *dolce stil nuovo*,[7] is expressed in comparatively long eight-syllable lines (24, 26, 28), helping to give the stanza the logical coherence that comes from a more sustained phrase. Meanwhile, the poet intersperses three-syllable lines ("par me foi," "je le croi") to continue the speaker's more personal-sounding effort at expressing confidence. This eight-line stanza follows a balanced, back-and-forth pattern in both meter and rhyme ($a^8b^3a^8b^3a^8b^3a^8b^3$) and creates a moment of stability in the poem, appropriately completed in the final two lines with a reference to the ideal of "atemprance" (30).

But as might be expected, any mention of this specific lady's "arroi" triggers a new set of emotional reactions in the lover, and stanza three shifts to a quicker, more nervous pace. Now, as the vocabulary leaves the abstract arena of the "fourme" and enters into a concentrated recitation of emotions, the ratio of short to long lines increases (*4,4,8,4,4,8...*) and the density of the rhyme pattern, which parallels the meter, intensifies (*aabaab...*). This time, the words expressing pleasure--"esjoïst," "resjoïst," "confort," "leece"--are clearly identified as antidotes (through the verbs "adoucist" and "esclaircist") to the "tristece" which underlies the love experience. But rather than dwelling on the obvious opposition which has been created, as one might expect in a poem based on tensions, the persona follows a more subtle associative link between the way the lady's bearing brightens his sadness and the way Love itself has improved his formerly rude and ignorant behavior (40). Instead of disappearing, the tension has shifted from one set of oppositions to another, laying groundwork for the next set of conventional--and thus again recognizably idealized--elements.

If the purpose of the *lay* is indeed to represent the tensions of the love experience, then it is important that the poem account for the full range of expressive modes, including not only the appropriate feelings and thoughts, but also the characteristic narrative moments associated with love in traditional literature. Having mentioned "jonece" in stanza three, Froissart's persona moves in stanza four--apparently through the trigger of memory--to a retelling of the first moment when he loved his lady, a reaction attributed, predictably, to the image of the lady's "semblant / Douls et riant" (52-53) and characterized as a form of voluntary servitude. With its unsteady rhythm (*3,4,7,7,3,4,7,7...*) and unevenly matched rhyme (*aaabaaab...*) the stanza hesitates and surges forward in a motion reminiscent of the uncertainty of youth, suggesting only through the presence of words such as "rendi" and "dangier" the underlying threat that the naive boy willingly endures. Indeed, his determination at this point in the poem is so strong that the fourth stanza is followed by another in similar form where conventional references to May and its catalogue of flowers--"roses, lis et glai"(65-66)--reassure the audience of the lover's familiarity with the conventional garden of Love.

And yet the intimate knowledge of Love brings with it, in the same stanza, a new tension, this time one that is central to the performative nature of the *lay* itself. For it is here that the persona is given a "trés douce ordenance" (71), a command to write which, like love itself, promises both difficulty and rewards. As the longest and most complex of the lyric forms, the *lay* holds within it the potential for earning relief ("aligance") from sufferings ("tous mes mauls"), seeming to offer an escape from the very tension that the poem recreates. The struggle for comfort is associated with the concept of deserving ("desservi" 78), providing momentarily the possibility that the dedicated poet/persona--the one who offers an ideologically pure and aesthetically pleasing representation of the love experience--can resolve his own dilemma.

It is no doubt for this very reason that the poem at this point takes its most dramatic turn toward the negative. After having spent the first five stanzas of the poem trying to focus on the joy of serving his lady and the hope that comes from loyal obedience, the poet who would continue to dwell optimistically on the chances of his own success would risk misrepresenting the true nature of love, and thus necessarily create his own failure. With the sudden introduction of "Fortune, li perverse / Et diverse" (80-81) at this point in the poem, the poet/lover avoids this error, not only continuing his careful depiction of the violent associative shifts that occur in the mind of a lover living in a heightened state of emotional tension, but also suggesting that *fin' amors* has a place in the larger context of human experience, interconnected with other issues of moral and spiritual significance. While the lover's concern that Fortune sets a man "en haut" and then sends him reversals (86-87) does not lead him to the total rejection of pursuits of pleasure that a more complete Boethian argument might urge, the reminder of Fortune as an irresistible force effectively draws upon the authority of a well-known philosophical doctrine that influenced many of the century's most important writers and thinkers. Furthermore, as the complaint against Fortune goes on for three full stanzas, it gathers rhetorical force, first through a rhythmically even stanza of hexameters introducing the example of a holy hermit in a pattern of feminine rhyme (96-111), and then in a catalog of ancients ("Absalom,/ Priamon / Ne le roi Lamedon ... 117-124) set in an insistent meter alternating three short lines with two longer ones *(3,3,3,6,6/3,3,3,6,6)* in all masculine rhyme. The resulting combination of emotional intensity, intellectual authority, and poetic virtuosity builds a convincing picture of a poet/lover who is indeed worthy of emotional relief.

With the difficulty of the enterprise now fully focused on the issue of Fortune, the tensions of the poem are carefully redefined in the concluding four stanzas. While at first the lover admits that his heart greatly fears ("s'effree" 132), his decision to give himself over completely to his lady ("ja donnee dou tout et voee" 148-49) creates a resolve that leads to philosophical triumph. Having now seen more clearly the nature of Fortune, the poet/lover realizes that remaining steadfast ("en fermeté" 177) and serving unfailingly ("sans partir" 179) without direct regard to outcome ("Quanque soit" 174) is in fact the way to enslave Fortune ("Fortune asservir" 181), creating a new kind of hope. His understanding at the end that he must honor his lady, lead a life of reflection, and speak of it always (193-204) lies within a system of oppositions even more intense than the one at the beginning of the poem, for now he is taking positive action in resistance to Fortune, which "attacks / And misleads / And deceives / And tortures so many hearts" (210-13). What is essential in the movement of this poem is that the exploration of the lover's experience has not merely led back to the same dilemma that the poet faced in the beginning. The final tension is defined not only through the opposition between personal joy and sorrow, which will remain as an inescapable element of any true lover's experience, but also through the now predominant battle to overcome Fortune through Hope. The complex structure and patterns of association that define the *lay* as a genre have allowed the poet to demonstrate how the subtle movements and shifting tensions of the lover's experience are part of a process that is never resolved, but continually moving towards a higher, ever more idealized, plane.

The governing principles illustrated in Lay 3 are important ones for anyone hoping to understand the function of conventional language in the medieval lyric system as a whole. Because the poet has many conventional words, images, and allusions to choose from, the overt signs of the lover's sufferings and comforts are never exactly the same in any two poems, giving the superficial impression that each of the *lays* treats an entirely separate theme. While in Lay 3 it is Fortune that acts as the primary obstacle to happiness and Hope that is the balancing consolation, other *lays* depend upon different combinations of forces. In Lay 4, for example, the Lady's refusals act as arrows wounding the heart, while comfort comes from the poet's contemplation of her beauty. In Lay 10, on the other hand, a lover who cannot find even the joy of a pitying look from his Lady imagines the comfort he would receive if only he could find a worthy confidant. The images and surface meanings of these two poems are quite distinct, yet underneath the expressed ideas in each case is the same fundamental pattern in which suffering and comfort are intricately interwoven. The noble lover demonstrates his worthiness on one level through his command of the conventions themselves, repeating, for example, the familiar litany of the "wound" that "invades" and "assails" his heart, which "cannot long withstand such attack" (4, 25-29). But, more importantly, the esoteric nature of the poem's structural arrangement allows the poet to demonstrate his understanding of a higher, much more difficult concept which, in its purity and nobility, defies direct expression. As the poet can show only through his sudden shifts from exultation to despondency and back again, the joys and agonies of love are interdependent, with each emotion heightening the other. It is only because the lover is totally enthralled by his lady's virtues that his vulnerability reaches the depths of his soul; the totality of his suffering, in turn, makes the beauty of the lady--or even the chance to talk about it with a friend--the only meaningful pleasure in life. In short, the true lover is in a constant and volatile state of tension between happiness and despair, and the associative structure of the *lay* provides the vehicle for conveying that tension poetically. Thus, as the poet chooses the particular experiences and images that make up the mosaic of familiar conventions on the surface of the poem, he must both develop a convincing picture of a single aspect of the conventional tradition and put the elements together in a way that communicates this essential higher truth.

The tension between joy and suffering in the *lays* is expressed in part by the intricacies of their stanzaic patterns, which sometimes include antithetical structures (mirror reversals) in the first and second halves of stanzas, as well as divisions into quarter stanzas and even smaller units. The identity of form between the first and last stanzas is often reinforced by the repetition in the final lines of an important opening image or idea, so that there is a sense of having returned to the point of origin,[8] though certainly by a complex and involved path. In Lay 4, for example, the poet begins by saying that Love has commanded him to compose a *lay* but that he does not know how he can do it with any joy, since he has been suffering for such a long time. Subsequent stanzas use such conventional images as the prolonged assault, the arrows of love, and the loss of health to express the poet's unhappiness. These images are balanced by occasional glimmers of hope, the "esperance, / Qui tous biens avance" (98-99). Nowhere in the poem's 238 lines does the poet ever make a second reference to his assigned task of writing a *lay*, but as the poem draws to a close, he gains more and more confidence in his lady's goodness, balancing his earlier despair with a feeling of contentment. In the final lines of the poem, it becomes apparent that in the process of reaching a resolution to the unhappiness that would have kept the poet from writing his *lay*, he has, in fact, written it:

> Ma dame adiés servirai,
> Car mieuls ne puis vraiement
> Tamps ne jouvent
> Emploiier. Dont de coer gai,
> Atendans son bon talent,
> Trés liement
> Nuit et jour je chanterai. (232-38)

> [I will serve my lady always,
> For truly I cannot spend
> My time or youth
> In any better way. And so with happy heart,
> Awaiting her desire,
> Most joyously
> I will sing both night and day.]

The link between the final word "chanterai" and the assignment of the song-writing task over two hundred lines earlier is, admittedly, strained by a ten-stanza separation, but the length of the poem and the meandering path it travels have their own significance, since, as all of these *lays* demonstrate, true love demands dedication, struggle, and patience.

Probably the most important thing that can be learned from the *lays* is that, for Froissart, the use of traditional conventions and motifs was not a limitation on his artistry but a means of drawing upon a complex system of closely interrelated ideas. The unity of these poems is not only that of a speaker's emotional experience but also that of the system of ideas itself, which, because it has been so carefully defined within the culture, allows the poet to assume the audience's understanding of basic concepts and pursue finer--and often more obscure--points of meaning. Froissart demonstrates his understanding of this function of form in the fact that he twice moves outside the usual system of ideas--that of *fin' amors*--and uses the *lay* form to convey the complexity of other spiritual experiences. In his elegiac "Lay de la Mort la Royne d'Engleterre" (Lay 7) he balances the conventional language of praise for a distinguished Lady with the language of a complaint against Death, suggesting the inseparability of love and grief. Similarly, in Lay 13, Froissart undertakes an expression of religious devotion, using the self-defined unity and balances of the poem's formal organization to free himself from some of the limitations of representational language and express his sense of the ultimate order that lies behind the apparent randomness of earthly life.[9] Although modern readers, with their differing cultural backgrounds and tastes, may never have access to all of the nuances of meaning conveyed in this way, Froissart's *lays* offer ample evidence of both his desire and his ability to achieve beauty and depth of thought, even within the most conventional and formalized of genres.

It is, then, within this context of a formal system that one can best approach a genre like the *chanson royale*. While the *lay* represents the most complex level at which the poet could attempt to communicate the dynamics of *fin' amors* as a whole, the *chanson royale*, like each of the shorter genres, serves a more limited, specific purpose, in this case providing a form for the highly polished rhetorical arguments of those who would wish to share their knowledge of appropriate attitudes and behaviors in love. If the *chanson* permits none of the variety of meters and rhymes that are characteristic of the *lay*, it instead requires a useful regularity within which the poet can make the audience aware of even the slightest variation in sound and phrasing. This fundamental formal difference in turn encourages an emphasis on word play and game that frequently puts the *chanson* into sharp contrast with the seriousness of most *lays*.

The fourteenth-century *chanson royale* is generally defined as a poem of five regular stanzas which ends with a short *envoi* addressed to an unspecified "prince." Though in its origin it appears to have been purely a song rather than a dance form,[10] the *chanson's* ten-syllable line and ten- to twelve-line stanza are similar enough to the line and stanza forms of the *ballade* that in some cases the *chanson* took on a refrain, as it does in Froissart's *pastourelles*. As its name indicates, the *chanson royale* was originally considered an elevated genre, having achieved a high level of dignity in the thirteenth century under Adam de la Halle.[11] By Froissart's time, however, it had become the most stereotyped of the fixed forms, and it was composed less often for a court audience than for competition at the meetings of bourgeois societies called *puys*, which were devoted to honoring the Virgin Mary.[12] It is the association of the poems with these celebrations that explains the use of the genre not only for secular love poems but also for the *chanson* "serventois de nostre dame." Froissart wrote *chansons* of both types, and the manuscripts indicate that all but one of his poems were "couronnés" as the winners of the competitions in which he participated.

Only three of Froissart's *chansons* are "chansons amoureuses," but even from such a small sample the distinctive characteristics of the genre are clear. Averaging around sixty lines, the poems are structurally arranged to provide, in each successive stanza, a slightly different treatment of the same central theme.[13] More specifically, the arrangement requires the poet to reveal a truth about the life of love in stanza one, provide supporting detail in stanza two, draw a conclusion about proper amorous behavior in stanza three, and summarize the lesson learned in stanza four. As this progression indicates, the genre tends to be didactic and the themes are easily identified. Froissart's three poems of this type include one which argues that the ennobling effects of love make it worthwhile whether the lover succeeds or not, another which shows that the lover's life is happy because of hope, and a third which maintains that a lover must avoid the dangerous assumption that a lady will be easily won just because she smiles and enjoys herself. As the controlling themes are presented in each of the poems, the rhetorical purpose of each stanza is often marked by a specific logical connector, such as the conjunction "for" ("car") to introduce the detailed restatement in stanza two and the phrase "in this situation" ("en cel estat") to begin the summary in stanza four. The beginning of stanza five is even more rigidly determined than the others, for at this point the speaker of the poem turns to address his lady, almost invariably with the words "Lady whom I love" ("Dame qui j'aim"). The main content of this stanza is a plea for mercy which takes the poem from a theoretical to a personal level, thus emphasizing the speaker's own involvement in the life of love, as well as balancing the mainly logical structure of the first four stanzas with a reminder of the emotional tension that holds a lover on the thin line between hope and despair. The whole poem is summed up, finally, in a three- to five-line *envoi*, which restates the main theme in terms of the speaker's own resolve to continue loving and to behave as a true lover should.

As this overview of the stanzaic structure indicates, both the range of possible themes and the manner of developing arguments are quite restricted. Moreover, there is hardly any more room for originality in the rhyme scheme, which, with the exception of Chanson 3,[14] follows a standard pattern of *ababccddede* for the five main stanzas and ends with an *envoi* repeating the pattern of the last five lines.[15] It is perhaps the very rigidity of the genre which made it so popular at the *puys*, for, as Poirion explains, it was not uncommon for inexperienced writers, wishing to imitate "les chefs-d'oeuvres," to copy only exterior form, naively believing that they had succeeded as poets if they could find enough proper sentiment and rhyming words to fill out the stanzas.[16] For Froissart, however, the genre's demanding patterns of versification were by no means merely an end in themselves; in poems of considerable complexity, he combined adherence to rules of form with carefully chosen rhetorical devices, clever word play, and graceful variations in rhythm, making his poetry as elegant and subtle as was the system of ideas within which he wrote.

Both Froissart's rhetorical skill and his command of rhythm are apparent in Chanson Amoureuse 2. In the first stanza, the main theme--that the life of love brings joy to the lover--is first plainly stated and then illustrated through enumeration:

> Trés gaie vie est d'amie et d'amant
> Qui justement le scet considerer,
> Car li parler, li signe, li samblant,
> Li douls regart, li venir, li aler
> Li vrai complaint, li maintient gai et gent,   5
> Li biel priier et li detriement

Sont ordonné pour tous coers esjoïr.
Dont, quant l'estat amoureus je remir,
Je di que c'est la plus trés gaie vie
Que bons coers puist prendre ne poursievir,   10
S'est euwireus qui jones s'i otrie.

> [The life of both the lover and beloved
> Is rightly considered a very happy one,
> For the discourse, the signs, the expressive glances,
> The tender looks, the meeting, the going away,
> The heartfelt sighs, the graceful and noble manners,
> The beautiful words of entreaty and sweet delay
> Are such as must bring joy to every heart.
> Therefore, when I consider the ways of love,
> I say it is the happiest life of all
> That a person with a pure heart can pursue,
> So he who yields to love in youth is fortunate.]

Car d'amours sont li fait si souffissant
Qu'on ne les poet prisier ne exposer;
C'est en aler, en penser, en priant,
Qu'on voit couleurs palir, taindre et muer,   15
Simple estre amant et amee ensement.
Par douls complains couvient l'amant souvent
Trés humlement eviers sa dame offrir
Corps, coer, penser, foy, entente et desir,
Et s'a tousjours esperance si lie;   20
Se de merci ne devoit ja joïr,
Se tient il bien sa painne a emploiie.

> [For the actions of people in love are of such
>   great consequence
> That they cannot be properly valued or explained;
> It is in the going, the imagining, the beseeching,
> That colors change and lovers grow pale and blush,
> Equally timid in loving and being loved.
> Often, in gentle complaint, the lover
> Must very humbly offer his lady
> Body, heart, thought, faith, will, and desire,
> And thus he always maintains kind hope;
> Even if he must not yet enjoy mercy,
> Yet he considers his pain worthwhile.]

Et lors qu'amans a le coer si engrant
De ses secrés humlement recorder,
Uns vrais desirs le muet. La aimme tant,   25
De si fin coer et de si vrai penser,
Que, quant il voelt parler trés sentamment,
Plaisance si habondament l'esprent
Que il ne puet parler ne bouce ouvrir;
La le couvient palir, taindre et fremir.   30
Vivre en cremeur, monstrer chiere asouplie,
Taire et servir, nuit et jour obeïr:
Tel sont li fait d'amant enviers amie.

[And when the lover's heart becomes so eager
To relate its secrets in humility,
He is stirred with true desire. He loves her so,
With such pure heart and with such true thoughts,
That when he wishes to speak with great feeling,
Pleasure catches him on fire with power so great
That he can neither speak nor open his mouth;
Then he must turn pale, blush and tremble.
To live in fear, show a saddened face,
Be quiet and serve, obey her night and day:
Such are the acts of the lover towards the beloved.]

En cel estat amoureus et plaisant
Vorroit amans toutdis sa vie user,   35
Et s'aucuns fais entreprent d'abondant,
Foible li sont et legier a porter,
Car li espoir de merci qu'il atent
Li donnent foi, vigeur et sentement
De ses grietés legierement souffrir,   40
Car vis li est que, s'il pooit venir
Au noble don que dame a en baillie,
Il ne poroit pour servir desservir
Les biens qu'aroit receü ceste fie.

[In this amorous and pleasing state
The lover should always wish to spend his life,
And even if he undertakes a great many feats,
They will seem small to him and easy to bear,
Because his hopes for the mercy he awaits
Give him the faith, energy and depth of feeling

To bear his pains easily,
For it seems to him that, if he could acquire
The noble gift that is in the lady's power,
He could not through any amount of service deserve
The riches that he would in such a case receive.]

Dame qui j'aim, ou tout bien sont manant,   45
Faite pour tous amans enamourer,
Voelliés en vous mettre pité, car quant
Priier vous voel, si crieng le refuser
Que povoir n'ai, avis he hardement
De vous priier si trés parfaitement   50
Que bien en ai l'entente et le desir,
Et se ne sai comment puisse avenir
A la merci de vous, dame agensie,
Se par pité n'en laissiés couvenir
Amours, ma dame, a cui mon coer s'afie.   55

[Beloved lady, in whom all goodness dwells,
Made to make all lovers fall in love,
Please put pity in your heart, for when
I wish to enteat you, I so fear your refusal
That I have no power, judgment or courage
To make my humble suit as perfectly
As I indeed intend and desire to do.
And so I do not know how I can attain
Your mercy, noble lady, unless in pity
You allow love to take its course,
My lady, in whom my heart trusts.]

Princes, espoir me donne souvenir,
Quoique ma dame ait refus sans partir,
Encor sera ma priiere essaucie:
C'est li confors qui me fait gais tenir
Et qui le plus me poet donner aÿe.   60

[Prince, hope leads me to believe,
Though my lady has refused incessantly,
My prayer will still be answered:
This is the source of comfort that keeps me happy
And can most surely give me the help I need.]

The catalog of features that characterize the amorous life in lines 3 through 6 provides a typical example of the technical skill that allows Froissart's *chansons* to rise above mere didacticism. The list is conventional in both its content and wording, but its placement in the stanza gives it particular rhetorical strength, building, as it does, from the simple opening statement that the life of love is a "trés gaie vie" to the much more intense assertion that it is "la plus trés gaie vie / Que bons coers puist prendre ne poursievir." The strong transitional "dont" and the introductory "Je di" before the second statement of theme add even more weight to the final four lines of the stanza, while also reminding the audience of the presence of a persona who is establishing his credibility through the strength of his art. The opening rhetorical argument accordingly ends on an emphatic, maxim-like generalization recommending love as the most "fortunate" of pursuits for any young man.

Much of this stanza's effectiveness depends on patterns of sound and Froissart's ability to make the most of the caesura, which, in the decasyllabic line, ordinarily falls after the fourth syllable.[17] Froissart uses the slight natural pause at the caesura to set off important words and to change the pace of lines, creating patterns of rhythm that reinforce the emphasis inherent in the rhetorical structure. In the very first line, for example, the caesura falls after "Trés gaie vie," a phrase which is particularly significant because it introduces a generalized image that will be clarified and expanded upon throughout the entire poem. Although the phrase appears to be very short, the pronunciation of the final "-e" on "gaie" slows the rhythm of the line; the resulting impression of length is reinforced by contrast with the repetition of sounds in the second part of the line, where the paired words "*d'*amie et *d'*amant" move along quite quickly. Once this rhythmical pattern is established in the first line, it is echoed in line two, a subordinate clause which is appropriately linked through its sound pattern with what has come before. Here again, the four syllables before the caesura move slowly in contrast to the alliterated second group of words, so that "justement" receives more emphasis than "le *s*cet con*s*iderer." Once more, the pattern of sound draws attention to the meaning of the line.

As the list of features characterizing the life of love begins in line 3, the alliterative pairing of the second line is repeated in "li *s*igne, li *s*emblant," maintaining a pleasing continuity of the sound combinations already established. At the same time, however, this third line marks the beginning of a new, three-part rhythmic pattern: now the line will be divided not only at the caesura (following "car li parler"), but also between syllables seven and eight, in the middle of the last "half" of the line. By creating an additional rhythmic unit, this arrangement allows the poet to draw attention to a greater number of the features of the amorous life, thus giving the entire passage more rhetorical weight. The three-part division is clearly marked in lines 3 and 4 by the commas and the repetition of "li," but the underlying two-part structure of the basic decasyllabic line is subtly maintained by the semantic pairing of the words following the caesura, first in "li signe, li semblant" and then in "li venir, li aler." With the pairing of the adjectives "gai et gent" in the fifth line, the sense of having three semantic units in the line remains, so that the shift back to a two-part rhythm, marked by the comma after "complaint," is almost imperceptible. As the sentence draws to an end, line 6, which is rhythmically regular and unalliterated, flows smoothly into the equally regular line 7, gaining momentum through enjambement and closing with finality on the important word "esjoïr."

The sudden stop at this point in the stanza marks a significant rhetorical break. The stop is made longer by the pause after "Dont," so that the emphatic restatement of theme in the final lines is set apart as a formal conclusion. In line 9, the phrase "trés gaie vie" again receives emphasis, this time because the staccato series of one-syllable words leading up to it ("Je di que c'est la plus . . .") minimizes the caesura and pulls the rhythm along to the end of the line. At this point, enjambement with line 10 allows the statement to continue unbroken through the strongly alliterated "*p*uist *p*rendre ne *p*oursievir," so that the simultaneous completion of the superlative assertion, the alliterated phrase, and the rhetorical pattern creates a climax and a short pause before the poet makes his final, more specific point about the value of the life of love for a young man. Here the word "euwireus" ("heureux" in modern French) is similar in position and significance to the words "trés gaie vie" in line one, and, like these earlier words, "euwireus" is placed before a strong caesura, this time one that gains emphasis from the fact that it marks the end of the main clause. The completion of this line with a relative modifier marks a return to more normal conversational rhythm, creating an effective contrast to the emphatic rhythms of lines 8 through 10 and bringing the stanza to a convincing yet graceful close.

In each of the stanzas that follow, Froissart displays similar skill in varying his rhythms and creating emphasis from the repetition of sound patterns and important words. In the third line of stanza two, for example, he returns to the three-part rhythm pattern introduced in the first stanza, using it this time to connect the outward acts of love already presented in stanza one to the more subtle, almost inexpressible, effects they are likely to produce. In line 14, the word "aler" is taken directly from the earlier list (line 4), while "en penser" and "en priant" recall the alliterated pair "li signe, li semblant" from line 3. The repetition of this familiar pattern is clearly useful for establishing the connection between the ideas in the two stanzas, yet, because the logical function of stanza two is to provide two distinct illustrations of the theme, beginning here with a tender image of timidity, Froissart does not extend the pattern into one climactic list, as he did in stanza one. Instead, he completes the idea of his first illustration quickly, using the sound repetition in "*amant* et *amee* ense*ment*" to draw attention to a thematically important phrase reminiscent of the words "d'amie et d'amant" from the poem's first line. The full stop at the end of line 16 marks the end of the first example; it is immediately followed by a second example of approximately the same length. With their conversational rising and falling rhythms, these two comparatively short clauses are well suited to the expository function typical of the second stanza in the *chanson royale*, preparing logically for the presentation of proper behavior in stanza three ("Taire et servir, nuit et jour obeïr" 32), the cleverly phrased lesson in stanza four ("Il ne poroit pour *servir* des*servir*" 43), and the plea to the lady in stanza five ("Voelliés en vous mettre pité" 47).

In this kind of fourteenth-century lyric poetry, the importance of being able to express such amorous "doctrine" in a style that is both rhetorically powerful and rhythmically graceful cannot be overestimated, for as the poet takes on the voice of the lover, he also takes on many aspects of the idealized lover's role. In conforming to his lady's often arbitrary demands and in going through all the proper stages and predetermined activities of the life of love, the perfect lover must still appear sincere, spontaneous, and adept at what he does if he is to be judged worthy of acceptance. Similarly, in composing his love poems, the poet assumes the arbitrary difficulties of form, but he must also write "selonc ce que mon coer sent"--in accordance with the feelings of his heart--as Froissart stresses in one of his *lays*.[18] The poet shows evidence of his sincerity both in his willingness to subject himself to difficult rules and in his apparent ease at overcoming the difficulty, for with a high enough level of inspiration and hope, the deserving lover can achieve a level of verbal skill allowing him to meet any challenge. As Froissart explains in Chanson 1,[19]

> Car souvenirs enracine en soi l'ente
> De vrai espoir; c'est li confors qu'il croit.
> Or vient avis, qui de sens le pourvoit,
> Et biaus parler ossi en lui descent. (37-40)

> [For the memory of sympathetic glances plants
> The seed of true hope in his heart; there is
>   comfort in this thought.
> Then   wisdom   comes,   and   provides   him   with   good
>   judgment,
> And eloquence descends on him as well.]

Only the lover who can master the art of expressing himself with passion while still remaining within the bounds of decorum has any hope of winning his lady; thus, on a symbolic level, graceful obedience to the rules that govern the writing of these poems is as essential to their artistic success as proper amorous behavior is to success in the game of love.

That the pursuit of love is often treated as an elaborate game suggests the potential for an element of play in the poetry of love as well, both in the attitudes expressed by the lovers and in the language that is an integral part of their relationship. Froissart incorporates both forms of play into Chanson 3, a poem denouncing the foolishness of any man who believes that a lady is easily won merely because she is pleasant and courteous:

Chanson Amoureuse 3

> Pour ce qu'on voit les dames deduisans
> En pluiseurs lieus et biaus samblans monstrer
> Par leurs bontés aux petis et aux grans,
> Et qu'on les voit humlement converser,

Rire en parlant, courtoisement jeuer,   5
Dient aucuns, par outrageus cuidier,
Qu'il ne faut fors hardiement priier
Qu'en dame lors ne soit merci trouvee;
Mais tels y vont a le fois assaiier
Aux quels elle est estragnement veee.   10

    [Because one sees ladies enjoying themselves
    In various places and seeming friendly
    In their goodness to both the humble and the great,
    And because one sees them conversing in a familiar
        way,
    Laughing in their talking, playing courteously,
    Some say, through outrageous presumptuousness,
    That it is necessary only to ask very boldly
    In order to find mercy in such a lady;
    But the ones who put this to the test are those
    To whom she is distantly forbidden.]

Car se dame est de soi esbanoians,
Humainne a tous, courtoise en biau parler,
S'avoec tout ce estoit merci donnans
Tout ossitost qu'on l'iroit demander,
Il ne fauroit jamais Amours merler   15
Dou don d'otroi que dame a a baillier;
Sens ne Cremeurs n'i aroient mestier,
Car sans honneur seroit mercis donnee.
Or voelt Amours, pour dames essaucier,
Qu'elle soit trop plus closement gardee.   20

    [For if a lady is making herself merry,
    Kindly to all, courteous in refined conversation,
    And if in addition she were granting mercy to
        everyone
    As soon as he would come asking,
    It would never be necessary to mingle Love
    With the permission to court that is the lady's to
        give;
    Neither Wisdom nor Fear would be involved,
    For mercy would be given without honor.
    But Love desires, in order to exalt the lady,
    That she be much more closely guarded in her behavior.]

Si que en dame est Sens et Cremeur poissans
Au los d'onneur pour merci refuser.
Quant dame jeue evoecques les jeuans
Et cuidans cuide en lui merci trouver,
Espoir anchois qu'il soit espris d'amer,   25
Dont fait refus ouvrer de son mestier
Sens et Cremeur, qui ont a consillier
Dame. Adont est si close li entree
D'otroi qu'il faut cuidant pourpos cangier,
Car falli a a sa folle pensee.   30

> [Thus Wisdom and Fear are powerful elements in a lady's
> Reputation of honor because of the way they refuse mercy.
> When a lady makes merry with other merry-makers
> And a presumptuous man presumes her easily won,
> He begins to hope before truly beginning to love,
> And therefore Wisdom and Fear, who have the task
> Of advising the lady, through their craft create
> Refusal. Then the access to amorous success
> Is so shut off that the presumptuous one must
>   change his plans,
> For he has failed in his foolish intentions.]

Ensi cuidiers fait abuser cuidans,
Car il proumet ce qu'il ne poet donner;
Dont qui le croit, il est moult ignorans.
Mais qui se voelt parfaitement fonder,
Il doit Amours servir, croire et amer   35
Dame, et s'elle est humle a esbanoiier,
Don de merci, qui tant fait a prisier,
N'est point pour ce sitost abandonnee,
Car il en sont Sens et Cremeur wissier,
Tant qu'Amours plest qu'a l'amant soit greee.   40

> [Thus presumptuousness deceives the presumptuous man,
> For it promises what it cannot deliver;
> So whoever believes it is full of ignorance.
> But whoever wishes to establish himself perfectly
> Must serve Love, believe in and love
> His lady; and if she is unassuming in amusing herself,
> The gift of mercy, which is so valuable,
> Is not because of this so soon given up,

For Wisdom and Fear are its doorkeepers,
Until Love pleases that it be bestowed on the lover.]

Dame qui j'ains trés belle et trés plaisans,
Li biaus deduis que vous savés monstrer,
Vos gratieus maintiens et avenans,
Me font souvent de desir embraser,
Mais quoiqu'ensi vous saciés deporter,   45
Vo mot sont si de refus coustumier
Qu'a cuidier n'ai que faire d'apoiier.
Or m'est d'amours plaisance presentee,
Si que j'en vifs en joieus desirier
En atendant merci la desiree.   50

[Most beautiful and pleasing lady whom I love,
The charming pleasures that you know how to show,
Your gracious and pleasing conduct,
Often make me burn with desire,
But although you too can frolic in this way,
You speak words of refusal so frequently
That I have no reason to behave presumptuously.
Now the pleasure of love is presented to me,
So that I live in joyous desire
Awaiting the mercy I desire.]

Li homs n'a pas science en lui fondee
Qui de dame cuide otroi eslegier
Sitost qu'en lui voit ne jeu ne risee.

[A man is lacking in wisdom and in knowledge
If he believes he has acquired a lady's favor
As soon as he sees her laughing or at play.]

Like Chanson 2, this poem begins with an assertion that is
expressed in graceful, rhythmic language, using concentrations of
similar sounds, like "*d*ames *ded*uisans," and natural pairs, like "aux
petits et aux grands," to reinforce his careful matching of syntax to the
phrasing created by the caesura. Also like the first stanza of Chanson
2, this one builds towards a rhetorical climax, here relying not on the
short list of behaviors in lines 5 and 6, but instead on the fact that the
stanza begins with a subordinate clause that is sustained through the

enjambement of the first three lines and not fully resolved until the completion of the main clause in lines 7 and 8. In fact, in setting up what will turn out to be a playful argument, the poet follows all the usual patterns, with the introduction of numerous logical connectors throughout ("mais" 9, "car" and "se" 13, "car" 18, "or" 19, "si que" 21, etc.) and an appropriate supporting explanation ("esbanoians" 11, "humainne" and "courtoise" 12) in stanza two. Even at the beginning of stanza three, the doctrine expressing the importance of "sens et cremeur" is exactly what the form demands, since, in order to maintain his status as a worthy lover, the poet cannot deviate from either the approved attitudes of *fin' amors* or the discipline required to express them.

But as a suffering lover whose sensitivities have been heightened through dedication to love service, what the poet/persona can do is to display virtuosity in his poetic skill and delight both himself and his Lady with the playfulness of language. This is what happens in lines 23-25, when the poet begins juxtaposing various forms of the words "jeuer" and "cuidier," setting up a pair of lines where the lady "jeue evoeques les jeuans" and the "cuidans cuide en lui merci trouver," leading to the cleverly balanced result that the misguided suitor of the example "begins to hope before truly beginning to love" ("*Esp*oir *an*chois qu'il soit *esp*ris d'*am*er"). Because the presumptuous lover is clearly in error, the tone of foolishness created by the poet's lighthearted language is entirely appropriate and even serves to reinforce the impression of the poet/lover's clarity of vision. Similarly, in the next stanza, Froissart continues playing with the word "cuidier" and uses the emphasis gained to introduce a surprisingly blunt statement of opinion:

> Ensi cuidiers fait abuser cuidans,
> Car il proumet ce qu'il ne poet donner;
> Dont qui le croit, il est moult ignorans. (31-33)

> [Thus presumptuousness deceives the presumptuous man,
> For it promises what it cannot deliver;
> So whoever believes it is full of ignorance.]

There is no lack of seriousness in the message, but rather, since the speaker must prove himself superior to the "ignorant" ones he denounces, his delivery gains power from a display of wit.

By the time the poet addresses his lady in stanza five, he has firmly established the foolishness of any fellow who would dare be presumptuous, and he has made it clear that he is not himself that sort of fool. But the word play that has dominated earlier parts of the poem has really been only a preparation for a more subtle bit of psychological playfulness at the end. For once the poet has offered his lady the traditional high praise for her charm and gracious conduct, the "biaus deduis" (42) that has been the inspiration for his desire, he suddenly reveals, with a wonderfully understated irony, the disturbing paradox of his personal situation :

> Mais quoiqu'ensi vous saciés deporter,
> Vo mot sont si de refus coustumier
> Qu'a cuidier n'ai que faire d'apoiier. (45-47)

> [But although you too can frolic in this way,
> You speak words of refusal so frequently
> That I have no reason to behave presumptuously.]

Although the poet has spent the entire first four stanzas of his poem building his case against the temptation to be presumptuous, he now reveals the sad truth. For him, there is no danger of overstepping the bounds of propriety because his lady has left no room for misunderstanding. Given the futility of his situation, Froissart has his speaker omit the direct plea for mercy typical of the fifth stanza in other *chansons*, allowing the juxtaposition of his own highly respectful attitude and his lady's apparently unnecessary harshness to speak for itself. With the oblique approach of one who understands game-playing very well, he concludes with the simple comment that he will continue to live in "joyous desire" while "waiting" for the mercy he so obviously deserves.

As this example illustrates, the strict conventions of the fixed-form lyrics allow the poet to rely on the audience's expectations to provide a context for interpreting even the smallest deviations from tradition. The importance of the audience's knowledge of the accepted forms is particularly apparent in another standard version of the *chanson*, the *chanson serventoise*, for the poet's task in these poems is to express praise and devotion to the Virgin Mary while following the same order of ideas--and even some of the same conventional wording--as in the love poems. In some of the local *puys*, the rules were so restrictive as to require that a *chanson serventoise* be based on a particular *chanson amoureuse*, with the poet borrowing the first and last lines of each successive stanza and using his virtuosity to turn the meaning of the interior of the stanzas from the secular to the religious.[20] Froissart's two *chansons serventoises* use the language of secular love only for the first line of each stanza, rather than for the first and the last, and there is no known source for his opening lines, which may simply follow familiar phrasing that could be common to any number of poems. But even in this less restricted format, the pleasure of the audience must have come in large part from hearing the poet turn the well-known language of love away from its accustomed direction and apply it to another very popular subject. The honor that was intended for the Virgin would no doubt have been enhanced by the poet's success in playing a challenging and quite serious game of language:

Chanson Serventoisc 6

Pour grasce acquerre, honneur, loenge et pris,
Doient tout coer servir devotement
La Virgne en qui dignement fu compris
Li Fils de Dieu, par le promovement
De la trés sainte et pure deïté.   5
Et ce fu trés divinement ouvré,
Car, sans avoir en lui corruption
Ne sentement de generation,
Conchut le Fil de Dieu, no fois l'afie,
Qui pour nous prist l'aministration   10
D'umanité, char, sanc, substance et vie.

[In order to obtain grace, honor, praise and
    worthiness,
All hearts must devotedly serve
The Virgin in whom the Son of God was worthily
Contained, at the instigation
Of the most holy and pure deity.
And this was accomplished in a most divine way,
For, without having in her the corruption
Or the desires of carnal knowledge,

She conceived the Son of God, as our faith affirms,
Who took upon himself for us the governing
Of mankind, flesh, blood, human form and life.]

Se doit amans qui d'amer est espris
Loer ceste oevre et la Virgne humlement,
Et croire ossi que li Sains Esperis
Enama plus la Virgne entierement,   15
Pour sa parfaite et grande humilité,
Qu'il ne fesist pour sa virginité,
Car Dieu servoit de vraie entention;
Vie tenoit de contemplation,
Tous tamps estoit humle, devote et lie,   20
S'en a es chieus tele perfection
Que elle en est roÿne intronisie.

[And so a lover who is set afire with love
Must praise [God's] work and the Virgin humbly,
And believe also that the Holy Spirit
Began to love the Virgin even more
For her complete and endless humility
Than he did for her virginity,
For she served God with a pure heart;
She led a life of contemplation,
Always humble, devout and full of joy,
And therefore she attained such perfection
That she has been enthroned as heaven's queen.]

Or doit amans mettre entente et avis
A vous servir, Virgne, parfaitement
Et croire ossi qu'en es sains paradis   25
Fustes de Dieu essaucie ensement
Qu'en ou Lyban sont li cedre eslevé,
Ou que la palme en Cadés prent sousté,
Ou que la rose a sa plantation
En Jherico; car par election   30
Fustes ensi es sains chieux essaucie,
Et Sapience en fait bien mention,
Qui ces parlers approeve et segnefie.

[Now a lover must apply his will and desire
To serving you perfectly, Virgin,
And believe also that in holy paradise

You are exalted by God in the same way
That the cedars were raised in Lebanon,
Or that the palm in Kadesh took sustenance,
Or that the rose had its planting
In Jericho; for by divine election
You were thus exalted in the holy heavens,
And the Books of Wisdom, which announce and declare
These words, indeed make mention of it.]

S'est pour tous coers amoureus grans pourfis
De vous servir, Virgne, et savoir comment,   35
Puis que vos Fils fu en la crois transis
Et es sains chieux montés divinement,
Resgnastes vous cha jus en pureté,
Et puis vous fu par l'angle revelé
Que vos douls Fils, Peres d'une union,   40
Avoit ja fait vo preparation
Ens es sains chieux ou estiés dediie,
Car poëstés, virtus et treble et nom
Desiroient la sus vo compagnie.

[Thus it is a great advantage for all amorous hearts
To serve you, Virgin, and to know how,
After your Son died on the cross
And arose divinely into the holy heavens,
You reigned down here in purity,
And then it was revealed to you by the angel
That your gentle Son, together with the Father,
Had already prepared a place for you
In the holy heaven where you were consecrated,
For authority, virtue and the Trinity
Desired your company up there.]

Noble et plaisans en qui j'ai mon coer mis,   45
Virgne royaus, j'ai bien ce sentement
Que quant vos corps fu es sains chiex ravis,
Li douse apostle y furent proprement;
Par le plaisir de la divinité,
D'une nuee y furent aporté   50
Et furent tout a vostre assomption,
Et o vo Fil par consolation
Fustes es chiex solempnement ravie.

Chils vous donna la coronation,
Qui vous assist a sa destre partie.   55

> [Noble and pleasing one in whom I have placed my heart,
> Royal Virgin, I indeed believe
> That when your body was ravished into the holy heavens,
> The twelve apostles were there as they should be;
> At the pleasure of the divinity
> They were carried there on a cloud
> And were all at your assumption,
> And into the presence of your Son, your consolation,
> You were solemnly taken up to heaven.
> The one who performed your coronation
> Is the same one who set you at his right hand.]

Princes, la Virgne est la d'entention,
Resgnans es chiex en domination.
Or li prions qu'elle nous face aÿe,
Car bien poons par sa promotion
Des chieux avoir la glore auctorisie.   60

> [Prince, the Virgin is there for a purpose,
> Reigning in dominion in the heavens.
> Now let us pray to her that she will help us,
> For we can indeed, through her intervention,
> Have the praiseworthy glory of the heavens.]

The rhetorical parallels betweeen this poem and the *chansons amoureuses* are apparent both in the stong assertion of doctrine in stanza one and in the logical transitions that dominate the argument that follows. Stanza two, beginning with "Se doit," reinforces the admonition to serve the Virgin by focusing on the example of her humility, referring to her life of contemplation, and describing her as "humle, devote, et lie" (20), thus fulfilling the audience's expectation for a stanza of supporting explanation. Stanza three, beginning with "Or doit," turns to the issue of proper behavior, recommending that the devotee must apply his will and desire ("entente et avis") to serving perfectly and believing fully in the Virgin's exaltation. Likewise, stanza four follows the usual pattern of summarizing the lesson by beginning with the phrase "S'est pour tous coers amoureus grans pourfis / De vous servir," and stanza five turns directly to the lady (Virgne royaus") with a personal testimony of the speaker's devotion ("j'ai bien ce sentement"). Even the *envoi* serves its usual purpose of expressing resolve, asking the "Princes" to join in a prayer for assistance ("or li prions qu'elle nous face aÿe" 58). In all of its major features, the *chanson serventoise* replicates the formal perfection of the *chanson amoureuse*, appearing on its surface to be only a highly skilled expression of devotion.

What gives the form its power, however, is the implied comparison that continually takes place between religious and earthly love. In stanza three, for example, where the form might create an expectation for a list of flowers from the garden of love, the poem provides instead a scene of religious glory that includes the cedars of Lebanon, the palms of Kadesh, and the rose of Jericho (27-30).[21] In stanza four, where the secular Chanson 2 provides an explanation of the relationship between hope and endurance, this poem reminds the reader of the resurrection and the rewards that awaited the Virgin in return for her goodness and service on earth. Perhaps most striking of all, however, is the way that each stanza retains the language of secular love in its first line, with such references as the "amans qui d'amer est espris" (12) and the "coers amoureus" (34). By juxtaposing the different spheres of language, the poet creates moments of disorientation in which the audience must move back and forth between a concern for secular love and a desire for the exaltation of the Virgin. Although the heightening of consciousness created by the form is in complete harmony with the overt message of the poem, its subtlety makes it perhaps the more powerful reminder of the lover's need to look beyond earthly love for true virtue.

Just as the *chanson serventoise* creates meaning through the interplay between religious imagery and courtly form, the *chanson sotte*, a third type of *chanson royale* which had become popular in the festive atmosphere of the *puys*, is grounded in the juxtaposition of two existing literary traditions. In this case, the formal stanzas of the *chanson royale* are used as a framework upon which the poet builds an anti-courtly *descriptio* of excessive ugliness, creating a burlesque of the traditional head-to-toe portrait of beauty so common in medieval literature. The result is a full-scale parody of amorous conventions and poetic forms. Froissart's single example of the *chanson sotte* is typical in its depiction of "a lover who has chosen to love someone no one else could love."[22] In the opening lines, the poet introduces the same kind of wordplay used in his *chansons amoureuses*, though, appropriately, without the usual attempt at subtlety:

Chanson Royale 4 (Sotte)

Amours, par qui les lourdes et le lourt
Sont bien rataint de lourdement amer,
M'ont pourveü depuis un terme court
De dame amer ou il n'a qu'amender,
Car ses corps est ossi douls q'uns cierens.   5
Euwireus sui qu'elle a perdu les dens,
Car autrement ne m'euïst demoré
Drapiel entier; tout euïst deschiré.
Un usage a tel qu'a moi hape et tire,
Et quant par lui sont mi drap debieffé,   10
Elle ne sance apriés de moi maudire.

[Love, by which dull-witted women and men
Are surely condemned to love stupidly,
Has recently provided me a lady to love
Who cannot be improved in any way,
For her body is as gentle as a hackle.
I am lucky that she has lost her teeth,
For otherwise I would no longer have
A piece of cloth intact; she would have
        shredded it all.
She has a habit of grabbing and pulling on me,
And when my clothes have been torn to pieces,
She still doesn't stop cursing me.]

Je le trouvai l'autre ier en une court
Sus un fumier, preste pour remuer,
Et je li dis: "Ma dame, il fait la gourt;
Or vous voelliés un petit reposer   15
Et nous parrons d'amours tout a bon sens."
Et celle dont li estas est plus gens
Que d'un pourciel ort et embegaré,
M'a en soudain telement regardé
Que je vosisse adont estre en l'empire,   20
Car contre moi a un fourquié levé,
Et puis me dist: "Or cha, que voes tu dire?"

[I came upon her the other day in a courtyard
On a dunghill, ready to hurry away,
And I told her, "My lady, it is soft there;
Now be so kind as to stay and rest a little
And we will speak most sensibly of love."
And that woman whose condition is more noble
Than a soiled and filthy little pig's,
Suddenly looked at me in such a way
That made me wish to be far, far away,
For she raised a pitchfork towards me,
And then she said: "Now then, what do you wish to say?"]

"Dame," di jou, "Amours en mon coer sourt,
Car je le sens en mon corps haleter
Et je m'en doi aler a un behourt;   25
Pour vostre amour m'i vorrai esprouver,
Mais dittes moi, que crirai sus les rens?
Car je serai, je croi, de cheuls dedens."
Elle dist: "Fait criier a l'estonné,
Et se le pris conquers, j'ai volenté,   30
M'amour aras, qui est ossi entire
Que mi drapiel, qui sont tout ranoé.
Or soies preus, il te doit bien souffire."

["Lady, I said, "Love wells up in my heart,
For I feel it panting in my body
And so I must go away to a tournament;
There I will wish to prove myself for your love,
But tell me, what will I shout on the sidewalk?
For I believe I'll be among those in the lists."
She said: "Make the man you beat cry out,
And if you win the prize, it is my will that
You will have my love, which is as whole
As my clothes, which are all patched.
Now be valiant, this must be enough."]

"Dame," di jou, "vous serés sus un hourt;
La me verés les horions donner,   35
Mais se je truis le kokin et le sourt
Lequel on dist qu'il voet mes oes humer,
Je li donrai tel cop entre les gens
Qu'il s'en ira en sa maison dolens."

Lors dist ma dame: "Et qu'as tu en pensé?   40
S'a trestous ceuls qui ont a moi parlé
Tu voes avoir le debat ne l'estire,
Il te faudra, saches pour verité,
Plus q'un martir recevoir de martire,"

   ["Lady," said I, "you will be on a platform;
   There you will see me strike blows,
   Provided I find the beggar and the fool
   Who is said to want to sup on my eggs,
   I will give him such a blow between the legs
   That he will go away to his house grieving."
   Then my lady said, "And what are you thinking?
   If you wish to start a struggle or dispute
   With every one of those who've spoken to me,
   You will, truly, have to be willing to take
   More martyrdom than a martyr."]

Adont vei la le kokin qui acourt;   45
A ses nus bras vint ma dame acoler.
Lors m'avisai que, s'on ne le secourt,
Je li vodrai trop bien le dos fautrer,
Car je me tieng de lui trop mal contens.
Des nouviaus aus, dou pain et des herens,   50
Matons et bure, oes et bacon salé
A en l'escourc de ma dame aporté.
Quant cela vei, je n'euc talent de rire,
Ançois li di: "Ma dame, or ai prouvé
Que chils fols chi nostre amour fort
     desquire."   55

   [And then I saw the beggar running up;
   He came to embrace my lady with his bare arms.
   I thought to myself, if no one came to save him,
   I would like to thrash him soundly on his back,
   For I was really very unhappy with him.
   Some fresh garlic, and some bread and herring,
   Soft cheese and butter, eggs and salted bacon—
   My lady had brought [him] these things in her apron.
   When I saw that, I had no desire to laugh,
   But rather I said: "My lady, now I have proven
   That this fool here totally destroys our love."]

Princes, Amours m'ont lors se escaufé
Et parfette sotie, Diex leur mire,
Que j'ai ma dame et le kokin rué
En un ruiot, et la les laissai gire.

[Prince, I was then so enflamed by Love
And perfect foolishness, God bless them both,
That I hurled my lady and the beggar
Into a gully, and left them lying there.]

Although the opening lines have the syntactic structure of perfect
amorous discourse, the substitution of the words "lourdes," "lourt," and
"lourdement" for the expected courtly diction emphasizes the
heavy-handed satirical intention of the poem. In the phrase "de dame
amer," the Old French pronunciation of the final "r" allows the
possibility of a pun on the adjective "amer," suggesting that the subject
of the poem is a "bitter lady," although the poet does not see through
her faults until later in the poem. The aggressive, toothless woman,
who, we learn, is standing on a dung heap, provides an image in
striking contrast to the conventional beloved lady.[23]

Froissart's *chanson sotte* does not show the crudeness that often
characterized poems of this genre, and, since he included only one in
his collection, it seems likely that he did not take much interest in the
kind of blunt humor they required. But the typical characteristics of the
chanson sotte may have had some influence on his invention of the
historical *pastourelle*, for both use drama and dialogue to tell stories
from the point of view of a "roturier," creating either a contrast with
or a new perspective on aristocratic activities. In this particular poem,
the ridicule falls most strongly on the peasant lover, whose avowed
willingness to fight in a tournament for his lady ends abruptly when he
discovers that she has brought an apronful of his favorite foods to share
with his rival:

Des nouviaus aus, dou pain et des herens,
Matons et bure, oes et bacon sale
A en l'escourc de ma dame aporte.
Quant cela vei, je n'euc talent de rire . . .
(50-53)

[Some fresh garlic, and some bread and herring,
Soft cheese and butter, eggs and salted bacon—

My lady had brought [him] these things in her apron.
When I saw that, I had no desire to laugh]

The peasant's love, it turns out, can be destroyed merely by his jealousy over a homely gift, leading him, in the *envoi*, to the equally undistinguished act of throwing both his rival and his former lady into a gully. This conclusion, in direct contrast to the conventional *envoi* in which the poet resolves to continue loving in the most noble way possible, works particularly well as satire, since the speaker can comically claim to be "escaufé" (aroused or enflamed) by the power of love. As in his description of the unlovable lady, Froissart relies here on a type of humor that is far beneath the subtlety displayed in some of his *pastourelles* and *rondeaux*. But even though this poem is not typical of his style, the very fact that Froissart participated in the bourgeois satirical tradition is significant, for working with a form which relied so heavily on the audience's thorough knowledge of conventions no doubt contributed to his ability to see the subjects he was writing about from more than one perspective, even when he chose to stay within the boundaries of proper, formal poetic presentation.

Although Froissart's *chansons amoureuses* demonstrate considerable skill and grace, one problem with the genre in general is that the obligatory five-stanza structure allows the poet more space than is really necessary to develop the limited themes considered appropriate to the form. Often there is very little difference between what the poet says in his opening declaration of theme and in the four stanzas of variation which, to use Poirion's terminology, "radiate" from the same center.[24] If the audience delights in clever sound patterns and relishes the minute psychological distinctions made through the language of love--as Froissart's audience certainly did--then the *chansons amoureuses* can be judged successful as poetry. Even Froissart himself, however, chose to include only six *chansons* in his manuscripts, indicating perhaps that he found the rules that governed the genre too restrictive, the themes too didactic, or the substance of the poems a little thin. In contrast, by including dramatic dialogue, rather than mere amplification and examples, in the *chanson sotte* and the *pastourelles*, Froissart opened the door to livelier presentations with more of the density of meaning generally thought to be characteristic of good poetry today. As F.S. Shears has pointed out, the shorter lyrics likewise have a pleasing concentration of meaning, for "although we may not care for the lover's protracted companionship throughout a work of five thousand lines, his confidences arrest us when confined to the three strophes of the ballade or the seven lines of the rondelet."[25] These shorter genres, which are studied in Chapter 4, combine the linguistic skill demonstrated in the *chansons* with a succinctness of thought that is well suited to the expression of a lover's mood, the effusion of sentiment that comes from a pitying glance, or the glimpse of wisdom achieved through the experience of suffering. In these condensed poetic contexts, the mention of commonplaces such as lovesickness or the assaults of Cupid's arrows can call up in a few words a whole complex system of ideas, thus allowing the poet's single statement of theme in the refrain to take its place very neatly in the familiar context of the love experience as a whole.

Still, despite the attractiveness of the short forms, it would be a mistake to dismiss too quickly those lyrics that are by nature more diffuse, for even the *chansons royales*, with their predetermined logic and set themes, represent an important part of the overall aesthetic system within which Froissart moved and worked so comfortably. If the *lays* provide the groundwork for understanding the way that the poet could represent through form the complex web of relationships that shaped an entire system of thought, the *chansons* provide the first example of how certain elements of that system could be selected and patterned to reflect a particular, more narrowly defined, authorial stance. As the remaining chapters demonstrate, Froissart's artistry in all the fixed forms can be said to fulfill and expand upon these two fundamental functions.

Notes: Chapter II

1. Bastin, 16.

2. McGregor, 33.

3. Jean Maillard, *Evolution et Esthétique du lai lyrique des origines à la fin du XIVème siècle* (Paris: Université de Paris, 1961), 21. This published dissertation from the University's Séminaire de Musicologie provides a lengthy discussion of what is known about the origin and many varieties of *lays* in the Celtic, German, and Provençal languages, as well as in French.

4. Maillard, 23.

5. Poirion, 410-11.

6. McGregor's text reads "m'avoit"; he finds this line "unintelligible." Scheler suggests "m'anoit" for "m'avoit," and I have followed this suggestion in both my text and my translation.

7. One finds, for example, in Dante's *Vita Nuova*, Chapter XIX, a *canzone* in which Love says that the lady "is the best Nature can achieve, / And by her mold all beauty tests itself" ("ella è quanto de ben pò far natura; / per essemplo de lei bieltà si prova" 49-50; trans. Mark Musa, Bloomington: Indiana University Press, 1973). A similar idea is developed in Froissart's Ballade 38, where the lady is characterized as being made by Nature "pour regarder" (11) and being the "mesure" by which even Pygmalion would model beauty (19-21).

8. Poirion reserves the term "encerclement" for the *rondeau* and *virelay*, song-like forms in which the return of the refrain is much more evident. In writing about the "repetition progressive" of the *lay*, he is referring less to the movement of ideas than to the complicated schemes of rhyme and rhythm which change "progressively" in each stanza. For example, if the first stanza of a *lay* follows the rhyme pattern *aa bb cc dd*, the second stanza might multiply the pattern to get *aaaa bbbb cccc dddd*. For further discussion of this subject, see Poirion, 400-406.

9. For a more thorough discussion of this *lay* and its relationship to narrative context in Froissart's last *dit*, see Alice Planche, "Du Joli Buisson de Jonece au Buisson ardent: Le Lai de Notre-Dame dans le Dit de Froissart" in *La Prière au Moyen-Age: Littérature et civilisation* (Aix-en-Provence: Université de Provence, 1981), 395-413.

10. The origin of the *chanson royale* has not been clearly determined. Leonard E. Arnaud, in "The Sottes Chansons in Ms. Douce 308 of the Bodleian Library at Oxford," *Speculum*, 19 (1944), describes the genre as a variation upon the religious *serventois*, a form that was developed by minstrels belonging to benevolent organizations called *charités* (beginning as early as the year 1120) for the writing of poems in praise of the Virgin. As prosperous burghers joined the organizations in the twelfth and thirteenth centuries and the societies (now called *puys*) became more secular in nature, emphasis shifted away from adoration of the Virgin. Thus, though the religious poems had precedence historically, by Froissart's time the poems to the Virgin were clearly modeled after the love poems rather than the other way around.

11. Poirion, 362.

12. McGregor, 46. These bourgeois literary societies were quite widespread in Picardy and Flanders in the fourteenth century. Froissart's manuscripts indicate that his poems won prizes at Valenciennes (2, 5, and 6), Abbeville (3), and Lille (4).

13. Poirion refers to "un principe de rayonnement" according to which each stanza comes back "à la même suggestion du rhythme ou à la même idée du refrain" (361). Froissart's *chansons* do not have refrains, but the rhythm follows the same strict pattern in each stanza. More importantly, the ideas seem to be arranged "autour d'un centre virtuel, comme en une rosace," with each variation helping to complete the meaning of the central theme.

14. Chanson 3 uses a ten-line stanza, rhymed *ababbccdcd* with a short *envoi* rhymed *dcd*. Davidson, 229, quotes a passage from Eustache Deschamps' *Art de Dictier* indicating that the chanson royale

could have stanzas of ten, eleven, or twelve lines; Froissart does not use the twelve-line type.

15. The five-line *envoi* is the standard form as described by Deschamps. As indicated in note 12, Chanson 3 has a three-line *envoi*; Chanson 4, the only *chanson sotte* in the collection, has an *envoi* of four lines.

16. Poirion, 362.

17. See Baudouin, pp. xlix-lxi, for a more complete discussion of versification.

18. Lay 6, l. 21.

19. For the complete text and translation of Chanson 1, see Appendix A.

20. Poirion, 363. In *Themes and Images in the Medieval Religious Lyric*, Douglas Gray notes that there was a *puy* or *confrérie* in London in the fourteenth century which had functions similar to those in France, most likely including presentation of religious lyrics (n.9, 236). For examples of how the "erotic language of courtly literature" was used for religious expression in the less formally restrictive English tradition, see Gray's chapter on "Christ and the Virgin Mary," especially 91-94.

21. For a discussion of the traditional image of Mary as a rose, as well as other marian figures, see Gray, 88-90.

22. McGregor, 47. For a detailed discussion of the history and characteristics of this ironic subgenre, which can be traced back to Matthew of Vendôme's twelfth-century portrait of Beroe, see Jan Ziolkowski, "Avatars of Ugliness in Medieval Literature," *Modern Language Review* 79 (1984): 1-20. For background on the traditional formal description of beauty, see Derek S. Brewer, "The Ideal of Feminine Beauty in Medieval Literature, Especially 'Harley Lyrics,' Chaucer, and Some Elizabethans," *Modern Language Review* 50

(1955): 257-69, and Edmond Faral, *Les Arts poétiques du XIIe et du XIIIe siècle* (Paris: Champion, 1924), 75-84.

23. While the language and imagery of Froissart's poem are restrained in comparison to that of other poems of this type, certain features are quite typical of the tradition as Ziolkowski describes it. Particularly noticeable are the reliance on antithesis ("ossi douls qu'un cierens" 5), comparison to an animal ("un pourciel ort et embegaré" 8), and the suggestion that physiognomy reflects one's moral state ("m'amour aras, qui est ossi entire / Que mi drapiel" 31-32). For a contemporary example of the ironic *descriptio* carried out in full detail in Middle English, see John Lydgate's "Hood of Green" (incipit "My fayr lady, so fresh of hewe") in *Percy Society*. Vol. 2. *Early English Poetry, Ballades, and Popular Literature of the Middle Ages*, ed. James Orchard Halliwell and J. Payne Collier (London: Percy Society, 1840), 199-205.

24. Poirion, 361.

25. Shears, 217.

III

Pastourelles:
The Art of Multiple Perspectives

While the persona of the *chanson royale* may be said to represent Froissart's version of the worthy lover who proves himself through didactic elegance, the persona of the structurally similar *pastourelle* represents a more complex authorial stance that allows the poet to move beyond the narrow confines of *fin' amors* and explore other aspects of aristocratic life. Often praised but never analyzed in depth, the *pastourelles* combine lyric form with narrative and dramatic content, revealing more than any other poetic genre the poet-historian's keen eye as an observer of human behavior. In evaluating Froissart's works, most critics have shown interest only in the seven historical *pastourelles*, which, according to Ernst Hoepffner, constitute "un tout autre genre, tout nouveau . . . et inconnu avant Froissart."[1] But while Froissart's inclusion of historical subjects is significant, such a narrow focus does not do justice to his larger vision as a poet, for it fails to reveal how purposefully he adapted what was essentially an outmoded tradition to the job both of entertaining sophisticated patrons and of contributing to his broader message of chivalric revival.[2] The twenty known *pastourelles* include light-hearted satires of peasant life, idyllic visions of pastoral simplicity, and serious depictions of aristocratic responsibilities, as well as playful celebrations of the joys of living and a variety of respectful tributes to kings and patrons. Through his skillful handling of diverse subjects, perspectives, images, and tones, Froissart created a body of poems depicting the harmony of an idealized social structure that is both a pleasure to imagine and a thoughtful response to the changes taking place around him.

In choosing the *pastourelle* as a poetic vehicle, Froissart set himself apart from Machaut and other important poets of the day, for the traditional *pastourelle* was not among the "formes fixes" that so appealed to fourteenth-century tastes. Having flourished in both folk and courtly versions during the twelfth and thirteenth centuries, the *pastourelle* was judged by many in Froissart's day to have exhausted its potential for freshness, largely because of its limited subject matter. As William Powell Jones describes it, the traditional Old French *pastourelle* dramatized the "meeting of a knight and a shepherdess in the fields or near a wood, his proposals of love, and the subsequent success or failure of his attempt" to win her over.[3] The shepherdess herself was, as Jones points out, the "one constant element" in all poems in the genre; other typical elements included an early morning setting on a beautiful spring day, the image of the shepherdess singing or making a crown of flowers, and the popular motif of the ruse, which often allowed the girl to escape the knight's advances.[4]

By the time Froissart began writing poems in this mode, a number of court poets had already experimented with variations on the basic plot, the most important of which transformed the knight from an active participant into a disinterested aristocratic observer. In some of these poems, for example, the upper-class narrator stops to watch rustics at play and provides his audience with a description of their customs, music, and games, while in others he witnesses a love scene, a debate, or a quarrel.[5] It is this later tradition that Froissart both followed and expanded upon, using the contrasting perspectives of the observer and the observed as a point of entry into his subject. At the same time, Froissart reinforced the importance of the aristocratic perspective by setting his poems into what is essentially a *chanson royale* form: five regular stanzas of eleven to sixteen lines each, followed by an *envoi*, usually addressed to the traditional "prince."[6] These poems differ in structure from Froissart's own *chansons* in that they are in octosyllables and have a refrain at the end of each stanza, features which give the poems a livelier pace and more potential for irony. But even with these variations, the regularity of fixed-form stanzas helps create the kind of elevated tone necessary for depicting an idealized society where nobles and peasants live in a harmonic relationship extending from the most traditional activities to the most specific contemporary events of daily life.

Froissart's basic techniques for creating entertaining and nuanced narratives can easily be seen in Pastourelle 7, a poem with a strictly conventional theme. This poem treats the familiar subject of a rustic celebration, with all its costumes, feasting, and music. But Froissart adds complexity to the perspective by making the narrator only an indirect observer of the festivities. Instead of having the narrator describe events as they occur, the poet brings him onto the scene immediately after the celebration has ended so that his impressions are based solely on what he can glean from the shepherds and shepherdesses talking excitedly about the details of the day. Thus the narrator has "heard it said" that a prize was given to the group best prepared for the occasion, and he merely witnesses the intense feelings of the losers, who at first can barely manage to hold back their "angry words" at having been bested in the competition:

Pastourelle 7

Entre le Roes et le Louviere
Vi awoen desous un ourmel,
Ensi qu'a basse remontiere,
Mainte touse et maint pastourel,
Car on avoit la un jeuiel   5
Donné, ensi que dire oï;
S'en estoient moult esbahi
Li pastouriel d'oultre le bos,
Et en tenoient leurs gros mos
De ce qu'il leur fu escapés,   10
Més li pris eut esté donnés
A sen droit, ce me dist Thieris,
Car onques més ens ou païs,
(Ce tesmongnoient li plus sage)
On ne vit bregiers si faitis   15
Selonc le bregerois usage.

[Between Roeulx and La Louviere
On a recent late afternoon,
I saw underneath a small elm tree
Many shepherd girls and shepherds,
For a prize had just been awarded there,

As I overheard them say;
The shepherds from beyond the woods
Were greatly disturbed about it,
And struggled to hold back their angry words
At having let the prize escape them,
But the prize had been given justly,
As Thieris told me,
For never before in that country
(As the wisest testified)
Had anyone ever seen shepherds so fine
According to the way shepherds do things.]

"Or m'en recordés le maniere,"
Di je a celi, "pour Saint Marsel."
--"Volentiers," dist chils, "par Saint Piere.
Il estoient tout d'un hamel,   20
Et avoit cascun un jupel
De toille long et le vesti,
Et estoient sus çaint par mi
A replois ou ventre et ou dos,
Holetes portans a leurs cols   25
Et eurent solers takenés
A quatre noiaus reversés,
Wans, wages, caperons petis
Et capiaus sus leurs testes mis,
Qui leur acouvroit le visage.   30
N'estoit ce mie uns bons habis
Selonc le bregerois usage?

["Now tell me all about it,"
I said to one, "by Saint Marcel."
--"Gladly," he said, "by Saint Peter.
They were all from the same village,
And each one was wearing
A long tunic
And there were hooks going up to their necks
From the belt around their middles
Along the folds on the stomach and the back
And they had shoes with ornamental leather[7]
With four small reverse knots,
Gloves, leggings, and little hoods
And caps placed on their heads,
Which covered up their faces.

Now wasn't this an excellent way to dress
According to the way shepherds do things?]

"Riens n'est qui au mestier afiere,
Qu'il n'euïssent tout de nouvel:
Sakiaus, trellis et panetiere   35
Lacie au costé d'un cordel,
Aloiiere, bourse et coutel,
Escorgies, boistes ossi
Et clokettes de Saint Remi,
Pipes, canemiaus et flaios   40
Et musettes a bourdons gros,
Tamburs et esclifes trauwés,
Feces de soilles et de blés,
Ongement a oindre brebis,
Chiens en laisse, colers, rivis,   45
Et se parloient un langage,
Onques si bons ne fu oïs
Selonc le bregerois usage.

["There was nothing they had for herding sheep
That wasn't completely new:
Small bags, lattices and bread sacks
Laced up on the side with a rope,
Travelling pouches, purses and knives,
Leather belts and boxes, too,
And little bells from Saint Remy,
Pipes, reed instruments, and little flutes,
And bagpipes with droning bass,
Drums and carved out fiddles,
Stalks of rye and wheat,
Ointment made of sheep oil,
Dogs wearing leashes, collars and ropes,
And they were speaking in a language so good
That a finer one had never been heard
According to the way shepherds do things.]

"Et pour faire le feste entiere
Et mieuls avenir a revel,   50
Cascuns bregiers eut sa bregiere,
Arree gentement et bel
De blanc cainse et de court mantel,
Qui leur avenoit jusqu'a chi,

Et mis un chapelet joli   55
De perselles et de pavos,
Et portoient godés et pos
Ou dou buvrage avoit assés,
Tous tels qu'il keurt parmi les prés.
Et quant il se furent assis,   60
Wastiaus saquierent et pain bis,
Aus, porions, sel et froumage.
Ne deurent chil avoir le pris
Selonc le bregerois usage?

> ["And to make the festivity complete
> And lead to even greater joy,
> Each shepherd had his shepherdess,
> Elegantly and beautifully dressed
> In a white chemise and a short cloak,
> Which came down to here,
> And they all wore pretty crowns
> Of bluebottles and poppies,
> And they carried glasses and wineskins
> With more than enough of all such drink
> As flows freely in the meadows.
> And when they had all sat down
> They took out cakes and brown bread,
> Garlic, leeks, salt, and cheese.
> Now shouldn't they take the prize
> *According to the way shepherds do things?*]

"Et chiaus que tu vois la derriere,   65
Qui s'assamblent en un tropel,
Il sont de Thier et de Triviere
Et ont juré Saint Daniel
Pour ce qu'on donra un agniel
Dimence a le feste a Givri;   70
Dou wagnier se sont ahati,
Se bienfaires poet avoir los,
Car nuls ne sara leurs pourpos,
Si les vera on acemés.
Ossi tu vois a l'autre lés   75
Chiaus de Seneffe et des Bastis,
Qui prendent entre yauls un avis
Comment il feront ce voiage,

Et en yauls desgisant toutdis
Selonc le bregerois usage."   80

    ["And those that you see behind there,
    Who are gathering into a group,
    They are from Chierq and Trivieres
    And they've sworn an oath to Saint Daniel
    Because a lamb will be given
    Sunday at the feast at Givry;
    They hurried away after winning the prize,
    And this wise action is praiseworthy,
    For no one will know their intention
    Until they see them adorned.
    Also you see on the other side
    The ones from Hainaut and Les Batis,
    Who are deciding among themselves
    How they will make this voyage,
    Always disguising and hiding themselves
    According to the way shepherds do things."]

Princes, j'en jurai Jhesucris
Que pour despendre cent parsis
Et de laiier me cloke en gage,
Je verai les jeus dessus dis
Selonc le bregerois usage.   85

    [Prince, I swear to Jesus Christ
    That if I have to spend a hundred gold coins
    And put my cloak in hock,
    I will see those festivities that were spoken of here
    According to the way shepherds do things.]

    The shepherds' emphasis on the importance of the prize makes plausible the detail and enthusiasm of the description that comprises all of stanzas two through five, allowing this part of the poem, independent of the frame provided by the first stanza and the *envoi*, to provide a traditional kind of courtly entertainment based purely on spectacle. The shepherd's voice in itself, sustained over four full stanzas, creates a strong dramatic image of naïve rustic enthusiasm, while the content of the speech provides surprisingly detailed visual imagery, ranging from the ornamental leather of the shepherds' shoes to the flowers in the shepherdesses' hair. Indeed, almost every line offers the audience a different object or person for consideration, as Thieris' account hurries along in the excited syntax of a person who can't be bothered with putting ideas in careful order. In lines 20-23, for instance, he starts with a statement about how the winning group all came from the same village and then jumps directly into a slightly garbled observation about how (translated literally) "each one had a long tunic of cloth and was wearing it. . . ." For a full eleven lines, the description tumbles out in one long, breathless sentence.

Likewise, in stanza three, Froissart emphasizes the dramatic intensity of the shepherd's story by implying a physical gesture to accompany the words. In describing each shepherdess as wearing a short cloak "qui leur avenoit jusqu'a chi" (51-54), the poet encourages the reader (or perhaps the person reciting the poem) to interpret exactly how Thieris is delivering his lines, bringing his presence as a character into sharp focus. At the end of each stanza Froissart further emphasizes the emotional vitality of the scene by placing the words of the refrain within either a rhetorical question or a superlative statement. The poem leaves no doubt of the shepherd's certitude that the details he describes add up to the best possible example of pastoral taste: "Now shouldn't this take the prize / According to the custom of shepherds?" (63-64).

But while the words of the refrain are sincere and heartfelt in the mouth of Thieris, they take on a second layer of meaning in the context of the aristocratic frame. The very fact that the festivities are judged wonderful and elegant "selonc le bregerois usage" implies that by some other standards--in particular those of the narrator and the audience--the same celebration will appear quaint and unsophisticated. As the elaborate details of courtly celebrations in both the *Chroniques* and the historical *pastourelles* reveal, Froissart and his audience were fascinated with matters of taste and took great pains to achieve the highest possible level of refinement.[8] In this social atmosphere where refinement was prized as a distinguishing mark of gentility--an attitude reflected in the very existence of the fixed form lyric--members of the court must have been both curious to hear about the rustic, more "natural" version of their own pageantry and quite amused to imagine shepherds who considered it the height of achievement to be equipped with a new set of bagpipes and a fresh supply of sheep ointment as a part of their holiday finery (40-44). By the same token, the shepherds' delight in "disguising" themselves ("acouvrit le visage" 30 and "en yauls desgisant toutdis" 79) creates a homely image that contrasts sharply with the elaborate masquerades that sometimes took place in aristocratic circles.[9] Most telling of all are the contents of the feast, which include "cakes and brown bread, / Garlic, leeks, salt and cheese" (61-62). This stereotypical peasant meal is a sure mark of the simplicity of rustic tastes, a point reinforced by the fact that Froissart has Thieris mention it immediately before the reference to "bregerois usage" in the refrain.

The idea of using the *pastourelle* to describe the simple charms of a rustic celebration was, of course, in itself nothing new for the genre, but what makes Froissart's poem especially effective is the skill with which he handles two different levels of meaning. On a literal level, the poet expresses the point of view of the shepherds themselves, offering a wealth of naturalistic detail without ever slipping into a tone that would contradict their mood of enthusiasm. At the same time, however, he chooses the narrator's words so carefully that they also accommodate the aristocratic point of view which the audience is sure to adopt. When the narrator enters the scene in stanza one, the poet provides no clues about his attitude towards the shepherds: he simply "saw" a group gathered under a tree, "heard it said" that a prize had been given, witnessed the high emotions of the losers, and began to hear the story from Thieris. On the surface, the dramatic intensity of the scene itself provides sufficient motivation for the narrator's interest in hearing the full details of what has occurred, so that it would appear, at least from the shepherds' point of view, that the narrator is properly impressed by their reports to him. Similarly, at the end of the poem, the narrator seems literally to be echoing the enthusiasm of Thieris and the others when he declares that he would "spend a hundred *parsis* and put his cloak in hock" to see the kind of competition the shepherds have described (81-84)--an attitude which again, if one were a shepherd, would seem quite natural, since it would be hard to imagine any better entertainment or source of amusement than a fine rustic celebration.

But it is, of course, the comic distance between the two points of view that creates a second level of entertainment for the poem's aristocratic audience. What Froissart and his audience must see in the bountiful display of quaint clothing and simple foods is a childlike ignorance of what it means to stage an elaborate celebration. The shepherds' foods, their music, and even their fascination with disguises are mere shadows of the festivities that Froissart and the members of the court know so well. When Froissart has his narrator express an exaggerated desire to see a rustic celebration for himself ("I swear to Jesus Christ . . . I will see those games"), he captures perfectly the tone of an aristocrat who can be certain he will not be misunderstood. These peasants are delightful precisely because they are both idealized and limited, a perfect reflection of the theoretical social order that was most comfortable to the aristocratic mind. The exaggerated approval in the poem's narrative frame invites the audience to share the pleasure of a familiar inside joke, rounding out a point of view that is in itself as entertaining (and reassuring) as the poet's account of unsophisticated rustic life.

Froissart takes a similarly light-hearted approach in several of the other *pastourelles* which treat conventional subjects,[10] but the satirical point of view is by no means the only one he chooses. In a second, quite different category of poems, he develops an idyllic image of pastoral life and writes from the perspective of one who apparently envies the shepherds' ability to experience pure, uncomplicated love. On first impression, these two treatments appear inconsistent, the one growing out of a critical perspective and the other out of admiration. But in fact their coexistence demonstrates Froissart's understanding of aristocratic ambivalence towards the rustic condition, at least as aristocrats wished to imagine that condition to be. On the one hand, as the previous poem shows, the shepherds are like children, full of charm but lacking the sophisticated sensibilities that are part of a noble's very essence. On the other hand, the simple life of the shepherd offers an escape from the pretense and politics that often made life difficult for members of the court, especially in matters of love and marriage. Froissart strikes a careful balance between these two points of view by choosing to laugh only at those specific features of rustic life that help define the superiority of aristocratic tastes, while at the same time allowing characters such as Thieris to be generally likable in their openness and lively demeanor. Froissart makes Thieris the object of humor because he is so naïve about good food, good music, and good costumes, but he also shows him to be both energetic and sincere, a character with the kind of pure spirit and unadulterated motives that the aristocratic fantasy of love requires. Froissart's characterizations thus support W.T.H. Jackson's contention that one of the *pastourelle*'s primary functions is to allow the audience's desires to be acted out: in matters of taste, the shepherds' deficiencies let the aristocracy enjoy a sense of their own refinement, while in matters of love, their simplicity lets the audience fantasize about being free to act on their true feelings.[11]

One of the main differences between the satirical *pastourelles* and those that present love fantasies is that in the first the members of the audience are expected to identify only with the narrator, while in the second they are encouraged also to share the feelings of the rustic characters themselves. Froissart's awareness of this difference in point of view is evident at the beginning of Pastourelle 4, where, instead of emphasizing the aristocratic frame, he makes the narrator's role as unobtrusive as possible:

Pastourelle 4

Entre le Louviere et Praiaus,
L'autre jour deus bregiers oï,
Si entendi que li uns d'iaus
En complaindant disoit: "Hé mi!
M'amie se voelt marier,   5
Et point ne m'i voel acorder;
Or sera nostre amour desfete,
Se je ne fai ce qui li hete.
Conselles m'ent." Et respont chieus:
"Et puis qu'avoir poes la tousete,   10
Oserois te demander mieus?"

[Between La Louviere and Preaux,
The other day I overheard two shepherds talking,
And I heard one of them say
Plaintively: "Ah, me!
My sweetheart wants us to marry,
But I don't wish to at all;
Now our love will be destroyed
If I don't do what she wants.
Give me some advice." And the other answered:
"Since you can have the girl,
Would you dare to ask for more?"]

"Je ne sçai," chi respont Ansiaus,
Car mi parent m'ont dit ensi
Que j'arai a ces quaremiaus,
Més qu'a leur gré m'ordonne ossi,   15
Abit pour moi renouveler,

Coroie, espee et bouqueler,
Gans, wages, jupel et houcete
Et cote a mon point trés bien fete.
Se tu avoies tels hostieus,   20
Si en euïsses le disete,
Oserois te demander mieus?"

> ["I don't know," answered Ansel,
> "For my parents told me
> That at the next carnival time,
> If I do as they wish, I'll get
> A whole new suit of clothes,
> A leather belt, a sword and buckler,
> Gauntlets, leggings, tunic and cassock
> And an overcoat made exactly to my taste.[12]
> If you could get such clothes,
> And had never had them before,
> *Would you dare to ask for more?*]

"Et s'ai, que brebis et qu'agniaus,
Environ un cent et demi;
On dist qu'il n'i a jusqu'a Miaus   25
Nul plus rice bregier de mi,
Ne qui mieuls se doie assener."
--"Va," dist chils, "qu'on te puist tuer,
Més que ce soit d'une bourlete;
Quant la trés douce bregierete   30
Tu refuses, c'est grans orghieus:
Se tu poes avoir la tousete,
Oserois te demander mieus?"

> [And also I have about one hundred fifty
> Sheep and lambs;
> They say that between here and Meaux
> There is no shepherd richer than I am,
> Nor any who is likely to marry better.
> "--Go away," the other said,
> And may you be killed with a club;
> If you refuse the gentle shepherdess,
> It will be an act of arrogant pride:
> Since you can have the girl,
> *Would you dare to ask for more?*"]

De ce que dist Thieris li Viaus,
Ansiaus forment se resjoï,   35
Et li bregiere as blons cheviaus,
Qui gardoit maint mouton joli,
Les fist de celle part tourner.
Thieris le prist a regarder
En apoiant sus se holete,   40
Et dist au fil dame Noirete:
"Di moi, plus lours q'uns kokevieus,
Se elle voet estre t'amiete,
Oserois te demander mieus?"

> [Ansel greatly rejoiced
> At what Thieris li Viaus had said,
> And the blonde-haired shepherdess,
> Who was watching her pretty sheep,
> Made them turn her way.
> Thieris began to look at her
> Leaning on his crook,
> And said to the son of Noirete:
> "You are dumber than a cuckoo;
> Tell me, if she is willing to be your lover,
> *Would you dare to ask for more?"*]

Li tousete o tout deus capiaus   45
Vint la, s'en baille un son ami.
Adont y fu grans li reviaus,
Car cascuns le prist endroit li,
Et puis prisent a caroler,
Et la bregierete a chanter   50
Une canchon moult nouvelete,
Et disoit en se canchonnete:
"Di moi, Ansel, si t'aït Dieus,
Se je voel estre t'amiete,
Oserois te demander mieus?"   55

> [The girl came over with garlands for both,
> And gave one of them to her sweetheart.
> Then there was great merriment,
> For each one took her near him,
> And then they began to dance a round,
> And the shepherdess started to sing
> A brand new song,

And she said in her little song:
"Tell me, Ansel, so help you God,
If I am willing to be your sweetheart,
Would you dare to ask for more?"]

Princes, je les vi, lés le frete,
Tous trois seoir sus l'erbelete,
Et chantoient par mos gentieus
Avoec une basse musete:
"Oserois te demander mieus?"   60

[Prince, I saw them, beside the ridge,
All three resting in the short grass,
And they were singing with noble words
To the sound of a low bagpipe:
"Would you dare to ask for more?"]

Unlike the narrator in Pastourelle 7, the observer in this poem does not
interact with the rustic characters at any point in the narrative. Instead,
the poet limits his function to reporting changes in speaker and
describing significant movements and gestures. The effect of this
narrative restraint is to focus interest entirely on the debate between the
two shepherds, whose opposing viewpoints are clearly defined in the
first stanza where one fellow resists the idea of marriage (5), while the
other has a more imaginative view of what it means to "have the girl"
(10). For an audience familiar with the traditional *demande d'amours*,
the structure of the rest of the poem is easy to predict: while each
character will have a chance to present his arguments, only one will
prove to have a true understanding of the spirit of love. Thus, the
audience must decide not between the point of view of an aristocratic
observer and that of a rustic, but rather between the points of view of
two shepherds, who will reveal their attitudes in a lively dramatic
scene.

One might expect that in using two rustics to represent opposing
attitudes towards love, Froissart would choose the more "aristocratic"
of the two as his winner, distinguishing, for instance, between one
fellow who is refined in his sensibilities and another who is simply a
churl. But instead, with his ever-present sense of irony, Froissart has
Ansel, the loser of the debate, base his objection to marriage on his
hope of making a better match, thus placing him in the company of
many a rich bourgeois or ambitious courtier. Ansel reveals his

obsession with material goods in a lengthy description of the fine clothing and equipment he hopes to receive from his parents ("A strap, a sword and buckler, / Gauntlets, leggings, tunic and cassock . . ." 18-19), and completes his argument with a direct reference to his status in the community, including his belief that "there is no shepherd richer" and none "likely to marry better" (26-27). Ansel's inclination to choose "having" the goods rather than "being" the lover is the kind of behavior that could occur at any level of society, giving the question under debate a universality quite different from the issue of aesthetic tastes in Pastourelle 7.[13]

Of course, in the larger picture of class differences, the fact that a mere shepherd like Ansel is tempted to let his concern for advancement interfere with his chance to marry the lovely shepherdess could easily lead to a narrowly satirical treatment of his character as a member of the lower class, especially since he measures his worth by only a single suit of clothes and one hundred fifty sheep. But Froissart does not allow this difference between aristocratic and rustic perspectives to cloud the issue. His second shepherd, Thieris, quickly speaks up to define the real problem with both force and clarity, comically insisting not only that his friend deserves--quite specifically--to be beaten to death with a club ("Qu'on te puist tuer...D'une bourlete," 28-29), but also labeling his friend's material concerns as "grans orghieus" (30-31). The question to be answered is not just whether Ansel the shepherd is too proud, but whether pride should be permitted to override love--and in the clear light of the rural countryside, the answer is unequivocally "no." Rather than directly criticizing the material interests that had come to dominate the aristocratic way of life, the poem invites its audience temporarily to abandon that life and imagine another where practical considerations can be abruptly dismissed, where beauty and love can take precedence over money and status. It takes only a few strong words from Thieris for Ansel to see the error in his judgment and "rejoice" at the thought of the lovely blonde shepherdess; from that point on, the characters sing and dance and revel with a joy that celebrates the rewards of following one's heart.

Since a convincing picture of the spirit of love is central to the meaning of this poem, Froissart makes the most of the *pastourelle*'s potential for dramatic presentation. From the start, Ansel and Thieris have distinct personalities, marked by Ansel's verbosity in explaining all the details of his dilemma and Thieris' directness and certitude in giving advice. Indeed, Thieris bothers to explain himself only once, in the passage where he states that refusing the girl would be "orghieus"; more often, he seeks to convince his friend through the power of insults ("plus lours q'uns kokevieus" 42), as if the error of Ansel's way is too obvious even to deserve serious consideration. Thieris' spirited retorts add a comic element to the scene, as well as giving dramatic credibility to the fact that Ansel comes to agree with his confident friend after only three stanzas of discussion.

But even more surely than these characterizations, Froissart's handling of physical stance and gesture brings the poem to life. At the very moment when Ansel begins to "rejoice" at what Thieris has said, an image of the "bregiere as blons cheviaus" herself intervenes to provide the most convincing argument of all--the power of her presence, which immediately makes them "turn her way" (36-38). As Thieris leans thoughtfully on his crook, he becomes totally absorbed in gazing at the pretty girl. The single detail of his posture communicates how powerfully the girl affects him, freezing the scene in a moment of pure admiration. He does not need to present any new arguments to Ansel because, in the context of his friend's gaze, Ansel--and the audience as well--cannot help but finally understand what it means for Thieris to ask, "Oserois te demander mieus?"

In addition to emphasizing dramatic elements, Froissart also draws on the *pastourelle*'s potential for musicality, using the lyricism of the form to build towards the idyllic mood of the final stanza. Like the *ballades* and *rondeaux*--genres which had recently evolved from dance forms and were still often set to music--this *pastourelle* is developed mainly through subtle variations in the meaning of the refrain, a line which provides the poem's thematic center of gravity. Froissart's emphasis on the refrain first becomes apparent at the end of stanza two, where Ansel picks up Thieris' original question about the shepherdess and turns it into a commentary on his own materialism. In the context of describing the elaborate clothing he hopes to receive, Ansel diminishes the value of what was originally a spiritual question, now limiting the issue to the mere acquisition of fine clothes when he "had never had them before" (20-22). His reference to what he lacks--"le disete"--parallels the naming in stanza one of what he could have--"la tousete"--making the limitations of his argument more obvious.

Ansel's misuse of the central question is effectively countered throughout the rest of the poem. In stanza three, his friend's repetition of these same words in a moral context--after his reference to the sin of "pride"--lends the word "oserois" additional rhetorical weight. Even more significantly, when the refrain next appears in stanza four, it becomes the climax of the scene in which Thieris succumbs to the shepherdess' charms, a context which suggests that both shepherds are now moving away from argumentative logic and into the magic spell of love and beauty. And, indeed, in stanza five the seriousness of Ansel's dilemma is completely replaced by the pleasures of the moment, made all the more delightful by the clever shepherdess herself as she incorporates the refrain into her own original song:

> Et puis prisent a caroler,
> Et la bregierete a chanter
> Une canchon moult nouvelete,
> Et disoit en se canchonnete:
> "Di moi, Ansel, se t'ait Dieus,
> Se je voel estre t'amiete,
> *Oserois te demander mieus?"* (49-55)

By using the refrain line as the climax of the shepherdess' song, Froissart blends the music of the pastoral scene into the rhythms of his own poem, giving the whole *pastourelle* something of the character of popular folk music. Indeed, by this time the refrain has been uttered by each one of the characters at least once, so that it seems only natural that they all join together in the *envoi* to sing the words of the refrain together:

> Princes, je les vi, les le frete,
> Tous trois seoir sus l'erbelete,
> Et chantoient par mos gentieus
> Avoec une basse musete:
> *"Oserois te demander mieus?"* (56-60)

In spite of the fact that they are singing to the tune of a rustic "musete," the shepherds and shepherdess sing with "mos gentieus," for their song has become the symbol of the aristocratic fantasy of simple, idealized love. As the refrain is repeated for the last time, the question of deciding whether to marry fades into the background and the audience becomes free to join in with the musical sentiments, which now seem firmly focused on praising an unattainable, yet highly desirable, way of life.

Froissart's skill in developing points of view that can allow both sympathetic and satirical treatments of rustic scenes is the key not only to his poems on traditional subjects but to those dealing with less conventional matter as well. In choosing new topics for his *pastourelles*, Froissart went well beyond the love stories and celebrations that the members of the aristocratic audience would expect, often inviting them to see themselves and their own customs through new eyes. Indeed, one of the most important unifying element of these poems is the way Froissart used them to raise the question of how the various elements of the aristocratic world would appear outside of their own highly structured context. As with the poems on traditional subjects, those that treat topics of contemporary interest both celebrate and seek to refine the concept of nobility in a witty and entertaining fashion.

The most striking example of a poem with specific contemporary detail is Pastourelle 1, where Froissart uses the stereotype of rustic naïveté to develop a double-edged satire of the latest style in cloaks, an extravagant garment known as the "houpellande." Like the poem on marriage, this one plays with the idea of rustic tastes, beginning with the declaration of a shepherd who has just seen riders in *houpellandes* for the first time and has decided that wearing such a garment--with huge sleeves and a full hemline--is his one desire:

Pastourelle 1

Entre Aubrecicourt et Mauni
Priés dou cemin, sus le gaschiere,
L'autre jour maint bregier oï,
Ensi qu'a l'eure de prangiere.
La disoit Levrins Cope-osiere: 5
"Signeur, veïstes vous point hier
Chevauceurs par chi chevaucier
Ne houpellandes deviser?
J'en vi cascun une porter,
Mais j'en euch joie si trés grande   10
Qu'onques puis ne fis que viser
A vestir une houpellande.

[Between Aubrecicourt and Mauny
Near the road, upon fallow ground,

The other day I heard shepherds talking
Around the hour of noon.
And Levrins Cope-osiere was saying:
"Gentlemen, yesterday didn't you see
Men on horseback riding by
Or hear talk about houpellande cloaks?
I saw each man wearing one of them,
And the sight brought me such great joy
That, ever since, I've done nothing but wish that I
Could dress in a houpellande.]

"Houpellande, vrais Diex, hé mi!"
Ce li dist Willemes Louviere,
"Et que poet estre, or le me di!   15
Bien cognois une panetiere,
Un jupel et une aloiiere,
Unes wages, un agillier,
Un lievre, un coler, un levrier,
Et se sçai bien moutons garder,   20
Sainnier et le pousset oster;
Més je ne sçai, si te demande,
Qui te poet mouvoir de parler
A vestir une houpellande.

["A houpellande, dear God, oh my!"
Thus answered Willemes Louviere,
"And what can that be, now tell me that!
I know what a bread sack is, all right,
A tunic and a traveling pouch,
Leggings, a needle holder,
A hare, a collar, a greyhound,
And I know how to guard sheep well,
Care for them and get rid of disease;
But I don't have the slightest idea
What on earth could make you talk about
Dressing in a houpellande.]

"Je le te dirai, entent chi: 25
C'est pour le nouvelle maniere,
Car l'autrier porter une en vi,
Mance devant, mance deriere;
Ne sçai se li vesture est chiere,
Més durement fet a prisier;   30

Bonnes sont esté et yvier,
On se poet ens envoleper,
On y poet ce qu'on voet bouter;
On y reponroit une mande,
Et c'est ce qui me fet penser   35
A vestir une houpellande.

> [Listen, and I will tell you:
> It's because it's the latest style,
> For the other day I saw someone wearing one,
> One sleeve in front, another behind;
> I don't know such clothes are expensive,
> But they certainly are valuable;
> They are good both summer and winter,
> You can wrap yourself up snugly inside,
> You can put whatever you like in there;
> You could easily hide a wicker basket--
> And *that's* what makes me think about
> *Dressing in a houpellande.*]

"Par ma foi," dist Ansiaus d'Aubri,
"Je sçai bien qu'au temps cha arriere
Bregiers les portoient ensi,
Més c'estoit de toille legiere,   40
Car encor ai je le premiere
Qui fu a mon taion Ogier."
Dont dist Adins, li fils Renier:
"Ansel, pour le corps Saint Omer,
Voelliés le demain aporter,   45
Se metterons sus no viande,
Car ossi puis je desirer
A vestir une houpellande."

> ["By my faith," said Ansel D'Aubri,
> "I am sure that some time ago
> Shepherds used to wear cloaks of that kind,
> Except theirs were made of light cloth,
> For I still have the very first one
> That belonged to my grandfather Ogier."
> Then Adins, son of Renier, responded:
> "Ansel, by the body of Saint Omer,
> Please bring it with you tomorrow;
> We will use it to cover our food,

For I might also decide that I wish to
Dress in a houpellande.]

"Signeurs," dist Aloris d'Oisi,
"Et foi que je doi a Saint Piere,   50
G'irai a Douay samedi,
S'achaterai une aulne entiere
De drap, se ferai le plus fiere
Qu'on vit ains porter sus bregier.
En aroi je assés d'un quartier   55
De drap pour faire ent une ouvrer?"
—"Nennil; il t'en faut pour doubler
Noef aulnes d'un grant drap d'Irlande."
—"Haro! trop me poroit couster
A vestir une houpellande."   60

["Gentlemen," said Aloris d'Oisi,
By the faith that I owe Saint Peter,
I will go to Douai Saturday,
And buy an entire ell of cloth,
And I will make the most excellent cloak
That anyone has ever seen a shepherd wear.
Will I have enough cloth to have one made
And have a fourth left over?"
—"My, no; to line it you will need
Nine ells of broad Irish cloth."
—"Alas! It would cost me too much to
Dress in a houpellande."]

Princes, la les vi aviser
Et dire entre yauls et deviser:
C'est bon qu'a tous bregiers on mande
Que cascuns se voelle acorder   65
A vestir une houpellande.

[Prince, I saw them thinking it over
And talking among themselves and making plans:
It would be good to require of all shepherds
That every one of them should agree to
Dress in a houpellande.]

The incongruity of the first shepherd's ambition would, of course, be immediately obvious to an aristocratic audience familiar with the garment's sumptuous proportions, but Froissart emphasizes the irony of the situation even more by having a second shepherd respond in a speech reminding the audience of the stereotypical rustic point of view. As Willemes Louviere rattles off his list of familiar objects and skills, from breadsacks to sheep cures (16-24), what he is really doing is defining the limits of his own world, making the contrast between his own ordinary expectations and the first shepherd's ambitious plans as obvious as possible. As a result, the first speaker's response to the question about what could possibly motivate him seems all the more out of place when he announces that he is talking about the *houpellande* because it is the latest style ("le nouvelle maniere" 26)--a matter he is hardly qualified to discuss, no matter how impressed he may have been by what he saw. By so firmly establishing the contrast between the world of the shepherds and the world of the riders, Froissart has created a disparity in point of view that allows him to explore the details of the garment and its significance without the encumbrance of any prejudices or preconceptions.

As one might expect, since styles and clothing involve matters of taste, Froissart takes every opportunity to let his audience enjoy the shepherds' display of foolishness. Locked into the simple-minded literalness of a practical life, the first shepherd follows his reference to "style" with an explanation that is based solely on his assessment of the garment's usefulness as protection against the weather or as a covering for hiding baskets (31-36), thus entirely missing the point of what it means to follow "la nouvelle maniere." To make matters worse, another shepherd confuses the new aristocratic garment with an old-fashioned cloak his grandfather used to wear, as if the difference between "light cloth" (40) and the rich, heavy fabric of a *houpellande* were of no consequence at all. Froissart's depiction of rustic naïveté reaches its climax in stanza five, as one enthusiastic shepherd completely misjudges the amount of material such a garment would require, thinking that he might even have some left over if he buys "an aulne entiere" (52). The shepherd's sad closing words, deploring the fact that "it would cost . . . too much" to dress in the wonderful cloak, underline the point that unsophisticated rustics can only end up looking silly when they wish for the kind of fine things that belong exclusively to members of the upper class.

The satire on the shepherds is not, however, the only effect the poet achieves, for the dynamics of the poem allow him to expose the absurdity of what the shepherds see as well as the inadequacy of how they see it. Froissart's decision to have his characters comment on a specific current fashion provides a fresh viewpoint on the kind of subject that might otherwise be too close to the heart of the average aristocrat to allow for much objectivity. While those who blindly followed the new style might never before have given a second thought to the excessive material they were wearing, the image of a shepherd trying to hide a wicker basket underneath makes it apparent that the garment, far from being practical, was designed mainly for the purpose of ostentatious display. As Elizabeth Sage points out in her study of the history of costume, the *houpellande* developed during a period when aristocrats were passing sumptuary laws to prohibit members of the wealthy middle class from imitating the elaborate costumes that had previously been the exclusive mark of nobility.[14] As a result of this kind of competition, the garments not only required huge amounts of cloth, but also incorporated magnificent fur trim along the sleeves and hemlines, making them indeed "cost too much" for anyone but those willing to use their clothing as a symbol of unlimited wealth.

Like the more traditional poem about Ansel's reluctance to marry, this poem on a contemporary subject has potential for making a statement about the aristocrats' own values, again consistent with Froissart's more idealistic view of a nobility based on true refinement rather than materialism. The satirized shepherds lack the sophistication to perceive the true purpose of the cloak's large proportions. But like the children they resemble, the shepherds have the capacity to reveal a good deal of truth in their words, simply by saying exactly what they think. If, indeed, the *houpellande* is nothing but an expensive version of an oversized cloak that was popular among shepherds of an earlier generation, its supposed elegance may be nothing but an illusion of those caught up in displaying their wealth. In the context of this possibility, the *envoi* takes on a particularly heavy irony as the narrator suggests a requirement for all shepherds that "every one of them should agree to / Dress in a houpellande" (64-65). On one level, it is certain that the narrator is laughing at the prospect of seeing a countryside populated with overdressed rustics using their fancy cloaks like tablecloths. But on a second level, his suggested requirement raises the question of whether the *houpellande* itself is not such an absurdity that any plan for its widespread use would expose it for the affectation it really is.

The two perspectives in this poem, which show how the rustics look to the aristocrats and how the aristocrats look through the eyes of reason, fit together without much difficulty because there is no inherent conflict between the "truths" that each perspective reveals. The very fact that shepherds are unaware of the complex motives that lie behind changing styles is what makes it possible for them to present an unbiased view of what they see. In some of Froissart's other *pastourelles*, however, the handling of perspective is a good deal more complex because the shepherds' understanding of the subject at hand is neither entirely naïve nor entirely complete. In these cases, Froissart solves the problem of conflicting perspectives by carefully limiting the degree to which the opinions of the characters are to be taken seriously.

This situation is particularly well illustrated in Pastourelle 17, where Froissart presents a debate over whether the daisy is indeed the most beautiful of all flowers. As the favorite flower of many fourteenth-century poets, the daisy--the "margherite"-- had often been used symbolically in poetic narratives or treated allegorically in such debates as Machaut's *Dit de la fleur de lis et de la Margherite*.[15] The aristocratic audience was thus very familiar with the flower's conventional virtues and could generally be expected to know beforehand what arguments would be raised, their appreciation of any given daisy poem depending more on the beauty of execution than on originality of thought. Like most poets of the day, Froissart had contributed his share of poems of this traditional type,[16] but what makes his *pastourelle* different is the fact that he is dealing with rustic characters who cannot reasonably draw on the rich literary tradition behind conventional arguments. If a shepherd girl like Isabel is to prove the superiority of the daisy, then she must do it in a way that makes sense within her own world. At the same time, however, if the poem is to be effective for the aristocratic audience, the poet must be careful that the shepherdess' arguments neither conflict with what the audience already believes nor imply such a highly developed aesthetic sense that the rustic characters encroach upon the exclusive domain of the upper class. Because of these restrictions, there is a good deal of complexity in the way Froissart develops the characters in this poem, as well as a strong reliance on humor to create the appropriate balance:

Pastourelle 17

Pastourielles et pastouriaus
Vi l'autrier en une vallee
Garder brebis, moutons, agniaus,
Et la oÿ touse senee
Qui dist comme bien avisee: 5
"Toutes et tous, voelliés oÿr,
Ma mere a cui doi obeÿr
M'envoia orains a flouretes;
Or en ai toursiaus et bougetes
De pluiseurs diverses coulours   10
Mais trop sui mal de mes serours,
Car je soustieng une querelle
Et certefi entre les flours
La margherite a la plus belle."

[The other day in a valley
I saw shepherds and shepherdesses
Watching ewes, rams, and lambs,
And there I heard a sensible girl
Who said in a very knowledgeable way:
"Please listen, all you shepherds and shepherdesses,
My mother whom I must obey
Has sent me just now to gather flowers;
Now I have both bouquets and basketfuls
In a variety of different colors,
But I've had a falling out with my sisters,
Because I insist on my point of view
And avow that among all the flowers
The daisy is the most beautiful."]

Adont li respondi Ansiaus,   15
Qui fu homs de grant renommee,
Et dist: "Belle, par mes ceviaus,
Ceste matere fort m'agree
Et chi sera determinee,
Se jusqu'au fons je sçai venir,   20
Mais il le vous fault esclarcir,
Car les voies sont trop orbetes.
Pourquoi laissiés vous violetes
Et roses, qui ont bien leur cours
Et qui font pluiseurs biaus secours   25

A mainte dame et damoiselle,
Et vous nommés chi et aillours
La margherite a la plus belle?

> [Upon this, she was answered by Ansel,
> A man of great renown, and he said:
> "Pretty lady, by the hairs of my head,
> This subject greatly pleases me
> And the dispute will be settled here,
> But first you must make it clearer,
> For the pathways are too obscure.[17]
> Why do you neglect violets
> And roses, which are certainly fashionable
> And which make so many beautiful trains
> For the dresses of ladies and maidens,
> And instead name both here and elsewhere
> *The daisy as the most beautiful?*]

"On en voit paré ces praiaus;
On en aroit une caree,   30
Voire quatre, pour deus roiaus,
Et vous l'avés tant alosee,
Et point ne nommés en pensee
Trois aultres flours qu'on doit cerir,
Faites pour l'omme et Dieu servir: 35
Bled, vin et lin; ces trois sont nettes.
Encor en y a des parfettes,
Sans nommer ne ronses, ne hours,
Ne genés dont on cauffe fours:
Le lis, pione et la perselle;   40
Cestes ne tenront a nuls jours
La margherite a la plus belle."

> ["You can see the meadows adorned with them;
> You could have a whole cartload,
> Indeed four cartloads, for two gold coins,
> And yet you have praised this flower so much,
> And do not even mention
> Three other flowers that deserve to be loved,
> Made to serve man and God:
> Wheat, wine, and flax; these three are clear.
> And there are still other perfect ones,
> Without mentioning blackberries or holly,

Or broom-shrub to heat the oven:
The lily, the peony, and the cornflower;
These flowers won't agree on any day that
The daisy is the most beautiful."]

"Ansiel, Ansiel," dist Ysabiaus,
"Quant la violette est fenee
Et roses dont on fait capiaus,   45
Et il vient froit temps et gellee,
Lors ai tantost une esculee
De margherittes, sans mentir,
Se jusqu'au camps je voel courir;
J'en troeve en cemins et en fretes,   50
Et lors entre nous bregheretes
En faisons capiaus as pastours;
Adont se doublent les honnours,
Quant on en a en temps qu'il gelle;
Lors tiennent amant par amours   55
La margherite a la plus belle.

["Ansel, Ansel," said Isabel,
"When the violet has been cut
And the roses that garlands are made of,
And the cold and freezing weather comes,
Right then I can have a bowlful
Of daisies, it is no lie,
If I wish to run to the field;
I find them in roadways and ditches,
And then among us shepherdesses
We make crowns out of them for the shepherds;
Then the honors double,
When one has them in freezing weather;
Then those who are deeply in love will believe
The daisy is the most beautiful.]

"Plus avant, Cepheÿ li biaus,
Nés de Thessalle la contree,
Pour qui Heros reut par ruissiaus
Plours et larmes . . ., en Galatee,   60
La fu premierement trouvee
La margherite sans falir;
La le fist hors de terre issir
Jupiter, li diex des planetes,

Qui l'aourna de ses saiettes;   65
Zephirus li donna oudours.
Entent, Ansiel, se tu n'ies lours,
Grant matere te renouvelle
Pour soustenir en toutes cours
La margherite a la plus belle."   70

   ["Furthermore, the handsome Cepheus,
   Born in the country of Thessaly,
   For whom Hero[?] cried streams
   Of tears, . . . in Galatia,
   There was the place where one first found
   The daisy in abundance.
   There Jupiter, the king of the planets,
   Who adorned the daisy with his arrows,
   Made it come forth from the earth;
   Zephyrus gave it its scent.
   Listen, Ansel, if you're not dull-witted,
   I am repeating matter of great substance to you
   In order to uphold in all courts
   The daisy as the most beautiful."]

Princes, adont li dist Guibours,
Ossi fisent Guis et Raimbours:
"D'or en avant tenrons, pucelle,
Par camps, par villes et par bours,
La margherite a la plus belle."   75

   [Prince, then Guibours said to her,
   As did Guis and Raimbours:
   "From now on, maiden, we will consider,
   In the fields, in the towns and in cities,
   The daisy as the most beautiful."]

Like many of the *pastourelles*, this poem is made up almost entirely
of dialogue, with very little commentary from the narrator. The few
comments that he does make, however, are essential for establishing his
point of view. While most opening sections refer simply to "many
shepherds" or some "pretty shepherdesses," this one introduces a
"touse senee" ("sensible girl") who speaks as if she is "bien avisee"
("very knowledgeable"). Considering how little Froissart's rustics know
about most subjects, it is difficult to judge from these words alone

whether the narrator's opinion is to be taken seriously. But as the shepherdess begins to speak, Froissart has her immediately establish her trustworthiness through the fact that she is going to take the side of fashionable aristocrats by arguing in favor of the "margherite":

> ..."je soustieng une querelle
> Et certefi entre les flours
> La margherite a la plus belle." (11-14)

The initial credibility of the shepherdess is boosted by contrast with the shepherd Ansel, whom the narrator describes as an "homs de grant renomee" (16). This designation, unlike the words referring to Isabel, is less the narrator's own judgment than a statement of reputation, a characteristic feature of Froissart's chivalric world that, transferred into a rustic context, is likely to be ill-founded. And Froissart shows that this is indeed the case as Ansel begins to speak, for although the shepherd is pleased by the subject of discussion ("Ceste matere fort m'agree") and quite willing to settle the dispute ("chi sera determinee"), he really doesn't understand what Isabel is talking about: he says she must "make it clearer" because her reasoning is "obscure" (21-24). Like the Ansel in the poem on marriage, this Ansel is on the wrong side of the debate and is destined to be taught a lesson as the poem proceeds.

Having clearly established the narrator's preference for Isabel's point of view, Froissart entertains the audience by using Ansel, the character who is less "knowledgeable," as a focus for satire. Ansel's first argument against the daisy is perhaps not totally unacceptable, mentioning, as it does, the fact that roses and violets are the most fashionable flowers for the trains on ladies' dresses (24-26). But after he makes this first point, each succeeding reason he offers strays farther and farther from the kind of symbolic interpretation that the audience's knowledge of literary tradition prepares them to expect. Not only does Ansel worry about the fact that daisies are too common to be of much value, but he goes so far as to estimate their price at "four cartloads for two gold coins" (30-31), as if they were to be measured out like sacks of flour instead of being appreciated for their individual or symbolic beauty. He reveals his ignorance even more when he offers a list of other flowers that he believes should be cherished, including not only "wheat, wine and flax" but also "blackberries," "holly," and "broom-shrub" (34-39). Like the shepherds who assessed the value of the "houpellande," this shepherd is impressed more by a plant's practical value than by its symbolic signification.

In direct contrast to this, Froissart has Isabel base her opinion of the daisy on its ability to serve the cause of love. Although she acknowledges that violets and roses are the traditional flowers that shepherdesses use to make "capiaus" for their sweethearts, she considers daisies superior because they are still plentiful after other flowers have been destroyed by the "cold and freezing weather" (46). Contrary to what Ansel has said, the fact that the daisy is a common flower is not to be held against it, since its availability is what makes it distinctive: all one must do to get them is "run to the field" and begin to "make crowns" for the shepherds (49-52). As her reference to these activities indicates, Isabel belongs not to the type of tasteless rustics whose judgments are so easily satirized, but rather to the tradition of idealized lovers, those shepherds and shepherdesses who are free to spend their time pursuing amorous pleasure.

Indeed, it is not her own judgment that Isabel is promoting in her argument so much as the judgment of Love itself, for, when she draws the stanza to a close, she concludes that "those who are deeply in love" (amans par amours") will then agree that the "daisy is the most beautiful" (55-56). Because Froissart has identified Isabel with one area of life in which rustic simplicity is an advantage, the aristocratic audience can take her point of view seriously and accept her argument as an additional reason to value the "margerite." As Isabel herself indicates, her purpose is to "uphold" the daisy's reputation "in all courts" (69), and, in effect, what Froissart has done is to let her show that the daisy is a fine enough flower to appeal to every level of society--"in the fields, in towns, and in cities" (74). In this sense, the poem is remarkably original, since it moves outside the narrow aristocratic context in which the "margerite" was ordinarily honored and shows the flower having a broader, more universal appeal.

With this accomplished, however, Froissart does not hesitate to exploit the remaining satirical potential in the poem. In fact, by developing the comic aspects of the personalities of both main characters, he resolves any inconsistencies that might have arisen from combining the satiric treatment of Ansel with a wholly idealized treatment of Isabel. For while Isabel's attitude towards the "margerite" falls into the tradition of idyllic pastoral love, the rest of her personality is more reminiscent of the earlier *pastourelle* tradition in which a clever shepherd girl would delight the audience by outwitting a foolish aristocratic suitor. In this case, the shepherdess prevails over the "renowned" Ansel and his friends not primarily because her opinion is correct (a point which the unsophisticated shepherds are hardly capable of judging) but rather because she argues aggressively and dominates them with the force of her personality. This becomes apparent in stanza five where Froissart has her abandon her previously logical mode of argument and begin instead to cite obscure mythological evidence:[18]

> "Plus avant, Cepheÿ li biaus,
> Nés de Thessalle la contree,
> Pour qui Heros reut par ruissiaus
> Plours et larmes . . ., en Galatee,
> La fu premierement trouvee
> La margherite sans falir;
> La le fist hors de terre issir
> Jupiter, li diex des planetes,
> Qui l'aourna de ses saiettes;
> Zephirus li donna oudours.   (57-66)

As Audrey Graham has pointed out in her study of Froissart's use of mythology, the story of Heres/Hero and Cepheus is unique to Froissart, appearing only in this poem, his *Dittie de la Flour de la Margherite*, and *Le Joli Buisson de Jonece* (ll. 3216-41).[19] According to the story in the *Joli Buisson*, which is Froissart's last and most detailed version of the myth, Cepheus fell from the tree where he was watching for his lady and was killed, causing the lady Hero to cry streams of tears from which sprang the daisy. With its parallels to the legend of Adonis and Aphrodite,[20] the story seems to have been a useful invention for Froissart, who was a devotee of both a lady and the flower named Marguerite. But while he used the myth in a traditional manner in the other two sources, here Froissart mixes names and allusions playfully, revealing Isabel to be more enthusiastic than accurate. While the lady in Froissart's *Dittie* is called Heres, in this poem she is Heros, a name just different enough that it seems to bring to Isabel's mind another pair of lovers, Hero and Leander. Apparently by association, Isabel decides to provide the names of specific places in her story, with Thessalle perhaps representing the Greek side of the Hellespont and Galatee (if it is a place) a location in Asia Minor.[21] All in all, the story seems to be garbled purposefully to produce just the kind of confident misinformation that a bright rustic with a smattering of knowledge would be likely to come up with.[22]

Listeners familiar with Froissart's mythology would no doubt by this point in the poem get the idea that Isabel is operating more on good instincts than true refinement, an impression that Froissart reinforces by having her suddenly turn to Ansel, insulting him and commenting on the fact that he has apparently lost interest in the whole debate:

> Entent, Ansiel, se tu n'ies lours,
> Grant matere te renouvelle
> Pour soustenir en toutes cours
> La margherite a la plus belle. (67-70)

Isabel's domineering tone, along with Ansel's apparently limited attention span, makes the whole scene appear suddenly quite absurd, creating a satirical view not only of this particular shepherd and shepherdess but also of the literary convention that allowed rustic characters to talk as if they had aristocratic educations. Although Isabel may have been right in principle about the beauty of the daisy, Froissart's light-hearted exaggeration of her range of knowledge suggests that the validity of her point of view is limited to that small area of concern in which shepherdesses have particular expertise.

Froissart's careful addition of just the right amount of humor in the character of Isabel is matched by a similar lightheartedness in the resolution of the poem's action. Since the central theme of this *pastourelle* is the beauty of the daisy, the most appropriate ending would be one in which all the characters finally agree with Isabel's opinion and thus confirm what the audience already believes to be true. At the same time, however, it is important to maintain the playful tone of what has come before, since the poem should not imply that the aesthetic judgment of shepherds is somehow to be taken seriously. Froissart accomplishes both of these goals by placing the lines in which Isabel scolds Ansel for not listening at the very end of stanza five, immediately before the *envoi*, where the other shepherds assure Isabel of their agreement:

> Princes, adont li dist Guibours,
> Ossi fisent Guis et Raimbours:
> "D'or en avant tenrons, pucelle,

Par camps, par villes et par bours,
La margherite a la plus belle." (71-75)

By juxtaposing Isabel's sharp words with this hardy chorus of compliance, Froissart leaves open the possibility that the shepherds have decided to support Isabel not because they have really understood anything she has said, but simply because they do not want to risk being chastised along with poor "dull-witted" Ansel. Their emphatic reference to the "fields," the "towns," and the "cities" is effective both as a final statement of the theme of broadened appeal and as a dramatic sign of how eager they are to satisfy Isabel and end the debate. The shepherds thus remain just as unsophisticated and amusing as ever, while still satisfying the audience's sense of how the question should be resolved. By combining these two layers of meaning, the poet brings the aesthetic and satirical points of view neatly together in the end.

In the poems examined thus far, Froissart demonstrates the extent of his ability to redesign the entire relationship between his characters and his audience with just a few subtle changes in detail and tone. His thorough understanding of how members of the aristocracy wished to see themselves, combined with his mastery of the satirical and fantasizing modes, allowed him to move easily from one subject to another, even when some of the unconventional subjects he chose required him to de-emphasize certain traditional elements or eliminate them altogether. This flexibility, more than anything else, made it possible for him to treat the historical subjects which were such an important part of his own experience. There is no doubt that the historical *pastourelles* are interesting for their content alone, as Scheler and others have indicated,[23] but here again, it is mainly Froissart's reshaping of conventional elements that makes the poems entertaining and effective as pieces of literature.

In developing a point of view for the treatment of historical subjects, Froissart continued to follow the general principle that *pastourelles* should present fantasies fulfilling the desires of the aristocratic audience. And from his experience in the court, he knew very well what desires lay behind the public actions he was documenting. During the many travels which he undertook to gather historical information, Froissart always found both princes and knights eager to tell their stories; often they would spend days travelling with him in order to convey every detail of their exploits that might serve to enhance their reputations.[24] Thus the poet was constantly aware--and supportive--of the ruling class's tremendous desire to obtain honor and glory, a desire which, much like their sophisticated aesthetic tastes, was one of the most important features distinguishing them from the lower classes. The rustic characters typical of a *pastourelle* could never properly emulate the chivalric behavior of their rulers, and they probably would not even understand it--but, on the other hand, it was unthinkable that they could fail to admire it. Thoroughly understanding this aristocratic attitude, Froissart consistently emphasized the awe and admiration his pastoral characters experience upon seeing important people pass by or hearing of something new they have done. By carefully blending this perspective with familiar rustic scenes and personality traits, he created a new sub-genre that was effective not only for simple poems in honor of a triumphal entry or marriage, but also for the more complex subjects he undertook in later years.

Froissart's means of adapting traditional elements for use in honoring his patrons and benefactors can be easily understood through a short summary of one of his earliest historical *pastourelles*.[25] Pastourelle 2, written in 1364, celebrates the voluntary return of the French king Jean le Bon to his captivity in England. Froissart begins with the traditional element of a festive celebration; as the narrator first comes upon the shepherds and the "mainte gaitice pastourelle," he sees all of them dancing "au son d'une canemelle" (5-7). This opening scene establishes the conventional situation of an aristocratic observer watching a quaint scene of rustic pleasure, but Froissart immediately introduces an important difference in the circumstances: these shepherds and shepherdesses are not dancing to celebrate a feastday or a marriage, but rather they are trying to "do their best" because they have heard that the one "qui porte les fleurs de lis" will soon be passing by (9-11). The introduction of this unusual subject gives the poem a surprising immediacy, for the arrival of the French king was a matter of great importance in the English court where Froissart was living at the time. The idea that even the people in the countryside shared the excitement is a particularly effective device for conveying the theme of universal admiration, and the traditional rustic activities of singing and dancing create a pleasant scene for those who would like to imagine that the lower classes shared the joy of the arrival of a great chivalric hero.

Still, the use of such current material also presents certain difficulties for the poet. As the characters respond to events in the real world, they risk becoming, in a sense, less fictional; thus, they could easily become less effective as purveyors of fantasy. Froissart responds to this problem by emphasizing stock characters and plot devices as he fills in the details of what the narrator sees. Upon the first mention of the "fleur de lis," for example, one shepherd fulfills the role of the typical fool who misunderstands. He wants to know whether the flowers are carried in a "panier" (14), and, in his excitement, he hopes to be given some of them in trade for the "cornuelle," the "musette," and the "flahutelle" with which he makes his music (27-29). In clearing up the misunderstanding, Froissart fits in a short speech that gives the other shepherds the opportunity to praise the "rois de noble lignie" and point out how "appropriate" it is for them to dress in new costumes in his honor (35-39). But, again, the reference to reality is shortlived. As the shepherds carry out their plans, Froissart draws on the stereotypes of rustic behavior to satirize the inadequacies of their efforts. Their new outfits include such items as a "grand loudier" (defined by McGregor as a "full-cut overcoat worn by people of low estate"[26]) and their music-making includes the sound of "a little white stick upon a small plank of wood" (47-51). With typical confidence in the wondrous spectacle they are producing, one shepherd finally declares what a shame it is that they "aren't . . . being seen now" by the king (54-55), thus completing the humorous picture of these typically fictional characters. Yet the effect of the praise is not lost, for in the *envoi* Froissart has his narrator explain that these shepherds were singing "a l'usage de leur pays" (57-58). Although their method of expressing honor is humorous, their message comes through all the same in the final lines: "Li trés bien venus ores soit / Chils qui porte les fleurs de lis!" (59-60). By introducing only a limited taste of reality into an otherwise recognizable fictional world, the poet makes full use of the pleasure the audience takes in escaping into a familiar fantasy and, at the same time, gives that fantasy an immediacy that makes it all the more convincing.

Froissart used such lighthearted rustic revellers to respond to a variety of historical situations, including the introduction of a new coin (Pastourelle 3), the entrance of Queen Isabella into Paris (Pastourelle 16), and two aristocratic marriages in the powerful family of the Duc de Berry (Pastourelles 14 and 15).[27] When the poet visited Gaston de

Foix in 1388, he likewise honored his host with two *pastourelles* (Pastourelles 8 and 9) demonstrating the interest and devotion of the people of the countryside. But even with all its ingenuity, this single type of historical *pastourelle* was not Froissart's only adaptation of the genre for historical purposes. For as an individual and as a historian, he understood the complexity of the role the aristocracy played and he experienced first-hand the suffering that wars for glory and honor brought with them. Though his *pastourelles* always remained basically celebratory in nature, focusing, for example, on either a victory or the return of a hero, those that deal with the results of war take on a surprising seriousness of tone, reflecting the poet's sense not only of the aristocracy's glorious exploits, but of their difficulties and responsibilities as well. In these poems in particular, it becomes clear how the *pastourelles* fit into Froissart's larger vision of a true nobility that lives up to idealistic standards.[28]

In the earlier of the war-related poems, Pastourelle 6, Froissart celebrates the return of his own patron, Duke Wenceslas, from a year of captivity. Knowing the pain that the Duke and his family have endured, and having sorely missed the Duke himself,[29] Froissart avoids introducing any element into the poem that might seem to make light of the situation, instead emphasizing the joy that comes from personal admiration:

Pastourelle 6

Entre Binch et le bos de Hainne,
En l'ombre d'un vert arbrissiel,
Vi bregieretes en grant painne,
L'autre jour, pour faire un capel;
Et la disoit la fille Ansel: 5
"Ce capelet, quant fait l'arons,
A cui or le presenterons?
Je le donrai endroit de mi
A Sohelet, mon douls ami,
Qui me dist her soir en riant   10
Que le duch ravons, Dieu merci,
De Lussembourch et de Braibant."

[Between Binche and the forest of Haine,
In the shadow of a little green tree,
The other day I saw young shepherdesses

Hard at work on a crown of flowers;
And the daughter of Ansel was saying:
"This crown, when we get it all done—
Who, then, will we offer it to?
As for me, I would choose to present it
To my sweetheart, Sohelet,
Who said to me last night with a smile
That, thank God, we will get back the duke
Of Luxemburg and of Brabant."]

Adont li respondi Helainne:
"Chil parler me sont moult nouvel,
Car on disoit l'autrier a Brainne   15
Qu'on le tenoit en un castiel,
Car il, de glave et de coutel,
Comme nobles et vaillans homs,
A cheuls de Jullers et des Mons
Et de Gcrlcs se combati,   20
Et li dux avoit avoec li,
En arroi noble et souffissant,
Maint chevalier preu et hardi
De Lussembourch et de Braibant.

[To this Helainne responded:
"These words are news to me,
For the other day some people at Braine
Said that he was being held in a castle
Because, with a lance and a short sword,
Like a noble and valiant man,
He fought against the troops from Juliers
And those from Gueldre and Berg;
And in the fighting the duke had with him,
In noble and distinguished array,
Many a valiant and courageous knight
From Luxemburg and from Brabant.]

"T'esbahis te se je me sainne   25
Quant on tenoit un tel jeuiel?
Que de Bar et de Lorainne
Et de Haynnau li plus isnel,
Et de Namur li damoisel,
De Franche et d'autres nations,   30
Escuiers, chevaliers, barons,

De combatre prest et garni,
Ensi que recorder oï,
Eut au jour dont on parla tant
Le dux, que tu ramentois chi,   35
De Lussembourch et de Braibant.

"Does it surprise you that I make the sign of the cross
When they were holding captive such a jewel?
For the most agile and swift from Hainaut,
From Bar and from Lorraine,
The young gentlemen from Namur,
From France and other lands,
Squires and knights and barons,
Ready and armed to fight
Were there, as I've heard it told,
On that day of great renown,
With the duke, who you were talking about,
Of Luxemburg and of Brabant.

"Or nous di qui le nous ramainne,
Car, foi que doi a Saint Marsel,
N'oï parolles de semainne
Qui me venissent si a bel."   40
Adont respondi Yzabel:
"Par le poissance le ravons
L'empereour, qui tant est bons,
Son frere, qu'onques je ne vi,
Mais on dist, et il est ensi,   45
Que chils que j'ai nommé devant
A la duçoise le rendi
De Lussembourch et de Braibant."

"Now tell us who's bringing him back to us,
By the faith that I owe Saint Marcel,
For I haven't heard any words for a week
More beautiful to my ear."
To this Isabel responded:
"We will have him back by the power
Of his brother the emperor,
An admirable man, though I've never seen him;
But it's said, and I think it is true,
That this one I've just told you about

Will restore him to the duchess
Of Luxemburg and of Brabant."

"Il n'est cose riens plus certainne,"
Che dist la touse dou Hamel,   50
"Que nous ravons no capitainne,
Le duch au corage loiiel,
Qui est issus de sanc roiiel;
Dont bien resjoïr nous devons,
Car nos brebis et nos moutons,   55
Sans avoir doubte ne soussi,
Garderons; car, pour voir vous di,
De sanc plus noble ne plus grant
Onques mais dou paÿs n'issi
De Lussembourch et de Braibant."   60

"There is really nothing more certain,"
Said the girl from Hamel,
"Than that we will get back our captain,
The duke with the loyal heart,
Who descended from royal blood;
And so we must surely rejoice,
Because now we can watch over our sheep
Without cares and without doubts;
For I tell you as absolute truth,
That no man of nobler blood
Has ever before come forth
From Luxemburg and from Brabant."

"Belles," di je, "je vous affi,
Jamés ne revenrai par chi,
S'arai veü par couvenant
Le duch et la duçoise ossi
De Lussembourch et de Braibant."   65

"Pretty ladies," I said, "I swear to you
I will never come by here again,
Unless I have most assuredly seen
The duke and the duchess as well
Of Luxemburg and of Brabant."

In order to escape the usual frivolity of the genre, Froissart carefully enhances the validity of the point of view expressed by his characters. He begins by describing a quiet scene "in the shadow of a little green tree" and then populates it with the most favorable of pastoral types--a group of "young shepherdesses hard at work on a crown of flowers" (1-4). The choice of this type of female character suggests that the poem will fall into the category of love poetry rather than satire, thus preparing the audience for an elevated, even dignified, presentation. The audience's expectation of a love theme is reinforced as the first shepherdess begins to speak, thoughtfully raising the question of who should receive this "capelet" when it is finished. When she mentions her choice, her "sweetheart" Sohelet, it seems likely that the poem will be comprised mainly of his praises, the shepherdess' adoring rehearsal of his virtues and fine qualities. Thus it takes only the slightest adjustment in the audience's attitude when they suddenly realize that it is not Sohelet at all who is to be praised, but rather the leader whose imminent return he has announced. Since the shepherdesses of such poems as this are normally concerned only with the personal pursuit of love, it is a special compliment to the Duke that she would award the envied crown to the one bearing the good news of his return. All the elements of the opening stanza suggest that instead of the mere fascination that shepherds in other poems experience, these characters will express a deeper, more heartfelt concern.

As the poem progresses, Froissart continues to make the kind of small adjustments that produce a more respectful tone without seeming alien to the genre. The most important of these is a change in the plot device used to further the dialogue. In this poem, instead of introducing an ignorant character who misunderstands (always a male in the other poems), the poet brings on a second shepherdess, Helainne, who questions what she hears simply because she has not received the latest information. The difference is a crucial one, since, as Helainne begins to speak, she demonstrates that she is not at all a laughable character, but rather one who shares the first shepherdess' deep interest in anything she can find out about the Duke. Indeed, even if she does not know the latest news, she seems never to tire of hearing or retelling the story of the Duke's imprisonment, how, as she heard "a Brainne," someone held him in a castle because "de glave et de coutel, / Comme nobles et vaillans homs . . . se combati . . ." (15-20). The reference to the people at Braine--and the fact that they too were retelling the entire story--indicates that concern for the Duke is widespread, a general sentiment shared by everyone. With this broadened perspective established, it seems only natural that Helainne will continue relating the details of the Duke's story, pleasing the audience with memories of the "escuiers," "chevaliers," and "barons," that joined him from many regions and "autres nations" (27-31). The length of Helainne's speech is comparable to the length usually reserved for the humorous misinformation that comes from a naive shepherd, but because of the change in character types, Froissart is able to use this major portion of the poem to present accurate background information that will both honor his patron and provide a well-balanced account of historical events.

In portraying the shepherdesses who hold such a high opinion of the Duke, Froissart begins by making use of the aristocratic assumption that rustics will naturally be awed by chivalric greatness. When Helainne speaks, her enthusiasm seems to stem entirely from admiration of the chivalric exploits she details; her devotion appears almost religious in nature as she begins one passage by asking the rhetorical question, "Does it surprise you that I make the sign of the cross/When they were holding captive such a jewel?" (25-26). Yet the abstract, "jewel"-like nature of the Duke is not the only reason he is important to these shepherdesses. As the girl "from Hamel" points out near the end of the poem, his return means that finally they will be able to feel secure again, to watch over their sheep "without cares or doubts" (55-56). In spite of their idealized emotions, on a practical level these are real shepherdesses who look to the aristocracy for protection. In the larger context of Froissart's works, this small detail is a reminder of his genuine concern for a social order that must be provided not by an arrogant, self-serving nobility, but by a nobility that must justify itself by fulfilling a whole range of social obligations.

The final adaptations that Froissart introduces in this poem, and certainly the most ingenious, involve a redefinition of his relationship to his audience. Both certain references in the dialogue and a change in the conventional form of the *envoi* make this poem especially suitable as an oral greeting to be delivered directly to the Duke and Duchess themselves, soon after his return. In stanza four, for example, the poet is careful to acknowledge the important role of the Duke's "admirable" brother Charles IV, Emperor of Germany, in arranging the release. The compliment is emphasized by the fact that Charles is the subject of an entire stanza, even though there is very little information disclosed in the midst of the characters' exclamations and transitional commentary. Likewise, at the end of the same stanza, the poet further personalizes the presentation as he shows his consideration for the feelings of the Duchess. Isabel's choice of words in saying that the Emperor will "restore" the Duke "to the Duchess" expresses the poet's awareness that she, also, has suffered during this ordeal. It is only after these important points have been made that the poet allows the shepherdess to mention her own hopes for a more secure future, and it is not until the *envoi* that the narrator's own point of view comes through. Here, Froissart makes his most radical departure from tradition,[30] for instead of stepping out of the dramatic frame and addressing the *envoi* to a "prince," as is customary, he has his narrator become a participant in the scene, making his own comments the climax of the discussion:

> "Belles," di je, "je vous affi,
> James ne revenrai par chi,
> S'arai veu par couvenant
> Le duch et la duçoise ossi
> De Lussembourch et de Braibant." (61-65)

Not only does this device show that the poet/narrator heartily agrees with everything that has been said, but it gives the delivery of the poem a self-fulfilling performative function. If, indeed, the poet is standing before his patron for the first time in over a year, the firm intention expressed at the end of the poem has been carried out, and fact and fiction have become one and the same. The fantasy, in this particular historical poem, is clearly a reflection of the poet's personal sentiments, and, as such, it takes on the complexity of existing in two different worlds at the same time.

The complexity of Pastourelle 12, on the other hand, is of quite a different kind. Based on events during the Flemish Wars of 1382, this poem uses numerous shifts in tone to present an image of war that acknowledges not only the particular victory that is the historical subject, but also the more generalized suffering of the peasants whose lives have been ruined. Froissart's growing concern for this aspect of war is apparent in the *Chroniques*, where he mentions the people of the countryside with increasing frequency as the years go by. In his description of these same Flemish wars, for example, he tells how the

Earl of Flanders orders the fields burned in an area near Ghent in order to cut off the final source of food for the rebelling commoners in the city. When this had been done, the chronicler says, it caused "les povres gens, qui vivoient de leur bestes tout parperdre et enfuir en Braibant et en Hainnau, et al grigneur partie mendiier" (SHF 10:201-202) ["the poor people who lived on the produce of their cattle . . . to fly into Brabant and Hainault, and the greater part to beg their bread"].[31] In most contexts, any mention of the suffering of the common people in a *pastourelle* would not fit into the aristocracy's idealized image of itself and its continual warring, but in this case the fighting has arisen not because of disputes between princes but because the rich cities of Ghent and Bruges have thrown off the rule of their "rightful" lord--that is, they have refused to acknowledge the value of aristocracy itself. This difference in circumstances makes it possible for the poet to portray the invading French king as the restorer of order who, by winning his battles, will "straighten things out" (28) and save the shepherds from ruin. In this context, depiction of the shepherds' losses is both appropriate to the poem's theme and consistent with allegiance to the court. Still, the attempt to achieve an effective balance between dramatizing the plight of the peasants, criticizing those who caused the war, and praising the young French king who has come to save them makes this poem particularly ambitious in its intent.

The degree to which the poem differs from the others becomes apparent in the opening stanza. Like the beginning of the *pastourelle* honoring Duke Wenceslas, this one incorporates the element of surprise. Here, however, instead of simply applying an old pattern to a new purpose, the poet actually contradicts the audience's expectations:

Pastourelle 12

Entre Lille et le Warneston,
Hors dou chemin en une pree,
Vi le jour d'une Ascention,
Droit a heure de relevee,
De pastoureaus grant assamblee,   5
Més pas n'estoient en revel.
La oÿ Oudin Willemel
Qui dist: "Beau seignour, cils fort erre
Qui aime ne desire guerre;
Car guerre nous a tous honnis.   10

Tant soloie avoir de brebis
Que ne les savoie ou bouter;
On n'en sauroie une ou trouver,
Et se n'ai eü nul marchant,
Fors ce, au vrai considerer,   15
L'orgoeil de Bruges et de Gand.

      [Between Lille and Warneton,
      In a meadow off the side of the road,
      One Ascension Day I saw,
      At the hour of changing guard,
      A great gathering of shepherds,
      But they were not at play.
      In that place I heard Oudin Willemel
      Who said: "Gentlemen, a man greatly errs
      If he loves or desires war;
      For war has dishonored us all.
      I used to have so many sheep
      That I didn't know where to put them;
      Now I wouldn't know where to find even one,
      And so I've had nothing to sell,
      Except, to be honest about it,
      The pride of Bruges and Ghent.]

"Més cils orgieus, qui sans raison
A duré entre euls mainte anee,
M'a fait perdre tamaint mouton
Et mainte brebis bien tousee."   20
—"Je t'en croi bien," ce dist Poupee,
"Aussi ai je, et tamaint agniel,
Maint boef, mainte vache et maint vel,
Je ne cognois ne B ne R,
Més je sçai bien qu'en celle terre   25
N'avera paix, ne ou paÿs,
Se le pooir des flours de lys
Ne vient la chose refourmer."
Adont oÿ dire a Gommer,
Un pastourel de Saint Venant: 30
"C'est fort qu'on voie ja cesser
L'orgoeil de Bruges et de Gand.

      ["But this frenzy, which without any reason
      Has lasted between them for years,

Has caused me to lose many rams
And many a thick-fleeced ewe."
--"I believe what you say," said Poupee,
"So have I, and I've lost many lambs,
And steers, and cows and calves, too;
I don't know a B from an R,
But I do know one thing for sure,
In this country we'll never have peace
Unless the power of the fleur de lys
Comes to straighten things out."
At this I heard someone tell Gommer,
A shepherd from Saint Venant:
"It's a difficult thing to bring to an end
The pride of Bruges and Ghent."]

"Car ce sont villes de grant nom,
Plainnes d'orgoel et de posnee,
Et li homme y sont trés felon,
Qui ne s'entr'aimment de riens nee.   35
Leur haÿne a en la contree
Fait ardoir tamaint bon hamel
Et fait trencier maint haterel
De mainte grosse riche here.   40
Com plus vient la chose, et plus serre."
--"C'est vrai," ce respondi Henris,
"Perdu y ai de mes amis,
Qui ne sont pas a recouvrer,
Et quanque je puis desirer,   45
C'est que je voie traire avant
François, pour faire ravaler
L'orgoeil de Bruges et de Gand."

["For these are famous cities,
Full of arrogance and pride,
And their men are cruelly treacherous,
Merciless to any living creature.
Their hatred in this country
Has caused many a good village to be burnt
And many a fat rich lady
To have her throat cut.
The longer this goes on, the worse it will become."
--"This is true," answered Henris,
"In the fighting I've lost some friends,

Who will never come back again,
And all that I can wish for
Is that I might see the French
March forward to lay low
The pride of Bruges and Ghent."]

"Or ferai ferrer mon plançon,"
Ce dist Robins de la Bassee,   50
"Mon camail et mon haubregon
Roller, et fourbir mon espee;
Més que j'aie la teste armee
Et au costé mon grant coutel
Et ou poing plommee ou martel,   55
Pour grasce ou pour honnour conquerre,
Telement les irai requerre
Qu'on dira que je sui hardis."
--"Je sui des tiens," ce dist Thieris,
"Car je ne puis orgueil amer,   60
Més nous devons de coer penser
Au roy Charle, ce jone enfant,
Comment il vient de coer oster
L'orgoeil de Bruges et de Gand."

["Now I'll have someone forge my spear,"
Said Robins de la Bassee,
"I'll have my coat of mail polished
And my sword refurbished;
Provided I've a helmet on my head
And a cutlass by my side
And a club or mace in my hand,
To win myself peace and honor,
I'll go forward to fight in such a way
That the world will call me bold."
--"I'm with you," said Thieris,
"For I cannot love pride,
But we must give heartfelt thought
To King Charles, that young boy,
Who is coming courageously to remove
The pride of Bruges and Ghent."]

"Beau seignour," ce lor dist Guedon,   65
"J'entenc que hier de la journee
Passerent de nos gens foison,

Car la riviere est conquestee;
A baniere desvolepee
Sont deça passé li roiiel   70
Et espars entre Ippre et Cassel."
Lors dist Rogier de Sauveterre:
"Riens que faire n'a d'euls acquerre;
Puisque gaagnié ont le Lis,
Je tienc Flamens pour desconfis,   75
Contre nous ne poront durer,
J'en voeil deus dousainnes tuer;
C'est fait, on en voit l'apparant;
A ces cops verés vous finer
L'orgoeil de Bruges et de Gand."   80

["My lords," Guedon said to them,
"I hear that yesterday
A great crowd of our men passed by,
For the river has been won;
The king's troops, with banner unfurled,
Have passed by on this side
And spread out between Ypres and Cassel."
Then Rogier de Sauveterre said:
"There's no need to attack them now;
Since the French have won the Lys,
I consider the Flemings defeated,
They cannot last against us,
I would like to kill two dozen of them;
It's settled, I can see it coming;
With these blows you will see the end of
The pride of Bruges and Ghent."]

Princes, puis oÿ dire Omer:
"Nos testes brisons au parler,
Brugois et Gantois sont si grant,
Que tousjours verés vous regner
L'orgoeil de Bruges et de Gand."   85

[Prince, then I heard Omer say:
"Though we rack our brains with talk,
The people of these cities are so grandiose
That you'll never see the end of the reign of
The pride of Bruges and Ghent."]

By having his narrator first mention a holiday and then refer to a "grant assemblee" in a meadow, the poet prepares his audience to expect a poem describing holiday festivities, with games and feasting and dancing. But suddenly in line six the pattern is broken with the narrator's very deliberate statement that the shepherds "n'estoient en revel." These are not, as everyone naturally would expect, the carefree, lighthearted rustics who ordinarily inhabit the world of the *pastourelle*. Indeed, the break from tradition is so abrupt that the listeners are faced with being unable to predict the content of the poem; instead, they must pay special attention to what the shepherds say. Thus it is all the more striking when Oudin begins his speech not with a reference to some recent event or upcoming celebration, but rather with a gravely expressed opinion on the nature of war as something that "nous a tous honnis" (10). Whether one does or does not value the opinion of a shepherd regarding matters of war and honor, in an age that still admires chivalry this statement demands attention. Therefore, the poet moves quickly to clarify his point, identifying the source of the problem with the words of the refrain, "The pride of Bruges and Ghent." The war under discussion is thus defined as being of a very specific, particularly detestable type, creating a context which allows the audience to consider the shepherd's point of view with some degree of seriousness.

Froissart further enhances the validity of Oudin's perspective by giving his words a sophisticated tone. He could have allowed Oudin to sound merely pathetic as he complains about how he "used to have so many sheep / That [he] didn't know where to put them all" and now hasn't a single one left (11-13), but instead the poet concludes the shepherd's comments with a sharp satirical twist on the idea of having "nothing to sell" but the pride of the noble cities (14-16). By allowing this shepherd to rise above his sense of suffering long enough to imagine excessive pride as a substitute commodity--abundantly available but not worth much on the open market--Froissart demonstrates that the opinion being expressed is not just a simplistic reaction but the product of a complex, multi-level point of view. Though the evidence of Oudin's loss is measured mainly in terms of "rams" and "thick-fleeced ewes," there is authenticity in his sense of the absurd. Even when his declaration is seconded by a shepherd who admits not knowing "a B from an R" (24), the effect is not so much to remind the audience of the shepherds' illiteracy as to indicate that the reality of the situation is self-evident: even the most ignorant person alive would have to agree that the "frenzy" which has gone on for years "without any reason" can only lead to further destruction unless it is stopped by whatever power is available to control it.

The reference to just such a power at the end of stanza two balances the dark images of the opening stanza and introduces to the poem the celebratory function typical of the historical *pastourelle* as Froissart conceived it. As the second shepherd concludes his speech, he identifies the fourteen-year-old French king, Charles--"le pooir des flours de lys"--as the only one capable of restoring order in what has become a land of chaos:

> Més je sçai bien qu'en celle terre
> N'avera paix, ne ou paÿs,
> Se le pooir des flours de lys
> Ne vient la chose refourmer." (25-28)

In saying that the country will never have peace without the help of French nobility, this shepherd phrases his comment negatively, emphasizing the likelihood of continued disaster if events follow their present course. But the effect of these lines on Froissart's contemporary audience would have been almost entirely positive, since they (unlike most of the shepherds in the poem) had surely already heard of Charles' success in crossing the river Lys.[32] In the context of this knowledge, even the third shepherd's response that it is "a difficult thing" to put an end to such pride (31-32) becomes positive insofar as it asserts the magnitude of the task this young king is accomplishing. Similarly, this shepherd's depiction of the horror and chaos ravaging the countryside serves both to reinforce the sense of universal suffering expressed earlier by Oudin and to make the man who comes to end it appear the greater hero:

> Et li homme y sont trés felon,
> Qui ne s'entr'aimment de riens nee.
> Leur haÿne a en la contree
> Fait ardoir tamaint bon hamel
> Et fait trencier maint haterel
> De mainte grosse riche here. (34-40)

By the time the next shepherd, Guedon, announces in stanza five that Charles' troops have indeed handed the Flemish a major defeat,

Froissart has heightened the level of emotion so much that a single French victory seems like an event of monumental significance. The image of the French army spreading across the land "a baniere desvolepee" inspires one enthusiastic shepherd to announce with absolute confidence that "with these blows" they would "see the end of the pride of Bruges and Ghent" (79-80). Like the rustic characters in most other historical *pastourelles*, this shepherd thinks in flattering over-simplifications, bringing the final full stanza to the kind of joyful and glorious end that the audience is sure to anticipate.

In this *pastourelle*, however, the happy conclusion to the celebratory theme is not the conclusion to the poem as a whole. Although the idea of honoring King Charles is maintained with consistency through the speeches of numerous characters, it never entirely dominates either the structure or the meaning of the poem. In fact, as each successive speaker offers his point of view, the overall perspective expands to include an almost unsettling number of attitudes, opinions, and levels of credibility. Not only does Froissart follow the sophistication of Oudin with the simple earnestness of the illiterate Poupee,[33] but he likewise moves directly from the brutal story of destruction in the cities to the very personal comments of the soft-spoken Henris, who sadly observes that he had "lost some friends, / Who will never come back again" (43-44).[34] In an even more surprising shift of tone, Froissart has the next fellow, Robins de la Bassee, play the traditional fool, showing his complete ignorance of what it takes to be a great knight. With exaggerated bravado, Robins recites the list of preparations he is ready to undertake "pour grasce ou pour honnour conquerre," including, in typical comic form, everything from polishing his "coat of mail" to equipping himself with cutlass, club, and mace (49-58). The use of this conventional kind of humor invites the audience finally to become comfortable with a recognizable use of the *pastourelle* genre, but again, before they have time to settle into enjoying their superiority over this fellow, another shepherd speaks up, reminding everyone to "give heartfelt thought" to the courage of the young king who must face such terrible adversity (61-64). The fact that so many different types of people agree about the need to end the war and to honor the heroism of King Charles gives these themes an effective sense of universality; at the same time, there is something unsettling about the fact that the poem does not distinguish clearly between characters who are to be taken seriously and those who are not.

In fact, the function of the poem's varying tones and shifting levels
of credibility becomes clear only in the context of the *envoi*, where the
significance of the refrain takes on its full power. For although the
themes of suffering and triumph have both figured prominently in the
thinking of the shepherds, in the end it is the question of the pride of
the bourgeoisie that distinguishes those who truly understand the
problem from those who do not. Throughout the poem, different voices
have successively identified the "orgoeil de Bruges et de Gand" as first
an overabundant commodity and then an evil to be "ended," "laid low,"
and "removed" (13, 31, 47, 63). Froissart has hinted through one
speaker--the shepherd most knowledgeable about the horrors of the
cities--how "difficult" such an undertaking will be, but for the most
part, especially among the simpler characters, the cause of the war is
subordinated, both grammatically and thematically, to the idea that
Charles will come to end it. Indeed, this happy sentiment receives its
strongest expression in stanza five, which is, not coincidentally, the
most consistently lighthearted in the entire *pastourelle*. It is here that
the character "Rogier de Sauveterre," whose name puns on the idea of
saving the land, declares with sudden and humorous bravery that he is
ready to go out and kill "two dozen" of the Flemish soldiers--now that
it appears to be no longer necessary.

As this shepherd draws the conclusion that Charles' advance will
bring an end to "the pride" of the cities, Froissart seems to be
producing exactly the mood and sentiment that would be most
traditional and most pleasing to the audience; it is almost possible to
forget for a moment the darkness of some of the earlier stanzas. But
with the words of the *envoi*, all of the warnings and examples of
suffering regain their power, destroying the simple confidence of
Rogier's prediction just as surely and abruptly as Oudin's words
destroyed the tranquility of the opening scene:

> Princes, puis oÿ dire Omer:
> "Nos testes brisons au parler,
> Brugois et Gantois sont si grant,
> Que tousjours verés vous regner
> L'orgoeil de Bruges et de Gand." (81-85)

Like the opening statement of the shepherd who spoke out against the
destructiveness of war, Omer's declaration that the problem will
"always" continue forces the audience out of the complacency of

pleasant fantasies, inviting instead a fuller, more sophisticated view of what is really a very difficult reality. The simpler characters of the poem are, as Omer points out, merely wasting their time with "talk" as long as they fail to recognize that there is more to this war than one king fighting off the territorial advances of another. Unlike the chivalrous battles that had allowed noble prisoners such as Jean le Bon to be treated with honor and respect, this conflict was caused by the collision of two entirely different visions of how society was to be structured and ruled. The world of the past--the world symbolized by the ideal of glorious chivalric triumphs--had been disrupted by a new class of people who, as Froissart says in the *Chroniques*, "n'acontoient riens à conte ne à baron ne à chevalier qui fust en Flandres" ["thought nothing of any earl, baron, or knight in Flanders."][35] In this context, the simple, idealized message of the typical *pastourelle* cannot ring true; it is only in disrupting the normal pattern of the poem with contradictions and tonal inconsistencies that the poet can fully convey the degree of disruption facing courtly society.

Such a daring use of the genre is in striking contrast to the subtle adaptations Froissart usually relied upon to maintain the fiction of the *pastourelle* world. But this single departure from the genre's usually consistent, self-confident tone serves only to make it clearer how well Froissart understood the power of the conventions he was so skillfully drawing upon. For as surely as he knew how to use the audience's strong sense of its own place in society to create amusing satires and pleasing fantasies, he also knew that any disruption in the traditional role-playing of the characters in a *pastourelle* was symbolic of a breakdown in the entire aristocratic vision. Carried beyond a single poem, such disruption would mean the end of the genre itself, for it would destroy the poet's ability to use traditional elements as the guideposts for an audience that must, if it is to enter the fantasy with any assurance, see immediately whether it is to choose a sympathetic or critical point of view. In contrast to the risks he takes in this single instance, the careful limitations that Froissart habitually places on such elements as the wisdom of the daisy-loving Isabel and the rusticity of the respectful citizens of Brabant demonstrate his awareness that he is working with powerful, yet ultimately fragile psychological symbols.

Thus, it is not surprising that in his later historical poems he returns to the kind of simple, lighthearted   characterizations that show shepherds and shepherdesses in their most idealized roles, making crowns of flowers, retelling with fascination the story of how difficult royal wedding negotiations were achieved, or preparing to play their simple musical instruments for the pleasure of any noble person who might pass by. The return to more traditional themes and characters is consistent with the pattern of artistry which Froissart reveals in his *pastourelles*, for his strength lay not in some concerted effort to develop the genre in a single direction, but rather in his ability to take any subject that captured his interest and adapt the available conventions to express whatever point of view was likely to create the most effective combination of entertainment and social reinforcement for his audience. In the poems with the most conventional subjects, this meant using the shepherds' reputation for both simple taste and pure love to fulfill the audience's fantasies of who they were and what they most desired. In poems focusing on less conventional situations and events, it meant using the eyes of shepherds and shepherdesses--with both their strengths and weaknesses--to create a fresh perspective on the clothing, the symbolism, and the attitudes that were such an important part of aristocratic life. Even in the historical poems, which come nearest to making up an identifiable "subgenre" on the basis of their subject matter, the most striking characteristic is the variety of different methods and devices the poet draws upon to show how a single event fits into the larger picture of class structures, stereotypes, and attitudes in the fourteenth-century world. In writing poems that range from light entertainment to serious social commentary, Froissart revealed a surprising range of potential in a genre which, in the hands of others, was little more than an amusing diversion.

Notes: Chapter III

1. Hoepffner, 32.

2. Froissart's use of the *pastourelle* would appear to reaffirm chivalric social relationships in a way that is similar to his use of romance to revive chivalric service and *ordenance* (see P. Dembowski, *Froissart and His Meliador*). The idealized portrayals of people at different levels of society all successfully fullfilling their roles reinforced standards of nobility in matters of taste, valor, generosity, and responsible governance.

3. William Powell Jones, *The Pastourelle: A Study of the Origins and Traditions of a Lyric Type* (Cambridge: Harvard University Press, 1931), 5. For a more detailed discussion of the origins and characteristics of the genre, see Edmond Faral, "La Pastourelle," *Romania* (1929): 209-217; for examples in Old and Middle French, as well as an extensive bibliography, see William D. Paden's edition and translation, *The Medieval Pastourelle*, 2 vols. (New York: Garland, 1987).

4. Jones, 6-7.

5. Jones, 21-22.

6. The *envois* in Pastourelles 6, 8, and 15 are addressed to "Belles." Hoepffner speculates that the change from the freeer arrangement of verses in earlier *pastourelles* to the regularity of Froissart's day was the result of the influence of the *puys*, the poetic societies in the north of France where Froissart's *chansons royales* often won prizes (30). He cites evidence that some *pastourelles* were presented there in a form identical to Froissart's, though there is apparently no direct evidence that Froissart's own poems were ever entered in competition. Given the content of Froissart's *pastourelles*, it seems likely that the tradition of addressing the "Prince," usually the person presiding over the competition, was redirected to honor the patron; when changed to the word "belles," the address refers to

characters within the dramatic frame. Whether Froissart himself was responsible at all for the other changes in form is perhaps not as important as the fact that the more structured, and therefore idealized, stanzas suited his purposes so well. An example of how the influence of the *puys*, including the use of the traditional *envoi* addressed to the prince, survived into the next century can be seen in the *ballades* of François Villon.

7. This translation follows Scheler's gloss of the word "takene" to mean that the shoes had pieces of ornamental leather attached to them.

8. See, for example, the description of Queen Isabella's entry into Paris, described in the *Chroniques* (Lettenhove 14, 5-25), as well as in Pastourelle 16.

9. See the *Chroniques* (Lettenhove 15, 84-92), where Froissart describes a masquerade in which a number of aristocratic young men died when their costumes caught fire.

10. Such poems include Pastourelle 19, in which a shepherdess resists the advances of a shepherd who wants her to award him a "capelet de margherites," and Pastourelle 20, in which the shepherds choose the shepherdess who is "la plus belle." The second of these is uncharacteristically harsh in its satire of beauty contestants who limp, stutter, and have mismatched breasts, more reminiscent of Froissart's Chanson Sotte (4) than of his other *pastourelles*. See Appendix B for a chronology and complete list of the subjects treated in the *pastourelles*.

11. W.T.H. Jackson, ed., *The Interpretation of Medieval Lyric Poetry* (New York: Columbia University Press, 1980), 148. Froissart himself indicates in the opening section of *Le Joli Buisson de Jonece* that his primary purpose is to write poems that will please the aristocracy:

> C'est que de faire beaus dittiers,
> Qu'on list et qu'on voit volentiers,
> Especialement toutes gens

Qui ont les coers discres et gens.
Ce n'est mie pour les villains. (37-41)

Poirion comments that this attitude was natural for someone who was financially dependent on aristocratic benefactors (210), a point that can hardly be disputed. But there is also an artistic consistency in the way that each genre, including the *Chroniques*, is focused and refined with an eye to making the audience more aware of what was potentially good in the theoretical concept of nobility. As Poirion correctly points out in the same passage, Froissart saw his poetry as a "service" which he had the honor of offering to his patrons. This concept of service seems to have included consistent efforts to inspire a purer concept of what it meant to be noble.

12. The translation of this line is problematic. As McGregor suggests, "a mon point" could mean either "in my size" or "just like I want." I have chosen the latter, since the idea of Ansel's being pleased with the results is clearly consistent with the main idea of the stanza.

13. See Poirion, 61-82, for a discussion of how the concepts of "agir," "être," and "avoir" define the problem of authenticity for the nobility of the fourteenth century.

14. Elizabeth Sage, *A Study of Costume* (New York: Scribners, 1926), 68.

15. Guillaume de Machaut, *Dit de la fleur de lis et de la Marguerite*, in *The Marguerite Poetry of Guillaume de Machaut*, ed. James I. Wimsatt (Chapel Hill: University of North Carolina Press, 1970), 9-64.

16. Most notable among these are Froissart's *Dittie de la flour de la Margherite*, the narrative *Paradys d'Amours*, and Ballade 8.

17. According to Cotgrave, the word "orbetes" means "blind or sightless." McGregor offers "obscure or difficult" as his translation.

18. Both Scheler and McGregor comment in their notes that the shepherdess' statement is abruptly cut off in the middle of line 60. They do not make it clear whether they consider this a deficiency in the

text (the line is apparently the same in both manuscripts), but it is possible that the break is simply further evidence of the confusion of the shepherdess, who seems to be making the story up as she goes along.

19. Graham, 31.

20. See O.M. Johnston, "Froissart's *Le Dittié de la Flour de la Margherite*," *Modern Language Notes* 33 (1918): 122.

21. The name "Galatee" itself may be merely another associative slip, since there are parallels with Galatea, the nymph who shed tears over the loss of Acis, who was changed into a river (Ovid, *Met.* 13, 734-87). Galatea is also the name of Pygmalion's statue which was transformed into a mortal woman (Ovid *Met.* 10, 218-97); no parallels with this story are apparent, except for the general theme of metamorphosis. Likewise, no connection has been discovered between the Cepheus of this story and the Ethiopian of traditional mythology; see A. Graham, "Froissart's Classical Allusions," 31.

22. By first inventing a story and then quoting it in different versions and contexts, Froissart appears also to be playing a rather sophisticated game of self-authentication. As Ribemont explains, "Le poète, en jouant, souligne son propre talent et s'affirme ici comme inventeur de mythologie" (135).

23. Scheler says in his Introduction (lii) that Froissart's *pastourelle* "sort tout à fait du caractère ordinaire de ce genre poetique" except that the "sujet s'est annobli [sic]." Like Scheler and McGregor, Whiting sees Froissart's use of historical subjects as his greatest innovation in any of the poems ("Froissart as Poet," 210).

24. Early in his career, for example, he visited the Scottish king David Bruce and then returned to England and toured that country in the company of Edward Despenser (McGregor, 12). His conversations with such people as Gaston Phebus, count of Foix and Sir Espaenge di Lion are documented in the *Chroniques* (SHF 12, p. 21 ff.; 12, p. 2).

25. For a thorough discussion of the question of chronology, see Hoepffner, 33-42. The events in Pastourelle 2 took place in 1363; McGregor points out that Froissart was "probably present" at Jean le Bon's arrival, since he was touring eastern England during those months. The complete text and translation of this poem appear in Appendix A.

26. MacGregor, 344.

27. The text and translation of Pastourelle 14 appear in Appendix A.

28. Throughout the historical *pastourelles* there are reminders of the specific behaviors that are expected of a true noble, including valor (Pastourelles 2, 6, 12), impressive ceremony and appearance (3, 14, 15, 16), generosity (8, 14), and protection of those lower on the social scale (6, 8, 12, 14). These expectations become especially important to the argument of the two war poems.

29. McGregor refers to Duke Wenceslas as being "a friend of Froissart" as well as his patron (13). Froissart was associated with the Duke from the time he first returned to Brussels in 1366 until the Duke's death in 1383. The two shared a love of poetry, and they are thought to have collaborated on the *Prison amoureuse* around the time of the Duke's imprisonment.

30. This is the earliest of the *pastourelles* to incorporate a change of address; the only others are Pastourelles 8 and 15.

31. The English translation is from *Chronicles of England, France, Spain, and Adjoining Countries*, trans. Thomas Johnes (London: Henry C. Bohn, 1852), 1, 694. Another notable passage describes the French preparations for an invasion of England in 1386. Although Froissart is extremely impressed by the grandeur of the ships and provisions, he comments that "tout paioient povres gens parmi le royaume de France, car les tailles y estoient si grandes pour assouir ce voieage, que les plus riches s'en doloient et les povres s'enfuioient" (SHF 13, p. 12) ["The poor of France paid for all: the taxes were so grievous in that country,

that the rich complained, and the poorer sorts ran away" (Johnes 2, p. 178)].

32. The composition of this poem can be dated quite precisely as having taken place between November 20 and 27, 1387, since, according to Hoepffner (34), it would be very unlikely that Froissart would glorify the crossing of the Lys after news came of the much more important victory at Roosebeke a week later.

33. Unlike many of Froissart's names, which as Hoepffner points out, usually refer to particular localities in Northern France (39), the name "Poupee," meaning "baby" or "puppy," should no doubt be taken as an indication of the innocence of this character. The name of another character in this poem, "Rogier Sauveterre," appears to be chosen as a humorous commentary on this particular shepherd's vision of himself as the hero who will "save the land." More study needs to be done on this subject, since the names in several of the more satirical poems have comic potential.

34. McGregor's reading, "Qui ne *f*ont pas a recouvrer," is probably a misprint. Scheler's text shows the word "*s*ont," which is the word that would be expected.

35. *Chroniques*, SHF 10, p. 235; trans. Johnes 1, p. 706. In a subsequent passage, after a description of the pillaging of Flanders, the Duke of Burgundy is quoted as saying that "ce n'est pas bon ne cose deue de tel ribaudaille, comme il sont ores en Flandres, laissier gouvrener un païs, et toute chevalerie et gentillèce en poroit estre honnie et destruite, et en consequent sainte crestiennetté" (SHF 10, p. 251) ["it is not to be suffered that such a set of scoundrels as are now in Flanders should govern that country, as in that case all knighthood and gentility may be destroyed and pulled down, and consequently all Christianity" (Johnes 1, p. 711)].

IV

Ballades, Virelays, and Rondeaux:
Rhetorical and Thematic Variations

Of all the genres which Froissart included in his collected poems, the *ballade*, the *virelay*, and the *rondeau* come closest to achieving the qualities that modern readers associate with the concept of "lyric" poetry. Unlike the *pastourelles*, which dramatize varying points of view, and the *lays*, which symbolically recreate entire systems of thought, the shorter fixed forms are particularly well suited to presenting clearly defined, narrowly focused themes expressed through the voice of the individual poet. The characteristic which contributes most to this more thematically unified treatment--and which likewise distinguishes these genres from the *chanson royale*--is the use, in each case, of a refrain as the main structural focal point and center of meaning. Whether this refrain presents an image, an expression of personal emotion, or a more generalized idea, its repetition in the varying contexts of surrounding lines and stanzas gives the poet the opportunity to reveal a multi-faceted response that gives depth and imaginative interest to his theme.

Froissart's ability to write with both charm and variety in each of the short fixed forms is based mainly on his clear perception of the differences among the three genres. For, despite the fact that the *ballade*, *virelay* and *rondeau* were all musical in their origins and made use, at least theoretically, of an alternation between individual and collective voices[1], their structural proportions and patterns of arrangement are quite distinct, making each genre especially suitable for a different type of thematic development. As Poirion points out, for example, the very short and repetitive *rondeau* allows only enough space for the poet to provide a single "gloss" for the generalization or image presented in the refrain; the *ballade*, on the other hand, with its three independent and fully developed stanzas, lends itself to a logical progression of ideas.[2] Similarly, the fact that the refrain of a *ballade* appears only at the end of each stanza, rather than in the opening lines, gives the poet a greater degree of freedom in providing imaginative variations on the main idea than is possible in either the *rondeau* or *virelay*. As the poems in this chapter will illustrate, Froissart was fully conscious of both the constraints and the rhetorical potential inherent in each of the fixed-form genres, and he used his awareness of the differences to create a varied body of poems which brought together traditional elements in distinctive and artistically imaginative ways.

As with the *lay* and the *chanson royale*, Froissart's success with the *ballade* begins with his mastery of its formal requirements. In its broad outlines, the form he preferred--known as the "ballade commune"--requires that each of the three stanzas follow an identical rhyme pattern and end with a refrain of one or two lines; in addition, the first four lines of each stanza are always equal to each other in number of syllables and are rhymed *abab*.[3] Beyond these basic rules, however, the poet enjoyed considerable freedom in his choice of both meter and rhyme. Indeed, because the *ballade* had only recently begun to escape its ties to musical form,[4] it was defined more by the relationship of its parts than by strict adherence to specific patterns. Thus, the number of lines between the opening quatrain (Section I of the music) and the refrain (Section III) could vary from as few as one to as many as nine,[5] and the fifth line of each stanza could be shorter than the rest, apparently as a means of marking the beginning of musical Section II. Taking advantage of these possible variations in stanzaic structure and rhythm, Froissart composed his forty-three *ballades* according to twenty different patterns, demonstrating very clearly his virtuosity in matters of technique.

Nonetheless, as Whiting has rightly indicated, Froissart's *ballades* demonstrate a "variety" that goes beyond the number of different forms the poems take.[6] The three-stanza structure encourages a progressive development that can not only recreate the basic rhetorical pattern of medieval discourse, with its statement of theme, amplification, and conclusion,[7] but can just as easily allow for a virtuoso display of popular rhetorical devices, such as enumeration, mythological comparisons, and conventional courtly metaphors.[8] By combining these various possibilities in many different patterns--and even, on occasion, using them to develop subjects other than the traditional lover's lament--Froissart achieves a surprising number of different effects. Just as importantly, in exploring the range of available options, he consistently maintains the even tone and graceful eloquence appropriate to a genre in which the poet's goal is to illuminate a single idea through a series of three carefully planned stages.

The pattern of thought most typical of Froissart's *ballades* is illustrated in Ballade 8, a poem treating the familiar subject of the *margerite*. The stanzas follow a pattern of introduction, amplification and affirmation, with stanza one relying mainly on the device of enumeration to lead up to the initial statement of theme:

> Sur toutes fleurs tient on la rose a belle
> Et en apries, je croi, la violette;
> La fleur de lis est belle et la perselle,
> La fleur de glai est plaisans et parfette,
> Et li pluiseur aimment moult l'anquelie,   5
> Le pionier, le mughet, le soussie;
> Cascune fleur a par li se merite:
> Més je vous di, tant que pour me partie,
> *Sur toutes fleurs j'aimme le margerite.*

> [The rose is considered the most beautiful of flowers
> And after it, I believe, the violet;
> The lily is beautiful, and the cornflower,
> The gladiolus is both pleasing and perfect,
> And most people very much like the columbine,
> The peony, lily-of-the-valley, and calendula.
> Each flower has by nature its own merit,
> But I tell you, as far as I'm concerned,
> *I love the daisy above all other flowers.*]

> Car en tous tamps, plueve, gresille ou gelle,   10
> Soit li saisons ou fresce, ou laide, ou nette,
> Ceste fleurs est grascieuse et nouvelle,
> Douce et plaisans, blancette et vermellette;
> Close est a point, ouverte et espanie;
> Ja n'i sera morte ne apalie;   15
> Toute bonté est dedans li escripte,
> Et pour un tant, quant bien g'i estudie,
> *Sur toutes fleurs j'aimme le margerite.*

[For in all weather—rain, hail or frost—
Whether the season be cool, or dark or bright,
This flower is always full of grace and fresh,
Sweet and pleasing, soft white and rosy red;
At just the right time it closes, opens and blooms,
It never will die or be made to fade;
Within it is written everything that is good;
And because of this, when I examine the question well,
I love the daisy above all other flowers.]

Mes trop grans doels me croist et renouvelle,
Quant me souvient de le douce florette;   20
Car enclose est dedens une tourelle,
S'a une haie au devant de li fette,
Qui nuit et jour m'empece et contrarie.
Més, s'Amours voelt estre de men aïe,
Ja pour crestel, pour tour ne pour garite,   25
Je ne lairai qu'a oquison ne die:
Sur toutes fleurs j'aimme le margerite.

[But a terrible suffering grows and wells in me
When I remember the sweet little floweret,
For she is walled up tight within a tower,
And someone has put a hedge in front of it
Which night and day impedes and opposes me.
Yet, if Love is willing to come to my assistance,
In spite of crenellation, turret and tower,
I will not allow an occasion to pass without saying:
I love the daisy above all other flowers.]

As the pattern of detail in the first stanza shows, Poirion's metaphor of
"rayonnement," which describes each stanza as "radiating" from the
same central idea,[9] refers more accurately to an abstract relationship
among the stanzas than to the actual progression of ideas. For, in
almost every case, rather than asserting a main thesis and moving
outward, the poet begins with a generalized suggestion of the subject
and moves inward towards the precise focus. Thus, in the first six lines
the familiar reference to the popularity of the rose alerts the reader to
the nature of the question being raised, and the list that follows narrows
the possible answers by process of elimination. Froissart's insistence on
the contrast between other people in lines one and five ("on," "li
pluiseur") and himself in line eight ("tant que pour me partie") brings

the main idea into still sharper focus until, finally, it is stated in precise, personal terms in the refrain: "Sur toutes fleurs j'aimme le margerite." As the poet begins each succeeding stanza from a different position on the "outer circle" of related ideas, the movement towards the center produces an effect that Poirion compares, in its final form, to a rose window.[10]

Although Poirion's metaphor refers mainly to the arrangement of proportionately equal parts around the same "geometric center," it suggests also that one criterion for a successful *ballade* must be the poet's ability to fill in each segment of the design with pleasing patterns and colors, balanced in a way that will make the poem as a whole seem full and complete. Froissart's use of the catalogue of flowers meets this requirement in a number of different ways. Not only does the multitude of images give the stanza a desirable richness, but the careful balance of rhythms and sounds demonstrates the precision of a well-planned design. In the first two lines, for instance, where Froissart introduces the idea of choosing a favorite flower, the rhythms move slowly, giving the reader time to focus on each example individually, one flower per line. The initial prepositional phrase, "Sur toutes fleurs," ends at the natural caesura, as does the first phrase of line two, and the pauses in each case are emphasized by other devices--the first by the repitition of the *t*'s in "Sur *toutes* fleurs *tient* on" and the second by the interrupting phrase "je croi" in the middle of the line.

Once the subject has been established, however, the pace increases and the poet introduces variety into his meter and thought patterns. Line three, for instance, presents two examples instead of one. The rhythm picks up speed as the poet pulls the reader through the natural break after syllable four, using the syntax of the simple sentence ("La fleur de lis est belle") and the smoothness of vowel and liquid sounds to delay the caesura until after syllable six. The speed of this line is further emphasized by the fact that syllable ten rhymes with syllable six ("belle . . . perselle"), so that the last sound of the line arrives with convincing finality. Froissart maintains the imaginative quality of his list by introducing a new device in almost every line: the pairing of "plaisans" and "parfette" in line four, the shift to a new subject ("li pluiseurs") in line five, the listing of three flowers in line six. Though in the works of a lesser poet enumeration could quickly grow dull, Froissart's skill with the flexible ten-syllable line keeps the movement of ideas lively and aesthetically pleasing.[11]

Indeed, Froissart's mastery of the art of lists is so refined that he uses it to good effect again in stanza two, simply by adjusting its application to suit his new point of departure. In this poem, as in many others, the "amplification" in the second stanza takes the form of a logical explanation in which the poet presents his reasons for taking the position introduced in stanza one. The transitional word "car" signals this purpose, and the device of enumeration becomes a means of fleshing out the general line of thought. Thus, in the first line of the stanza, the concept of weather is translated into imagery through both concrete verbs ("plueve," "gresille," "gelle") and adjectives ("fresce," "laide," "nette"). Likewise the virtue of the flower is expressed not merely in terms of an abstract ability to survive the winter, but also through references to the various pleasures it offers the eye and the spirit ("gracieuse," "nouvelle," "douce," "plaisans," etc). As in the previous stanza, the movement of thought goes from a broad picture into a precise statement of theme, so it is not surprising that the transition in line 17 performs a function similar to that of line 8, first summing up the logic of the stanza ("et pour un tant") and then insisting on the individuality of the poet's point of view ("Quant bien g'i estudie"). The fact that the poet can start with two entirely different sets of images and two distinct rhetorical purposes yet still arrive so precisely at the same idea makes the return of the refrain all the more satisfying.

Froissart's understanding of the technique of building anticipation in order to strengthen the refrain is demonstrated most clearly in stanza three, where he introduces a variation upon the standard pattern of logic.[12] Certainly, after presenting his choice of the *margerite* in stanza one and defending his reasoning in stanza two, the most obvious method of concluding would be simply to affirm his intention of "serving" the daisy for the rest of his life. But rather than moving directly into that idea, he first introduces the obstacle of the "tourelle," which, with its references to suffering and opposition, takes the stanza in a less optimistic direction of thought. The poet's emphasis, at this point in the poem, on his personal experience ("*me* croist," "*me* souvient," "*m*'empece") is typical of the way *ballades* often lead from general principles to individual cases. But the sudden shift to a negative attitude ("Mes trop grans doels") is a more unusual device which heightens the tension--and thus the level of interest--for the reader who knows that the stanza must somehow come back to an affirmative point of view. Furthermore, Froissart increases the literary resonance of the poem with his reference to the "tourelle" and the "baie," reminders of the allegorical pattern of the *Roman de la Rose*[13] which require the reader to reinterpret the "margerite" as something more than a beautiful, or even a symbolic, flower. The allusion to this famous piece of literature brings with it the rich associations of an entire system of courtly thought, with characters such as *Dangier* and *Jalousie* opposing the efforts of *l'Amant* and *Bel Accueil*. The result is that with only a few key words, Froissart is able to match the breadth of imagery provided by the enumeration in the previous stanzas and at the same time bring to the whole poem a new layer of meaning.

The expansion of the scope of the poem would, however, be unsatisfactory if the poet were not able to bring the focus neatly back to its previously established center of meaning. Froissart accomplishes this by turning to one of the more optimistic conventional ideas of the courtly literary tradition, the belief in the power of Love as a guide who can help the suitor surmount overwhelming obstacles.[14] The reference to "Love" performs several functions, both confirming the fact that the "margerite" is really a particular lady and providing evidence that the poet-lover is properly humble in acknowledging the limits of his own powers. But, most of all, Froissart uses it to transform the negative "doels" of line 19 into the kind of strong affirmation the poem needs to be complete. The love of the *margerite* which stanzas one and two treat as a matter of simple preference or provable superiority becomes, in the face of difficulty, the basis for an act of personal commitment. Once the lover has called upon Love for help, the obstacles between him and his lady are transformed into symbols of persistence, a reinterpretation which the poet emphasizes through his subordinated listing of the "crestel," "tour," and "garite" immediately before the final declaration of his intent to serve. The poem ends up, in the last two lines, exactly where one would expect, given the traditional nature of its theme, imagery, and overall structure. But Froissart's decision to increase the complexity of his final sequence of ideas gives the last repetition of the refrain an especially convincing ring.

That Froissart was consciously using the sequence of stanzas to create a particular effect is most vividly illustrated by the fact that he provides an alternate version of this poem for inclusion in *Le Paradis d'Amour*. This *ballade* appears late in the dream narrative (lines 1627-

53 in a poem of 1723 lines), after the poet/persona has been walking in the meadow with his lady, who asks whether he has composed anything new. When he says that he has, she asks to hear it and sits down, in the company of Plaisance and a number of other allegorical characters, to make him a chaplet of flowers. While the first two stanzas of the poem are identical to those in the collected lyrics, the third is altogether different:

> Et li douls temps ores se renouvelle
> Et esclarcist ceste douce flourette.
> Et si voi chi seoir dessus l'asprielle
> Deus coers navrés d'une plaisans saiette,
> A cui le deix d'Amours soit en aïe.
> Avoec euls est Plaisance et Courtoisie
> Et Douls Regars qui petit les respite.
> Dont c'est raisons qu'au capiel faire dire,
> *Sur toutes flours j'aimme la margerite.* (1645-53)

> [And now the pleasant weather comes again
> And sheds light on this gentle little flower,
> And also I see sitting in the meadow
> Two hearts wounded by one pleasing arrow,
> To whom the god of Love extends his aid.
> With them are Pleasure and Courtesy
> And Tender Glances who delays them just a bit.
> And so, as for chaplets, it is right to have it said,
> *I love the daisy above all other flowers.*]

Like the third stanza of the independent poem, this one moves the discussion from a matter of general principle to a more specific dramatic illustration. But rather than introducing a complication that would be inappropriate to the happy mood of the garden scene in which the poet is reciting his lyric, this stanza recreates in its images almost the very situation described in the narrative frame itself, a coincidence which apparently is the reason that Plaisance responds "tout en riant," and the lady herself begins to smile and laugh (1654-56). If, as is quite possible, the audience was already familiar with the earlier, independent version of the poem, the substitution of these self-referencing images from the narrative frame, still reminiscent of the allusion to the *Roman de la Rose* but altogether different in tone, would have been a delightful surprise. The carefully tailored changes in theme and imagery would have not only underlined the relevance of lyric content within the narrative poems, but would also have drawn attention to the poet himself as one who used his imagination to expand the limits of a predetermined, and very familiar, rhetorical structure.[15]

Although Froissart follows a similar sequence of theme, amplification, and conclusion in a large number of poems,[16] he is equally comfortable with developing the three-part structure of the *ballade* in other ways. One of the patterns he draws upon most frequently sets personal experience side by side with a familiar--often mythological--illustration, revealing parallels that lead to a better understanding of the poet's point of view. In Ballade 7, the speaker of the poem presents the details of his own dilemma first:

> S'onques amans rechut mort pour penser
> A ses amours, morir je deveroie,
> Car nuit et jour je pense sans cesser
> A ma dame, comment je le revoie.
> Més je ne puis veoïr sentier ne voie   5
> Qui deviers li hastieuement me mainne.
> Dont je voi bien que la mors m'est proçainne,
> Car je desir ce que ne puis avoir,
> Et ce ne poet souffrir nature humainne
> *Que d'estriver encontre son pooir.*   10

> [If ever a lover caused his own death by thinking
> About his love, then I must surely die,
> For night and day I think incessantly
> Of my lady, how I will see her again.
> But I cannot see any path or way
> Which will lead me quickly towards her.
> Therefore I see clearly that death is near,
> For I desire that which I cannot have,
> And human nature cannot long endure
> *To strive beyond the limits of its power.*]

> Prés d'Albidos siet de Hellés la mer
> Ou Leander qui fine amour mestroie,
> Toutes les nuis pour Hero visiter
> Noe a esploit, car la belle l'en proie;
> Més Oleüs qui Zephirus desloie   15
> Met les amans en une mortel painne,
> Car Bruidis souffle de tel alainne

Que Leander ne poet Thetis mouvoir.
La est peris: or n'est folours si plainne
Que d'estriver encontre son pooir.   20

[Near Abydos the Hellespont is found
Where Leander, who was governed by *fin'amors*,
Swam every night, with pleasure, to see Hero
Because this beautiful lady asked him to;
But Aeolus, whom Zephyrus unleashed,
Put the lovers into mortal pain;
For Bruidis, the wind, blew such a breath
That Leander could not escape the sea.
There he died: there is no folly so great as
To strive beyond the limits of one's power.]

A Leander me puis bien comparer,
Car volentiers tous perils endurroie,
Més que seürs je fuisse de trouver
Celle au rivage ou ariver vorroie.
Prendons ensi qu'ens ou peril mors soie,   25
Moult me seroit le aventure sainne,
Car je languis en terre ychi lontainne
Et sans espoir de li plus revoir:
Se me voult mieulx mort prendre, quant g'i painne,
Que d'estriver encontre son pooir.   30

[To Leander I can surely compare myself,
For I would endure all perils willingly
Provided that I were certain I would find
My lady on the shore where I arrive.
Supposing, then, that I would be in peril of death,
That would be the healthiest thing for me to do,
For now I languish here in a faraway land
Without hope of ever seeing her again;
Thus, it is better, since I suffer so,
To accept death *than to strive against its power.*]

Like the *margerite* poem, this one is quite traditional in its subject, relying primarily upon the convention of love-sickness and the idea that unrequited love will ultimately lead to death. With his references to the familiar images of the lover thinking of his lady "nuit et jour" and searching for whatever "sentier" or "voie" will lead him to her,

Froissart lets the reader know in very few words exactly how the relationship stands, making the nearness of death in line 7 a foregone conclusion. What makes the movement of the stanza interesting, however, is the way the concept of dying from a broken heart broadens, in line 8, into an example of the more generalized experience of wishing for what one cannot have. For while the symbolism and images of the poem, in this stanza and throughout, come from the experience of idealized love, Froissart's method of analysis has to do also with the workings of "nature humainne," as his transition in line 9 points out. The "pooir" which the speaker of the poem lacks is that of satisfying his desire to see his lady again, but the psychological ramifications of being thwarted are drawn from a broader range of human experience.

It is not, however, exactly this same insight that Froissart develops in stanza two. While the words of the refrain and the amorous motivations of the characters remain identical, the particular mythological illustration he has chosen emphasizes an exterior, rather than an interior, drama. As the lack of logical connectors between stanzas demonstrates, the poet's freedom to start over from a new direction is even greater in this type of *ballade* than in those that follow the pattern of logical discourse. In fact, the poet initially makes no effort to link his complaint to the story of Leander, providing by way of transition only the the names of "Albidos" and "Helles" to let the audience know that the scene has moved to the ancient world. Given the conventions of the *ballade*, however, this is enough to prepare the reader for a mythological story that must somehow lead back to the idea of "striving beyong the limits of one's power." Like the enumeration in other poems, the concrete details of the plot create an overall design which points towards the refrain as its center of focus.

The elements of the design, in this case, are calculated to emphasize both the parallels and the differences between the two stanzas. Like the poet in stanza one, who calls himself "amans," Leander is ruled by "fine amour"; just as the speaker of the poem is obsessed with seeing his lady again and thinks of her "nuit et jour," Leander risks his life "toutes les nuis" because he wishes to visit Hero. Beyond this point, however, the two stanzas diverge. The "amans" of stanza one can find no "sentier" to lead him to his lady and suffers from his desire, fighting an interior battle aganst his own endurance. Leander, on the other hand, takes physical action: he swims to his lady, battling the exterior forces of nature. Froissart emphasizes the power that Leander comes up against by personifying it as a host of characters--"Oleus," "Zephirus," "Bruides," "Thetis"--all conspiring to destroy him. Whereas the lover of the first stanza must ultimately die because of his emotional limitations, Leander succumbs to another aspect of human experience, his powerlessness to control the forces of the natural world around him. As the emphatic opening words of line 19 indicate, the result in either case is the same: "La est peris." Froissart labels the Greek hero's actions "folly" as he makes his transition into the refrain, but this is less a negative judgment than a means of clarifying the distinction between two versions of the same thing. The dedicated lover has the option of waiting powerlessly or acting foolishly, but either way he is "striving beyond the limits of his power."

The weighing of these two options quite naturally becomes the point of departure for the third stanza, which must somehow bring together the separate experiences presented in stanzas one and two. But rather than simply raising the question of which is better and building towards a conclusion, as might be expected, Froissart's persona immediately identifies himself with Leander and expresses his desire to take the more active--though admittedly the more overtly dangerous--role: "volentiers tous perils endurroie" (22). In using the conditional mood of the verb, and following it with the qualifying phrase "més que," however, Froissart takes another turn in his logic, making it clear that the speaker is not, in fact, in the position to act upon such a choice. For whatever reasons--including perhaps long-term separation, lack of communication, or failure to secure the lady's approval[17]--there is no direct route available for him to follow. Froissart thus eliminates a second likely possibility for concluding his poem, that of resolving to take the necessary risk and see the lady at all costs. Any question about the lover's course of action has been answered.

At the same time, however, the speaker's assertion that he would rather be like Leander creates a new tension in the poem, because this apparently illogical conclusion requires further explanation. If such behavior is "folours," as he himself has asserted, then why should he prefer it? The remainder of stanza three provides the answer: if he is going to suffer anyway, he may as well accept death and be done with it. The logical nature of the development in this part of the stanza is signalled by numerous transitional words, such as "prendons," "ensi," "car," "se," and "quant." In fact, the order of ideas in the last six lines is very similar to the pattern of discourse that governs the stanzaic structure of so many other *ballades*: first the poet introduces the idea of preferring immediate death (25-26), then he supports it with his reasons (27-28), and finally he draws his conclusion (29-30). Each part of the argument is carefully worded to suggest a reinterpretation of what has already been said. Not only is a death like Leander's now called "healthy," but the speaker's current experience takes on tones of despair as he "languishes . . . without hope" (27-28) of ever seeing his lady again. It is this ultimate sense of hopelessness that both explains the lover's attitude and leads into a new turn of thought in the final repetition of the refrain, for while the "striving" in previous stanzas has ostensibly been against one's own psychological and physical limitations, it is now clear that the opponent is ultimately death itself. By structuring his poem to present apparent alternatives and then demonstrating that they differ only in the amount of suffering they entail, Froissart makes a convincing case for the idea that the plight of the frustrated lover is dark indeed.

As the previous examples have demonstrated, Froissart is able to use his strong sense of the three-part *ballade* structure to achieve strikingly different overall effects, even when his subjects and his methods of development are in themselves quite conventional. The freshness of his approach arises mainly from his flexibility in applying rhetorical devices where they will be most effective. While the pattern of logical discourse governs the stanzaic structure of some poems, it is likely to appear only within the conclusion of others; similarly, enumeration, literary allusion, or mythological example may be the basis for overall organization, or they may appear only for emphasis in a key line. In Rondeau 9, for example,[18] where a female speaker confronts Cupid with the amount of suffering she has endured, the refrain itself is a list of the ladies to whom she compares herself: "Candasse, Helainne, Yseut et Tholomee." The overall structure progresses from the story of the speaker's first experience drinking at the fountain of Echo (stanza one), to a less personal narrative revealing the role of Mars in requiring lovers to pursue combat (stanza two), to a summation of the specific fates that befell the ladies named in the refrain (stanza three). Although the function of the enumeration in this poem is different from the usual concentration of imagery that occurs in so many *ballades*, it is effective because it is both emphatic and inventive, while still maintaining the very tight structural relationships that give the genre its characteristic identity.

In addition to bringing variety to his *ballades* through rhetorical means, Froissart experiments in four of his poems with a particularly difficult form, the *ballade équivoquée*. Also known as the *ballade à rime enchaînée*, this form requires that the rhyming word or syllable at the end of each line be repeated as the opening word or syllable of the line that follows, with the additional provision that the meaning of the second usage must be different from the first.[19] Obviously, this kind of *tour de force*, as Baudouin rightly names it,[20] limits the poet's ability to choose his content purely for its meaning or rhetorical value, and its difficulty often causes the poet to resort to unnatural syntax or the revival of obscure words. At their best, however, Froissart's *ballades équivoquées* have the delicate beauty of fine miniatures, pleasing for their precision and their carefully selected detail, though purposefully limited in scope.

The effectiveness of this kind of treatment can be seen in Ballade 26, where, as the opening stanza reveals, the poet pleads his case using the image of the consuming fire of love:[21]

> D'ardant desir pris et atains,
> Tains sui, et ceste ardeur m'afine.
> Fine dame. Je sui certains,
> C'ert ains que la vie en moi fine,
> I ne me poet estre autrement,   5
> Car je sui espris ardanment.

> [Captured and overcome by ardent desire,
> I am pale, and this passion is killing me;
> Fine lady, I am certain
> That this will be the way life ends for me.
> It cannot be otherwise,
> For I am set on fire with love.]

> Dame, en vos douls regars humains,
> Mains jointes et le face encline,
> Cline mes yeux tous soirs, tous mains.
> Au mains regardés ent le signe,   10
> Si ne m'eslongiés nullement,
> Car je sui espris ardanment.

[Lady, in the presence of your sweet and kindly glances,
Hands joined and face bowed down,
I lower my eyes every evening, every morning.
At least look at the sign they are sending you,
And do not, by any means, send me away,
For I am set on fire with love.]

Se par vous n'est chils feus estains,
Tains ardans, plus vremaus qui mine,
Minera mon coer, je m'en plains,   15
Plains d'ardeur, qui si m'examine.
En mi ne voi aliegement,
Car je sui espris ardanment.

[If this fire is not put out by you,
A blazing arrow, brighter than red lead,
Will threaten my very heart, I lament,
Full of the desire which is so tormenting me.
Within myself I see no relief,
For I am set on fire with love.]

As would be expected in this type of highly formal poem, the content
of the first stanza is very conventional, drawing entirely upon the
familiar language of a dedicated lover. In contrast to the *lai* and the
chanson royale, however, this poem does not achieve its effect by
demonstrating an encyclopedic knowledge of amorous convention.
Instead, the sentiment is trimmed to its most economical proportions
and carefully fitted into one of the shortest possible *ballade* structures,
a six-line stanza with eight-syllable lines.[22]   The simplicity of the
progression of ideas is startling: the lover states his condition in the
first two lines, apprises his lady of the inevitable consequences in lines
3 and 4, and confirms the theme in line 5 and the refrain. Yet in
combination with the *rime enchaînée*, this compact form and quick
movement of thought give the stanza a density of meaning that makes
it intellectually demanding. At the beginning of line two, for example,
while the reader--or listener--is still considering the word "atains"
("overcome") from line one, it is necessary to hold the word "tains"
("pale") momentarily in suspension until its meaning is made clear by
the addition of the first-person verb "sui." Likewise, at the beginning
of line three, the meaning of "Fine" cannot be clearly separated from
"afine" ("kill") until its context is established with the word "dame."

As both of these examples demonstrate, Froissart often juxtaposes meanings that are in tension with each other, evoking either unusual causal relationships or conflicting emotional responses. Because the reader must consider the implications of these tensions, as well as dealing with the continuous ambiguity of homophonic syllables, the stanza requires a much more thoughtful reading than the brevity of its content would suggest.

In contrast to the abstract and conventional line of reason in stanza one, Froissart provides, in stanza two, a concrete illustration of his speaker's plight. In keeping with the compact, understated nature of the form, the illustration is not a complicated mythological story, but rather a momentary glance at a scene in which the suitor's humble behavior is symbolic of the entire relationship between him and his lady. Building upon the traditional motif of the "regard" through which love enters the heart, Froissart has filled this stanza with images of looking and seeing. The lady's "glances" are gentle, giving no sign of the harsh refusal that plagues so many lovers, yet the speaker of the poem "lowers" his eyes, avoiding both the overwhelming effects of gazing directly on her beauty and the accusation of being overly bold if he were to do so. His powerlessness in her presence is revealed by the details of his posture, for he stands "hands joined and face bowed down," like a servant before his sovereign; it is this devotion he hopes that she will recognize when he asks her to "at least look at the sign" he is sending. By keeping the scene essentially motionless except for the real or implied movement of the characters' eyes, Froissart emphasizes the subtlety and refinement of their courtly behavior. Remarkably, even the movement of the sounds in the rhyme pattern of this stanza is more restricted than the elaborate *rime enchaînée* requires: the same syllable, "mains," appears not only at the end of line one and the beginning of line two, but at the end of line three and the beginning of line four as well.

If the external world of society is characterized by its restraint, the internal world of the lover's passion is just as notable for its violence. In stanza three, Froissart uses the power of this contrast to build the poem to a climax in which the conventional idea of burning with love takes on both physical and emotional force. As in the previous stanza, the poet focuses here on a single motif, ensuring through this parallelism the kind of balance that makes the movement towards the refrain especially effective. But this time, since the central image is fire, he has chosen language that is full of action and color. The flames appear in the form of a "blazing arrow," and this painful weapon is "brighter than red lead"; in contrast to the subtle external signals of the previous stanza, the passion in the lover's heart "torments" and "threatens" him. Even the syntax of this stanza reflects the violence of its imagery, for lines 14, 15, and 16 are broken in an uneven pattern, with short phrases of three or five syllables tumbling out in an awkward sequence. Everything in the tone of the stanza works towards confirming the lover's opening argument that he is headed towards certain death.

Still, the lover's complaint would be of little use if it did not allow room for some degree of hope through intervention by the lady. Froissart incorporates this aspect of the traditional argument entirely through transitional phrases, strategically placed for both psychological and artistic impact. The pattern begins in stanza one, where the transition leading into the refrain makes death appear totally certain: "I ne me poet estre autrement." Although the lady is addressed as "Fine dame" in line three, her role is not emphasized at all; the struggle is depicted as being entirely between the lover and his burning passion, and he seems sure to lose, as even the passive structure of the refrain implies. In stanza two, however, after Froissart presents the images of the lady and the lover, the importance of her role--and the possibility of hope--increases. She is asked to take the slightest of actions, to "at least look" and not "send . . . away" this poor fellow who is so humble and well behaved. His suffering deserves compassion because he has placed himself entirely at her mercy, a result, again, of being "espris ardanment." Indeed, by the time stanza three begins, the lover appears so powerless that the responsibility for seeing that the fire is "estains" has shifted entirely to the lady; the transitional "if"-clause makes her willingness to act the only alternative to the violent images which follow. As the final lines point out, the lover's own ability to escape the death he predicted in stanza one has not changed: within himself, he can "see no relief," for he is still "set on fire with love." But the progression of the lady's role from virtual absence, to passivity, to involvement in a possible course of action creates a persuasive picture of her potential responsibility for his fate. Though the argument in itself is neither complex nor innovative, the two main images which support it appear at critical moments, giving the development of the theme an intensity that is particularly suitable for the short, yet demanding stanzaic form of this type of *ballade*.

Froissart's mastery of this challenging form, along with all the popular rhetorical devices associated with the *ballades*, creates in itself an admirable variety of poems on conventional subjects. In addition, however, Froissart extended the range of his *ballades* in another important way with his movement towards more unusual topics and treatments. While the poems in this category are not numerous, they are generally quite appealing because they show Froissart developing a more distinctive persona, with attitudes and interests of his own.[23] Moreover, the types of topics he chooses, and the way he develops them, offer further evidence of the extent to which he had mastered the artistic mechanisms of the genre.

The kinds of freedom that Froissart exercises in his *ballades* include both very subtle and more obvious departures from tradition. In some cases, such as Ballade 33, the change is mainly a matter of tone. Built around the refrain *"Je n'ai nul bien se je ne dors"* ("I have nothing if I cannot sleep"), this poem argues against the proposition that sleep is a waste of time. Although it is still fundamentally a conventional lover's complaint, telling the story of how the speaker of the poem dreams of being loved by a lady who rejects him in real life, the speaker's voice is unusual because of the way Froissart has him insist repeatedly upon the personal nature of his point of view:

> On me dist, dont j'ai grant mervelle,
> Que de dormir c'est temps perdus.
> Tant qu'a moi, je m'en esmervelle,
> Car li dormirs me vault trop plus
> Que li veilliers. C'est mes argus . . . (1-5)

> [People tell me, to my great surprise,
> That they consider sleep a waste of time;
> As for me, I am amazed at that,
> For sleeping is worth much more to me
> Than being awake. This is my opinion . . .]

The frequent use of first-person pronouns--"me," "j'ai," "moi," "m'en," "me," "mes"--reinforces the idea that the speaker of the poem is setting himself up against common opinion ("On . . . dist"), expressing an individual rather than a conventional point of view.

Furthermore, Froissart has him take on a distinctively self-deprecating attitude, not only in the refrain ("I have nothing . . ."), but also in his appraisal of the quality of his life ("Sleeping is worth much more to me / Than being awake"); the result is an appealing, human vulnerability that makes his delight in his dreams all the more charming.[24] The light-hearted description of how the god Morpheus guides him in his sleep, even going so far as to whisper in the lady's ear that she should abandon her refusals, shows the dreamer to be an optimist in spirit, even if his experience in real life is less promising. All in all, the effect of the poem is to provide a fresh, and even slightly humorous, point of view on a dilemma common to courtly lovers.

Others of Froissart's *ballades* venture further from conventional subjects, taking on topics that seem to be naturally suggested by the rhetorical devices most common to the genre. Ballade 34, for example, uses the technique of enumeration to present the many "sights and sounds" through which the poet's "spirit is renewed" (9-10). Like the poem on dreams, this one has a distinctly personal tone, for the speaker expresses himself "without worrying about what others think" ("sans autrui querelle" 8), mixing commonplaces like flowers with the kind of idiosyncratic luxuries that must have been particularly appealing to a traveler like Froissart:

> Violettes en leurs saisons
> Et roses blances et vermelles
> Voi volentiers, car c'est raisons,
> Et cambres plainnes de candelles,
> Jeus et danses et longes velles,
> Et biaus lis pour li rafresquir,
> Et au couchier, pour mieuls dormir,
> Espesces, claret et rocelle.[25]
> En toutes ces coses veïr
> *Mes esperis se renouvelle.*   (21-30)

> [Violets in their season
> And roses white and red
> I gladly see, for this is natural,
> And rooms full of candles,
> Entertainment and dancing and staying up late,
> And beautiful beds for resting,
> And at bedtime, in order to sleep better,
> Spiced wine, claret and wine from La Rochelle.[25]

> At the sight of all these things
> *My spirit is renewed.*]

The standard progression of ideas, from many examples to a point of
focus in the refrain, seems exceedingly appropriate to a subject that
brings together all the "diverse and dissimilar" influences by which, as
Froissart puts it, a man is "forgiés" (3-5). The fact that there is no
particular lady mentioned to put this *ballade* into the category of love
poetry is hardly an issue when images of courtly life and sensibilities
are brought together so gracefully.

In Ballade 23, however, Froissart combines both an unusual subject
and a lighthearted tone to create a poem that stands apart from all the
others. Making use once again of the progression from common
wisdom to personal opinion--and accenting it with a liberal dose of
enumeration--he presents his version of what a man must do in order
to remain healthy:

> Pluiseur gens vont souvent au medecin
> Pour demander consel de leur besongne;
> Et li aucun, soit en jun ou en vin,
> Aient le fievre ou le goute ou le rongne,
> Ja ne vorront de medecine ouvrer.   5
> Or je n'en voel mie trop argüer,
> Car je ne sçai li quel sont li plus sage;
> Mais je sçai bien qu'il se fait bon garder
> *De froit, de fruit, de fame et de froumage.*

> [Many men go to the doctor often
> To ask for his advice on their problems,
> And some men, whether they are fasting or feasting,
> And whether they have the fever, gout or mange,
> Will never wish to put medicine to work.
> Now I don't wish to argue too much about it,
> For I don't know which men are the most wise,
> But I know for sure that it's good to be wary
> *Of cold, of fruit, of women and of cheese.*]

> Car frois qui vient de soir ou de matin   10
> Soudainnement porte as gens grant virgongne;
> Pour ce s'en fait bon aviser, a fin
> Qu'on soit garni de tout ce qu'il besongne,
> Par quoi on puist le froidure eschiever,

Et fruis est tels, on en puet bien parler,   15
Qui trop en prent, il fait un grant outrage.
Siques je di qu'il se fait bon rieuler
De froit, de fruit, de fame et de froumage.

> [For the cold which comes by evening or by morning
> Suddenly brings to men great injury;
> And so it's a good idea to think ahead,
> In order to be supplied with all those things
> By which one can avoid the chill.
> And fruit is such, one can certainly speak of it,
> That whoever takes too much does a great wrong;
> Therefore I say that it's good to use moderation
> *With cold, with fruit, with women and with cheese.]*

Et fames ont un douls samblant benin
Que nullement on ne crient ne ressongne,   20
Et poeent plus de painne et de hustin
Qu'omme ne font: de leur santé chi songne,
Car bon s'en fait legierement passer.
Et froumages est fors au digerer.
Ensi ne voi droit chi nul avantage   25
Qu'il face bon par nul outrage user
De froit, de fruit, de fame et de froumage.

> [And women have a sweet harmless appearance
> That no one fears or dreads in any way,
> Yet they can cause more pain and more trouble
> Than men do: I'm concerned here with their health,
> For a good man easily does without them.
> And cheese is hard to digest.
> Thus I honestly see here no advantage
> That proves it good to make any excessive use
> *Of cold, of fruit, of women and of cheese.]*

Following his usual practice, Froissart suggests the general topic of this poem in the first line with the word "medecin" but does not clearly define the focus until he reaches the refrain. The way he carries out the narrowing process, however, is not entirely ordinary, since he must both create a distinctive context for his uncourtly argument as well as establishing a suitable tone. For even though the word "medecin" is an appropriate conventional point of entry to a familiar courtly theme, it is not the poet's intention to fulfill the audience's expectation for a poem on lovesickness with the lady as the "true" physician. The alternatives "en jun" and "en vin" in line three are important for their role in beginning to define the physical nature of the illness, preparing the reader--at least in part--for the list of examples in line four. It is here, of course, that the poet reveals the game he is playing, for the illnesses listed are not the highly refined maladies of a suffering lover, but rather the everyday complaints of ordinary people: "fever," "gout," and even the lowly "mange." As indicated in the lines that follow, the speaker is not presenting his opinion because he is in the throes of passion, seeking an outlet for his pain--indeed, he "doesn't wish to argue too much about it" and he isn't expert enough to judge who is "most wise." But he knows what experience has taught him and can therefore, as a oddly practical incarnation of the lyric persona, speak with confidence on the down-to-earth subject of "cold," "fruit," "women," and "cheese."

The handling of the refrain itself likewise contributes to the lighthearted, almost parodic tone of the poem. While this refrain takes exactly the same enumerated form as the stately list of mythological ladies in Ballade 9, the playful alliteration of all four nouns--"froit," "fruit," "fame," and "froumage"--draws attention to the artificiality of building a poem around such a fundamentally unpoetic group of words. Indeed, any remaining notion that this is a traditional *ballade* must now be abruptly dismissed, since the "dame" who usually is so revered has been transformed into a much less elevated "fame" and wedged into the line between two kinds of food. Still, for the novelty of the poem to be enjoyed, its structure must match the traditional model very closely, so Froissart uses his unlikely list as the basis for organizing the rest of the poem, dividing his arguments concerning the four sources of disease evenly between the second and third stanzas.

The traditional function of stanza two, on the problems with "froit" and "fruit," is signalled not only by the introductory word "car" but also by a whole sequence of logical transitions, including "pour ce," "a fin / Qu'," and "par quoi." This insistence on the logic of the argument about the cold, however, serves only to draw attention to the fact that this is not a complex, esoteric question of spiritual love, but rather an everyday, mundane matter of common sense over which the speaker is apparently being unnecessarily studious. The subject of fruit, on the other hand, is handled more by evasion than over-attention. Although

Froissart has his speaker comment that "one can certainly speak of it," the effects of eating too much fruit are quickly passed over as a "grant outrage," without the addition of any more details that could destroy the delicacy of the genre.[26] The implication is more than enough to lead the speaker to the conclusion that "therefore . . . it's good to use moderation" under any of the circumstances suggested in the refrain.

Froissart continues to follow the pattern of treating each of his topics one at a time as he begins stanza three, but at this point the concern for balance gives way to the power of the subject under discussion, with "women" commanding a good deal more of the speaker's attention than does "cheese," at a ratio of five lines to one. As the primary focus of so many traditional *ballades*, the subject of women carries with it an array of ideas which the poet can approach in this poem from a fresh point of view. Thus the conventional "douls semblant," which usually has such power over the hearts of lovers, appears, when it is analyzed objectively in line 19, to be "harmless" enough, hardly the sort of thing to inspire "fear" or "dread" in someone who is not under its spell. Still, as the speaker matter-of-factly concedes, women cause more than their share of "painne" and "hustin," making them prime candidates for his list of potential sources of illness. The choice of words here reinforces the contrast in tone between this and more traditional treatments, for while "painne" occurs in many of Froissart's poems about refined love, the word "hustin" is unique to this *ballade*, carrying with it connotations of commotion and uproar which are much less dignified than the usual image of spiritual suffering.

In any case, whatever may be the lure or power of women, Froissart makes it clear that for his speaker, it is all a matter of "santé." Writing with the self-assurance of a confirmed heretic in a genre that promotes the worship of sovereign ladies, he simply concludes that "a good man can easily do without them"--adding, as if it is an afterthought required by the structure of the stanza, that likewise "cheese is hard to digest." With the obvious imbalance between the treatment of the two subjects, Froissart makes it clear that a main purpose of his poem is to look at the effects of women on men without the usual glorification inherent in courtly poetry. At the same time, by making an obvious point of completing the structural pattern, he not only reemphasizes the lowly company that "women" must keep, but also increases the irony of the fact that his very uncourtly treatise on health is expressed in fully acceptable, even masterful, *ballade* form.

The versatility demonstrated in Froissart's handling of the *ballade* is, as both the conventional and unconventional examples demonstrate, largely a result of the way the three-stanza structure provides a dependable framework on which the poet can build with a variety of different materials. Because the refrain is confined to a single line or two,[27] its significance is largely dependent upon the poet's ability to provide meaningful contexts; by choosing carefully among the various rhetorical devices and patterns of logic available for each of the separate stanzas, he can make the statement of theme or subject appear in progressively more revealing lights. This type of progression towards clarity is, however, much less characteristic of the *virelay*, which, as Poirion describes it, is more suited to "enthusiasm" or "exaltation" than to logic.[28] Although Whiting probably goes too far in simply dismissing Froissart's *virelays* as "few and conventional,"[29] the elements of their structure are so much more constrained than those of the *ballade* as to make distinctive rhetorical arrangements and thought patterns rare. With their long refrains and complicated rhythms, the *virelays* have an essentially musical foundation which leaves little room for intellectual complexities; it is thus not surprising that Froissart found them more suitable as lyric interludes within his narratives (twenty-six instances) than as independent poems (three instances).[30]

The *virelay* is distinguished from the *ballade* primarily by the fact that its refrain stands alone as a separate stanza and appears at the beginning of the poem as well as at regular intervals throughout.[31] In Froissart's *virelays*, the refrain stanza (Musical Section I) may be four, five, or six lines long and may include lines of alternating lengths; it is always consistent in using only two rhymes. The stanza which follows begins a new metrical pattern (Musical Section II), again restricted to two rhymes; here the number of lines must be even (Froissart prefers six) since the stanza is symmetrical, consisting of structurally identical opening and closing halves (for example, ccd:ccd). This section is followed by a "coda"[32] repeating the metrical pattern established in the refrain (Musical Section I) and then by the refrain itself. At this point the whole sequence is usually repeated,[33] resulting in an overall pattern of seven distinct units: Refrain, Rhythmic Variation A, Coda A, Refrain, Rhythmic Variation B, Coda B,

Refrain. As Poirion indicates, the constraining influence of the position and length of the refrain makes the genre more conducive to a "static accumulation" of commentary than to a linear progression of ideas.[34] Even with this limitation, however, Froissart often creates a pleasing structural balance in his *virelays* by matching the required shifts in versification to individual turns of thought, thus allowing arbitrary rules to become functional. In Virelay 4, for example, the unified statement of theme in the opening refrain is immediately followed by a stanza in which the opposing roles of the lover and the lady are neatly set into the two symmetrical halves of the rhythmic structure:

> *De tout mon coer vous fai don*
> *Entirement,*
> *Ma droite dame au corps gent,*
> *Et le vous don*
> *Pour tous jours en abandon*　　　　　　　5
> *Trés liement.*

> *[I make you a gift of my whole heart*
> *Entirely,*
> *My honorable lady with noble bearing,*
> *And I give it to you*
> *Forever, in total surrender,*
> *With great joy.]*

> Car vous estes mon desir,
> Mon sens, mon bien sans morir
> Et ma douchour;
> Et sui chils qui moult desir　　　　　　　10
> De vous layaument servir
> Sans nul faus tour.

> [For you are my desire,
> My wisdom, my undying goodness,
> And my source of delight.
> And I am he who greatly desires
> To serve you loyally
> Without deceit.]

Et il soit dou guerredon
         A vo talent,
Ou petit ou grandement,   15
         Com vous est bon,
Car il ne doit par raison
         Estre autrement.

         [And may I receive recompense
                  According to your will,
         Either little or great,
                  As it seems good to you,
         For it must not, of course,
                  Be otherwise.]

De tout mon coer vous fai don
         Entirement,   20
Ma droite dame au corps gent,
         Et le vous don
Pour tous jours en abandon
         Trés liement.

         [I make you a gift of my whole heart . . .]

Car plus ne poés merir
Que je ne puis desservir
         Par me labour,
Las! quant verai je venir
Le reconfort ou je tir,   30
         Et par honnour.

         [For you cannot repay me more
         Than I deserve
                  For my labor,
         Alas! When will I see
         The consolation I aspire to
                  So honorably?]

Je sui en vostre prison
         Tous liegement;
Et coers qui merci atent,
         Grasce et pardon,   35
Doit avoir, s'il vit fuison,
         Aliegement.

[I am in your prison
　　Completely bound to your service;
　　And the heart that seeks mercy,
　　　　Grace and pardon,
　　Must have, if it is to live for long,
　　　　Some comfort.]

De tout mon coer vous fai don
　　Entirement,
Ma droite dame au corps gent,　　　　　　40
　　Et le vous don
Pour tous jours en abandon
　　Trés liement.

[I make you a gift of my whole heart . . .]

Although the six lines of the refrain are in fact divided equally into two clauses, this logical division is offset by the rhythmic alternation of long and short lines (*747474*), which destroys any possible sense of two-part symmetry. Furthermore, the rhyme sequence of *abbaab* forms a separate pattern from the meter, so that the only way to perceive the refrain is as a single, unified whole. The lines which follow, on the other hand, are in every way divided into two identical units: the metrical pattern of *774:774*, the rhyme pattern of *ccd:ccd*, and the grammatical pattern of two equal clauses all draw attention to the division between the role of the lady and the role of the lover. Within this overall pattern, the poet reveals the elegant simplicity of his vision of idealized love by making a clear syntactic distinction between the two halves of the stanza. Whereas the lady's role is defined with a list of nouns that give her virtue unquestioned solidity and permanence ("mon desir," "mon sens," "mon bien," "ma douchour"), the lover's role is spelled out through verbs and adverbs ("moult desir," "loyaument servir sans nul faus tour") to reflect his intense striving.

In keeping with its repetition of the metrical pattern established in the refrain, the stanza which follows (Coda A) again focuses on a single idea, using the alternating long and short lines to reinforce the importance of individual phrases. The topic of the stanza grows out of the suggestion of striving in the previous lines, with the focus now on how the lady will respond ("ou petit ou grandement" 15), an issue again linked to the poet's sense of the lady's superior judgment ("A vo talent," "com vous est bon" 14, 16) It is at this point in the poem that the fundamental differences between the *virelay* and the *ballade* become most noticeable, for rather than presenting a line of thought that leads convincingly towards the refrain, this passage treats the already stated theme as a given, to be illustrated or applied, not proven. If indeed the speaker of the poem has given his "whole heart . . . in total surrender" as the refrain insists, there can be no doubt as to his need to defer to the lady's judgment—it cannot, "par raison," be otherwise. As Poirion explains, using the metaphor of dance, the development merely "encircles" the refrain, with the "solo" performer executing a quick "pirouette" during the stanza of rhythmic variation and then rejoining the tight circle of meaning in the coda.[35] Thus the definitions in lines 7 through 12 momentarily reach beyond the question of what it means to make a gift of one's heart, offering instead some insight into the nature of the relationship, but the coda interprets this new material in relation to the central idea, drawing only the approved, inevitable conclusions. The separate, almost overly repetitive phrases in the middle lines—"ou petit ou grandement," "com vous est bon"—illustrate the total powerlessness of the lover who takes his commitment seriously, bringing the whole train of thought back to where it began, with the idea of total surrender. The return to the point of origin is reinforced by the repetition of the refrain, "De tout mon coer vous fai don . . ."[36]

The subtle balance of the overall pattern becomes clearer as Froissart enters his second stanza of rhythmic variation. Again, he begins with the word "car," which allows him to turn aside slightly from the main focus, but this time, instead of emphasizing his devotion to the lady, he voices a typical lover's complaint that, while he deserves consolation, he has no expectation of receiving it. Although the lover has already conceded that he must defer to the lady's judgment, the issue of fair treatment is still a legitimate concern, for it represents the painful, negative side of a commitment which has, up to this point, been affirmed with blind faith. Froissart uses the two-part structure of the stanza to show the emotional volatility of his speaker, who begins with a down-hearted comment about the impossibility of his ever being overcompensated and then shifts, at the beginning of line 29, to an impassioned rhetorical question demanding to know when he will see his reward. As the final word of the stanza indicates, however, the whole question of justice depends upon the quality of the lover's devotion, the fact that he aspires "honorably"; even here, the movement of ideas must come back to the fact that the lover makes a "gift" of his heart, "entirely."

Appropriately, the second coda takes on the suffering tones of the previous stanza as it gives a final interpretation of what it means to give oneself in "total surrender." Combining the familiar motif of the prisoner of love with the concept of the languishing lover, Froissart restates the speaker's plea for justice in terms that emphasize his efforts much less than his total vulnerability. The word "liegement," emphasized by its isolation in the second line of the stanza, is well chosen for representing the total picture of the lover's situation, for it combines the high concept of "honor" and "loyal service" (lines 31, 11) with the vulnerability of depending entirely upon the "will" (line 14) of another. As Froissart builds upon this image of the lover in the next two lines, he simultaneously draws attention to its relationship with the refrain by coming back to the word "coer," which is now not only the gift offered in the first line of the poem, but also the center of consciousness which awaits the powerful gifts of "merci," "grasce," and "pardon" from the only person capable of granting them. With the mention of the possibility of death in line 36, the poet brings the idea of vulnerability to a climax and prepares for the most striking use of the short line in the poem: in contrast to all the uncertainty and anticipation the speaker has expressed, the resolution falls upon the single word "aliegement." As the refrain is repeated one last time, it is colored now not only by the depth of surrender illustrated in the first half of the poem, but also by a sense that the lover's noble sacrifice could easily be repaid.

In spite of the skill which Froissart demonstrates in *virelays* such as this, his collected lyrics yield no examples of poems where he puts the genre to a new use and only one where he introduces a distinctive point of view.[37] This restraint is hardly surprising, however, given the fact that the structure of the *virelay* is so overburdened with repetition. Whereas a full-stanza refrain works well in musical performance, offering the pleasurable repetition of a familiar melody, in spoken form it creates special problems for the poet, who must struggle against the static sameness of a theme which has already been fully expressed. Although the two sets of interior stanzas can add dimension to the ideas and images of the refrain, supporting it with both rhetorical and musical grace, there is still a sense at the end of the poem that it has not really gone anywhere, or at least that the distance travelled is disproportionately short in relation to the length of the poem.

In this respect, the *rondeau* clearly holds the advantage over the *virelay*, for its brief structure of eight or eleven lines[38] is perfectly suited to the presentation of a single idea from one sharply defined perspective. The two- or three-line refrain with which the poem begins is short enough to be cryptic, making its final return after only a few lines of commentary both welcome and necessary. At the same time, the repetition of a single line of the refrain in the middle of the poem allows the poet to emphasize or redefine an important phrase, or at the very least to place the line in the context of a fresh sound pattern. Although the overall structure of the *rondeau* is in fact even more constraining and repetitive than that of the *virelay*, permitting, for example, only three lines of commentary to accompany the refrain in an eight-line poem, its resulting compactness gives the genre a distinctive capacity for presenting individual observations, expressions of opinion, and bits of wisdom in a pointed and satisfying way.

Froissart's appreciation for the concentrated impact of the short *rondeau* form is demonstrated not only by the fact that the manuscripts include one hundred fifteen poems in the genre, but also by the fact that he chose the briefest possible structural format for all but six of the *rondeaux* in the entire collection. In this version of the form, each line of text represents a phrase of music, and repetitions of musical phrases correspond to the recurrence of a particular rhyme. Thus, the basic musical pattern of the *rondeau* (I,II,I,I,II,I,II) results in a rhyme pattern of *ABaAabAB*. As the capital letters indicate, both lines of the refrain occur at the beginning and end of the poem, with only the first line being repeated at line four. It is possible to expand the structure of the genre by including more than one line for each musical section (Froissart uses an eleven-line pattern on five occasions) but the entire poem is always limited to two rhymes. Following the precedent established by Machaut,[39] Froissart uses lines of uniform length; unlike Machaut, who chose a seven- or eight-syllable line for about one fourth of his *rondeaux*, Froissart uses a ten-syllable line for all the 107 *rondeaux* that were not written for inclusion in a narrative.[40] The choice of this relatively long line, with its strong caesura, contributes towards establishing a relaxed, thoughtful tone and also promotes a syntactic clarity which is very pleasing in such a short form.

The key to all of Froissart's *rondeaux*, no matter what type of ideas they express, is his skill at creating interplay between the refrain and the commentary. According to the rules of the genre, the commentary is always divided into two parts by the recurrence of the first line of the refrain; the resulting back-and-forth movement makes it possible to emphasize contrasts or to build towards a climactic revelation of meaning. Froissart achieves both of these effects in Rondeau 3,[41] a poem which begins with the conventional language of the lover addressing his lady and gains emotional depth through careful interconnections among ideas:

> *Pour vostre amour, plus belle que la rose,*
> *Vorrai je avoir le coer joli et gai.*
> Commandés moi, je ferai toute cose
> *Pour vostre amour, plus belle que la rose.*
> Pardonnés moi quant a vous penser ose,
> Vostre biauté m'a mis en cel assai.
> *Pour vostre amour, plus belle que la rose,*
> *Vorrai je avoir le coer joli et gai.*

> *[For your love, more beautiful than the rose,*
> *I wish to have a joyous and pleasing heart;*
> Command me, and I will do anything
> *For your love, more beautiful than the rose.*
> Pardon me when I dare to think of you,
> But your beauty has made me take this risk.
> *For your love, more beautiful than the rose,*
> *I wish to have a joyous and pleasing heart.]*

Although one might expect from the initial statement of the refrain that the "rose" or the "coer" would be the central focus of the poem, these two images are in fact only conventional elements supporting a more important concept linking the lady's beauty and the lover's will to please her. The seeds of this central idea exist in line two, where the speaker expresses what is, in a sense, a desire to remake himself, to learn to "have" the sort of heart that will be appropriate for the "love" he praises so highly in line one. But it is in line three that the real significance of this desire begins to become clear, when Froissart has the lover suddenly declare that he will do "toute cose" at the lady's command: his desire to display the right spirit of service in line two can now be seen as only a first step towards what must turn out to be total commitment. The importance of line three is skillfully emphasized by its enjambement with line four; the intonation and rhythms of the original opening phrases are now transformed, making what seemed to be a simple statement of topic at the beginning of the poem ("Pour vostre amour . . .") now become the focus of all the lover's energy: "je ferai toute cose / Pour vostre amour . . ."

After this forceful statement, Froissart begins the second part of the poem with a contrast in tone that represents, in the tradition of courtly poetry, a necessary balancing element to the lover's initial boldness. Having used the imperative form in line three with "Commandés moi," he now uses a parallel structure to ask forgiveness, beginning line five with "Pardonnés moi" and ending on a reference defining his offense, the word "ose." What this admission of guilt naturally leads up to, of course, is an opportunity for the lover to explain his behavior. Whereas the reference to beauty in the first line of the refrain had served quite neatly to draw the connection between the kind of love being pursued ("belle") and the kind of heart that was necessary for success ("joli et gai"), it is now clear that the lady's "biauté" also exerts a much more significant power that causes the lover to undertake even the risk of displeasing her with his attentions. With the complex role of beauty thus defined in this climactic line, the word "belle" in the final repetition of the refrain takes on special importance, echoing the sense of inspiration that lies behind both the lover's audacity and his will to please.

Poems such as this, in which the lover addresses his lady or expresses an emotional response to the state of his affairs, are numerous in the collected *rondeaux* and are most notable for the way they establish intricate connections among a small set of conventional concepts or images. Froissart's best poems in the genre, however, make use of the *rondeau*'s capacity for exploring the tensions between a preconceived, generalized idea, which is presented in the refrain, and the speaker's personal experience, which is the basis for the commentary.[42] Even in these poems, the subject always has to do with love, but Froissart shows his inventiveness by presenting many different aspects of the suitor's experience and by using a variety of rhetorical approaches. This habitual flexibility in his thinking contributes a pleasing freshness to poems which are already notable for their technical perfection.

The dynamics of Froissart's method of exploring tensions are especially well illustrated in Rondeau 41. This poem begins with a conventional truism (introduced by "on dist") and then counters it in a two-pronged attack:

> *On dist que c'est une trop plaisans vie*
> *De bien amer par amours loyaument,*
> Et li pluiseur l'appellent maladie.
> *On dist que c'est une trop plaisans vie,*
> Mais tant qu'a moi, je sçai bien, quoi c'on die,
> Plus y ai mal assés qu'esbatement.
> *On dist que c'est une trop plaisans vie,*
> *De bien amer par amours loyaument.*

> *[People say that it's a very pleasing life*
> *To love with passion and with loyalty,*
> And yet love is often called a "malady."
> *People say that it's a very pleasing life,*
> But as for me, I'm sure, whatever they say,
> I have more pain in loving than gaiety.
> *People say that it's a very pleasing life*
> *To love with passion and with loyalty.]*

Since the commentary in this genre is traditionally dominated by a first-person perspective, the use of the third-person phrase "li pluiseur" in line three gives the speaker's opening argument an unexpected source of strength, establishing, as it does, a conflict outside the experience of a mere individual. Indeed, Froissart shows that the paradox he is exploring is inherent in the very language of love poetry, for while the first two lines amass an entire collection of conventional words and phrases with positive connotations ("plaisans vie," "bien amer," "par amours," "loyaument"), line three draws attention to the fact that the word "maladie" has at least as much, if not more, currency among those who know love well.

With this conflict of opinion established, the partial repetition of the refrain in line four takes on a tentative tone, the phrase "on dit" now seeming to command much less authority than before. This decrease in the credibility of the original generalization prepares for the speaker's second argument, the assessment of his personal experience.

Using three separate short phrases in line five, Froissart emphatically draws a line separating the voice of the speaker ("tant qu'a *moi*," "*je* sçai bien") from the now doubtful voice of common opinion ("quoi c'*on* die"), building anticipation for the resolution in line six. Thus, when the speaker's judgment is finally verbalized, it needs no embellishment: the negative ("mal") is weighed against the positive ("esbatement") and the former is found to be clearly dominant. As the refrain comes around for the final time, the original tension inherent in its phrasing has disappeared: it may be true that "people say" the life of love is predominantly pleasant, but, in the experience of the speaker, they are simply wrong.

Although the kind of *rondeau* which explores contradictory ideas is often, like this one, phrased mostly in abstract, conventional language, Froissart sometimes uses a specific image as the center of focus. In Rondeau 10, for example, he builds upon a child's experience of the schoolmaster's rod to express the tension between an individual's youthful expectations and the reality which he discovers as an adult:

> *Quant je parti des verges d'ignorance,*
> *Je cuidai bien estre issus de dangier,*
> Mais depuis ai senti aultre poissance,
> *—Quant je parti des verges d'ignorance—*
> Car Amours m'a donné cops de plaisance
> Qui sont plus dur que de fier ne d'achier.
> *Quant je parti des verges d'ignorance,*
> *Je cuidai bien estre issus de dangier.*

> *[When I outgrew the schoolmaster's rod,*
> *I believed myself free from harsh authority,*
> But since then I have felt another power,
> *—Since I outgrew the schoolmaster's rod—*
> For mighty Love has dealt me blows of pleasure
> Which are more severe than blows of iron and steel,
> *When I outgrew the schoolmaster's rod,*
> *I believed myself free from harsh authority.]*

In its basic structure, this poem is very similar to the poem on the life of love. Just as the phrase "on dit" in the refrain of that poem creates the potential for contradicting a generalized opinion, the past-tense expression "je cuidai bien" in this one implies that the speaker's past opinion has been proven wrong. Likewise, to build upon this implication, Froissart again makes distinct use of the two parts of the commentary, first increasing the tension and then resolving it. The main mechanism in this case is the teasing vagueness in line three, where the transition seems to promise an explanation ("Mais depuis ai senti") but the final words refuse to identify the source of harsh authority in the speaker's life ("aultre puissance"). This delay tactic, along with the interrupting repetition in line four, increases the level of anticipation, giving the next two lines the climactic importance they deserve.

In addition to this structural technique, Froissart also develops a pattern of imagery that contributes to the tension and significance of the poem. The "schoolmaster's rod," with its physical power and universal familiarity, is first introduced as an appropriate symbol for the stage in life when a child has the least defense against being controlled by others; phrased as the "verges d'ignorance," it implies that learning and maturity will enable the child to move on to a stage of awareness where such pain can be avoided. But the heavily loaded meaning of the word "dangier" offers a strong initial clue as to why the poem's speaker is still suffering, for the same word that represents the simple concept of the "harsh authority" of the schoolmaster in childhood is even more frequently associated, in adulthood, with the tyrannical domination and unjust disappointments of the life of love. The fact that it is indeed the power of love that the poet has experienced is confirmed in line five with the word "Amours"; at the same time, interest in the central symbol is heightened by the potentially oxymoronic expression "cops de plaisance," which reveals the comparative complexity of the adult experience. The importance of the concrete image becomes apparent at this point, for it would seem that "blows of pleasure" should be less disagreeable than the canings administered at school. As the language of line six reveals, however, these blows are "more severe than blows of iron and steel," giving them a level of power that even the defenseless child never experienced. Indeed, rather than leading to a resolution of the uncertainty introduced in the initial refrain, the imagery of the poem builds to a new, higher level of tension that carries over into the meaning of the final word of the last two lines: while the "dangier" of the schoolmaster's rod is in fact a thing of the past, the adult concept of "dangier" is a complex, self-contradictory, and inexplicably powerful experience that threatens to stay with the speaker of the poem indefinitely.

The interplay of ideas in this poem, and others of its type, depends upon having a refrain that implies a possible contradiction, but Froissart sometimes takes a more direct approach and begins his poems with a question.[43] This technique, like the other, allows back and forth movement between a generalized idea that is under scrutiny and the speaker's personal response, but in this case there is more emphasis on the authority that arises from the speaker's experience as a lover. Thus, in one poem the speaker answers the question "Where does love come from?" (Rondeau 43) and in another he explains why the song of the nightingale is "thought to be so full of grace" (Rondeau 97).[44] Interestingly, however, Froissart shows in Rondeau 44 that even something as seemingly stable as playing the role of the authority can involve internal conflicts, making the very asking of the question a source of psychological tension:

> *Des quels des deus fait Amours plus grant cure?*
> *Ou de la dame ou dou loyal ami,*
> Quant cascuns d'euls en bonne amour procure?
> *Des quels des deus fait Amours plus grant cure?*
> Taire m'en voel, la matere est obscure,
> Si en lairai jugier autrui que mi.
> *Des quels des deus fait Amours plus grant cure?*
> *Ou de la dame ou dou loyal ami?*

>> *[For which of the two does Love have more concern?*
>> *Is it for the lady or for the loyal lover,*
>> When both of them devote themselves to love?
>> *For which of the two does Love have more concern?*
>> I wish to hold my peace, the subject's difficult,
>> So I'll leave it up to someone else to judge.
>> *For which of the two does Love have more concern?*
>> *Is it for the lady or for the loyal lover?]*

With its opening lines phrased in the form of a traditional *demande d'amour*, this poem would immediately remind the audience of such works as Machaut's *Le Jugement dou Roy de Behaingne*, a conventional courtly narrative which required the poet to take a position in the debate over whether, in this example, a woman suffers more from widowhood or a man from rejection. While in Froissart's poem the controversy is neither as specific nor as dramatically engaging as in Machaut's, the importance of the question itself is emphasized by the fact that the speaker spends a full four lines stating and explaining the exact nature of the dispute, using balanced structure in line 2 and a statement of conditions in line 3 before repeating the basic question in line 4. This change from Froissart's usual practice of using the third line of a *rondeau* to introduce the speaker's personal voice reinforces the formality of the discussion, in turn giving extra weight to the conventional expectation that the poet is capable of resolving a doctrinal issue with a clear and authoritative answer.

Thus the poem is likely to catch its audience off guard with the sudden appearance of an authorial voice that seems to have no confidence at all in expressing an opinion on the subject. Instead of addressing the traditional question that he has so methodically spelled out, the speaker raises the more self-conscious literary issue of how a poet himself might feel about having to play the authority when he really doesn't know what to say. The audience, of course, would have been aware that this was not merely a theoretical problem, since Machaut, after concluding in his *Jugement dou Roy de Behaingne* that the man suffered more, had been compelled to write a second poem, *Le Jugement dou Roy de Navarre*, favoring the woman.[45] With his casual dismissal of the difficult "matere" that he has been handed, Froissart's persona steps outside of his official role as lyric poet and assumes instead the voice of a more humanized individual who is comically frustrated by a literary tradition that does not take into account the conflicting interests of the real-life men and women listening to the poem. Although in its opening lines this *rondeau* looks the same as many others, the tension that is created is a playful one, built not upon the conflict between a convention and a response, but upon the inconsistency between the attitude of the speaker and the requirements of the genre the poet has chosen to express it in. Like the *ballade* on health and several of the *pastourelles*, this *rondeau* suggests an ironic authorial self-awareness that allows the poet to comment on his craft even while performing it.

In addition to creating overt tensions within poems by using direct questions and inherently doubtful opening statements, Froissart also frequently produces a more subtle tension by beginning his *rondeaux* with a familiar proverb in need of specific interpretation. Like the other opening devices, this one makes the formal structure of the genre functional, since it allows the poet to establish a voice of common wisdom in the refrain and interpret through the voice of an individual

lover in the commentary.[46] As Rondeau 29 demonstrates, Froissart
uses the interplay between the two voices to apply a general principle
specifically to the concerns of the life of love:

> *En trop haster n'a nul avancement,*
> *Et tels se cuide arrierer qui s'avance.*
> Amours, j'ai bien de tout ce sentement:
> *En trop haster n'a nul avancement.*
> Mieuls vault souffrir et vivre liement
> Qu'enprendre riens dont on se desavance.
> *En trop haster n'a nul avancement,*
> *Et tels se cuide arrierer qui s'avance.*

>> *[There is no progress when there's too much haste,*
>> *And the man who thinks he's set back is progressing well*
>> Love, this is a thought I fully share:
>> *There is no progress when there's too much haste.*
>> It is better to suffer patiently and live in peace
>> Than to undertake an act that might cause loss.
>> *There is no progress when there's too much haste,*
>> *And the man who thinks he's set back is progressing well.]*

Because the distinction between the two voices is so important,
Froissart emphasizes the proverbial nature of the refrain by using two
easily recognizable proverbial structures, the introductory preposition
"en" (which occurs in 51 of the 2500 Old French proverbs listed by
Morawski) and the subject "tel" (represented in 63 of the proverbs on
Morawski's list).[47] In contrast to this, line three introduces both the
first-person subject "je" and a noun of direct address, "Amours,"
creating a very specific context in which the speaker voices his
agreement. This change in point of view colors the partial repetition of
the refrain in line four, inviting the reader to reconsider it as a truth
having to do with the way one would best proceed--or avoid
proceeding--in matters of the heart.

As it usually does, the climax of the commentary appears in lines
five and six. The argument in this case does not refer directly to the
speaker's experience, as might be expected, but rather falls into the
category of what Whiting calls "sententious remarks,"[48] that is,
non-traditional comments with the moralizing tone of a proverb. Since
the context of love has already been established, key words such as
"souffrir," "liement," "enprendre," and "desavance" all automatically

take on specific conventional meanings having to do with the relationship between the lover and the lady, making the application of the original proverb to this particular set of circumstances quite clear. At the same time, however, these words are general enough in meaning that they fit the "sententious" tone that Froissart obviously was seeking when he chose to use the structural pattern "mieuls vault . . . que," which is so common in proverbs (Morawski lists 68 in this exact form and several others beginning "il vault mieux"). By maintaining what appears to be the same amount of personal distance in the commentary as in the refrain, Froissart gives the whole poem a uniform level of credibility while still making use of the two distinct levels of generalized and applied truth.

It would be a mistake to assume, however, that Froissart's use of a consistently impersonal tone in one *rondeau* of this type means that he stays rigidly within the same constraint all the time. On the contrary, the one quality that makes the entire collection of *rondeaux* most interesting is his ability to combine each of the different rhetorical approaches with a variety of tones and structural configurations. Thus, even among those poems that state a proverb and then gloss it, there are some, like Rondeau 81, which present a distinctly personal point of view:

> *On dist que drois a bien mestier d'aïe,*
> *Et bien le puis en amours perchevoir,*
> Car j'ai priiet tous les jours de ma vie.
> *On dist que drois a bien mestier d'aïe.*
> Onques ne peuch dame avoir ne amie;
> Or regardés dont se drois a dit voir.
> *On dist que drois abien mestier d'aïe,*
> *Et bien le puis en amours perchevoir.*

> > *[They say that justice has great need of aid,*
> > *And I am surely aware of this in love,*
> > For I've made entreaties every day of my life.
> > *They say that justice has great need of aid.*
> > And yet I can never have a lady or a sweetheart;
> > Now judge for yourself if the proverb speaks the
> > truth.
> > *They say that justice has great need of aid,*
> > *And I am surely aware of this in love.]*

The proverb that Froissart has chosen as the basis for this poem is both less well known than the proverb on "haste" and less easily connected to the subject of love. Cotgrave's dictionary cites a version with the very similar wording "Bon droist a bon mestier d'aide" and glosses it as "a Prouerb taxing th'iniquitie, and iniustice of our times; wherein good right hath oftentimes need of great fauour"[49]--an explanation which places the meaning primarily within a legal context. Nevertheless, Froissart chooses not to paraphrase or otherwise explain the proverb in line two as he did in the previous poem; in this case, his proof lies not in connecting concepts, but in revealing the way the speaker's own life has illustrated the central principle. Thus the function of line two is simply to provide the transition into the main body of material, with the word "amours" putting the proverb into its proper context and the first-person verb phrase "puis perchevoir" emphasizing the personal perspective through which the proverb will be judged.

With the transition already completed in line 2 of the refrain, it becomes possible for Froissart to use the natural two-part division of the commentary as a logical device demonstrating the lack of "drois" in the speaker's circumstances. Line 3 spells out what the speaker has done to deserve notice "en amours": not only has he sought love, but he has "entreated" a lady "every day of his life." After line 4 reminds the audience of the fact that justice is often not served, line 5 states the sad results of the speaker's dedication, the fact that he never gets the lady no matter how hard he tries. As in some of the *ballades*, the speaker here is clearly an underdog; his pitiful vulnerability is emphasized by the pairing of his exaggerated claim of diligence ("tous les jours de ma vie") with an equally powerful image of his rejection ("Onques ne peuch . . ."). Froissart makes the most of the strongly personal tone of this passage by turning line six into a direct plea, addressing members of the audience with a demand that they judge the case for themselves. The word "drois," which refers to the dependability of the proverb itself in this line,[50] ties the poem together with a possible double meaning, since the syntax is arranged not only to urge affirmation of the truth of the proverb but also to raise the question of whether justice has behaved in an honest or upright manner. Appropriately, the arrangement of the refrain places the final repetition of the proverb immediately after the speaker's plea to the audience and leaves the important last line to reemphasize the personal perspective in what the speaker can "perchevoir."

Poems such as this demonstrate Froissart's ability to use the *rondeau* form effectively within a wide range of themes, tones, and rhetorical strategies; whether he is writing from a broad or narrow perspective, working with abstract or concrete language, or choosing between proverbial and expressive subject matter, his careful matching of form and meaning are indicative of his sure sense of the potential impact of the genre and its structure. One final measure of his poetic awareness is to be found, however, not in individual poems but in a set of four *rondeaux* which appear consecutively in both manuscripts. Although these poems are in no way marked as belonging to a group, they all treat the subject of the lover's struggle to decide whether to speak out to his lady and declare his love. Like the individual voices in a debate, each of these *rondeaux* takes on its own personality as it defends a particular point of view; the tones, the rhetorical strategies, and the levels of personal expression are all pleasingly varied. Even more importantly, the balance and interaction among the four poems demonstrate just how effectively Froissart was able to use the compact form of the *rondeau* to express the essence of each single, unified line of thought.

The series of poems opens with Rondeau 82, where Froissart introduces his subject by emphasizing the emotional tension in the lover's situation. The central image of the "basse vois" captures the uncertainty and sense of risk experienced by the suitor who is caught between desire and fear:

> *A basse vois vous prie merchi, dame,*
> *Car je ne puis ne ose haut parler;*
> Si ai je bien cause de dire alarme,
> *A basse vois vous prie merchi, dame,*
> Car vostre amour me mainne tel, par m'ame
> Qu'il me faurra, ou voelle ou non, parler.
> *A basse vois vous prie merchi, dame,*
> *Car je ne puis ne ose haut parler.*

> *[I beg your mercy quietly, my lady,*
> *For I cannot and dare not speak out loud;*
> Truly I have cause to express alarm,
> *I beg your mercy quietly, my lady,*
> For, by my soul, love leads me to the point

> That I'll have to speak, whether I wish to or not.
> *I beg your mercy quietly, my lady,*
> *For I cannot and dare not speak out loud.]*

The expressive nature of this poem is reflected in the fact that a first-person pronoun is either stated or implied in every line of verse, giving the whole *rondeau* an insistently personal point of view. What really makes the tension convincing, however, is the way Froissart fills the lines with words having to do with language and sound while at the same time creating a continuous string of oppositions. The opposing pairs "basse vois" and "haut parler" in lines one and two are supplemented by both an additional verb of speaking, "prie," and the negative verbal phrase "ne puis ne ose" to create a refrain which dramatizes the speaker's ambivalence. In line 3, as Froissart begins to present the details of the speaker's state of mind, he continues the pattern with the phrase "dire alarme," emphasizing again the central role of verbal expression in this lover's emotional dilemma. By the time he comes back to the key word "parler" in line 6, it has become clear through the verb "mainne" and the exclamation "par m'ame" that the lover is losing control of his ability to make rational choices, and that some sort of speech will come out "ou voelle ou non." As this last expression before the refrain indicates, the speaker's decision to speak softly is at best a timid compromise made by a lover who is torn between unacceptable alternatives.

Rondeau 83, on the other hand, takes a more decisive approach. As if in reaction to the soul-searching and tentativeness of the first lover, Froissart has this speaker turn his attention outward and directly challenge a rule that threatens to make his life miserable:

> *Ne sçai pour quoi on n'ose dire voir,*
> *Quant on se voit de tout perdre en balance:*
> Dame, merchi, a vous tient dou savoir.
> *Ne sçai pour quoi on n'ose dire voir.*
> Pour vostre amour languis et main et soir,
> Et si m'en tais c'est moult dure ordenance.
> *Ne sçai pour quoi on n'ose dire voir,*
> *Quant on se voit de tout perdre en balance.*

> *[I don't know why men dare not speak the truth,*
> *When they see themselves in danger of losing all;*
> Lady, have mercy, I can find out only from you.

I don't know why men dare not speak the truth;
I languish for your love both night and day,
And the rule of silence makes life much too hard.
I don't know why men dare not speak the truth,
When they see themselves in danger of losing all.]

Unlike the first poem, this one is not entirely dominated by personal perspective. Although the refrain begins with the first-person "ne sçai," this verb of knowing directs the focus onto a question of general principle concerning why men behave in a certain--apparently irrational--way. Moreover, Froissart's use of oppositions in this poem does not create a mood of ambivalence as it does in Rondeau 82, but rather sets up distinct and clear-cut alternatives between an obvious good--"dire voir"--and an unmistakable evil--"tout perdre." In place of multiple verbs of speaking, Froissart introduces in this poem a pattern which emphasizes the speaker's interest in what he sees ("se voit") and what he hopes to understand ("ne sçai," "savoir"). As is indicated even in the section addressing the lady directly in line three, this speaker's idea of "merchi" requires that he be provided a reasonable explanation for all the suffering he is asked to endure.[51]

Froissart makes the difference in attitude and tone between the two poems equally clear in his handling of lines 5 and 6, where he has the speaker in each case make reference to his personal situation. Although both passages include the words "vostre amour" near the beginning, the syntax of Rondeau 82 leaves its speaker in a passive situation, being "led" by love, while the syntax of Rondeau 83 puts the speaker in control, acting "for" love. This second lover is, of course, "languishing" nonetheless, but the emphatic tone of phrases like "et main et soir" and "moult dure" show him to be less interested in obtaining pity than in driving home a point. By making the general structure of the two poems so nearly parallel, Froissart is able to use these kinds of subtle differences in tone, vocabulary, and syntax to make the two speakers strikingly distinct.

The last two poems in the set, Rondeaux 84 and 85, likewise form a matched pair, this time based upon a different type of rhetorical strategy that puts less emphasis on the dramatic situation of the speaker. In contrast to the first pair of poems in which the speakers address their ladies directly and have a single course of action firmly in mind, these poems each show the lover weighing his options, using a kind of interior dialogue to clarify exactly what is at stake. In

Rondeau 84, Froissart begins by having the speaker imagine what will happen if he tries speaking out:

> *Se je parolle et je ne sui oïs,*
> *Trop me sera parolle virgongneuse,*
> Et sans parler n'est nuls homs conjoïs.
> *—Se je parolle et je ne sui oïs—*
> Dont me faut il pour estre resjoïs,
> Dire et monstrer ma vie langereuse.
> *Se je parolle et je ne sui oïs,*
> *Trop me sera parolle virgongneuse.*

>> *[If I speak out and I am not heard,*
>> *My speaking will be a terrible shame to me,*
>> Yet no man meets Fair Welcome unless he speaks.
>> *—If I speak out and I am not heard—*
>> And so I must, to attain the joys of love,
>> Speak and reveal the langourous life I live.
>> *If I speak out and I am not heard,*
>> *My speaking will be a terrible shame to me.]*

Like the first two poems in the set, this one includes an important pair of opposing words which define the conflict as the speaker sees it: if he speaks unsuccessfully, his words will be "virgongneuse," but if he does not speak, he has no hope of being "conjoïs." This poem differs from the others, however, in that the opposing words do not form the basis for a single argument which can be stated in the refrain and supported in the remaining lines. Instead, the opposition is distributed throughout the poem, with one argument appearing in the refrain lines and the other in the "commentary," creating the kind of carefully balanced tension that keeps the lover's dilemma appropriately unresolved.

If the poem does not resolve the dilemma, however, it does clarify it. Although the back-and-forth movement of the arguments would seem at first to be weighing equal concerns, the poet's choice of words shows the fear of shame to be only a serious risk the lover undertakes "*if*. . . he is not heard," while the failure to be accepted is an absolute result ("*nuls* homs") of remaining silent. This difference, combined with the lover's natural desire to push forward, explains the point of view in line 5, where the words "dont" and "faut" show the speaker drawing a conclusion only about the option of pursuing his "joy" and not about giving up. Ironically, what begins as an affirmation of line 3 ("I must . . . / Speak out) becomes, as it continues, a revelation of why the dilemma is inescapable: in order to be "resjoïs," the lover must reveal his "vie langereuse" and thus expose himself to the very shame he fears. Although the weight of the rhetoric of the poem leans towards a decision to speak, the tone is decidedly discouraging, especially as the refrain comes back with a final, persistent reminder that the danger is unavoidable.

Froissart's handling of the balance between the arguments in this poem is revealing, in itself, of the way he could adapt the *rondeau* form for exploring, rather than merely defending, a line of reasoning. In conjunction with the final poem of the series, however, it also shows his awareness of how one set of initial assumptions can shape an entirely different line of reasoning from another set of assumptions, even though both may be equally valid. By using exactly the same opening syntactic structure in Rondeau 85 as in Rondeau 84, the poet emphasizes both the similarity of his general approach and the difference in his point of departure:[52]

> *Se je me tais on ne fait de moi cure,*
> *Et se ne suis bien enlangagiés.*
> Que ferai dont? Ceste vie m'est dure.
> *Se je me tais on ne fait de moi cure;*
> Taire me vault trop mieulz et tout endure
> Que de parler et puis soie escachiés.
> *Se je me tais on ne fait de moi cure,*
> *Et se ne sui pas bien enlangiés.*

> *[If I remain silent, no one will care about me,*
> *Yet I am not blessed with the gift of eloquence.*
> So what shall I do? My life is hard.
> *If I remain silent, no one will care about me.*
> It's better for me to be silent and endure it all
> Than to speak out and then be sent away.
> *If I remain silent, no one will care about me,*
> *Yet I am not blessed with the gift of eloquence.]*

Instead of beginning by having his speaker consider what might happen if he speaks, Froissart has this lover think first of what will happen if he doesn't speak. This difference is important, since, as the previous poem demonstrated, failure to advance with the lady is a certainty, not just a risk, for the lover who remains silent. Moreover, when this speaker examines the other side of the issue, imagining what will happen if he speaks, he is faced not with the usual risk, identified by the previous speaker, but by another inescapable fact, his belief that he lacks eloquence. Whereas Froissart showed the other lover to be in a state of tension between the idea of the refrain and the idea in the commentary, he demonstrates this lover's doubly difficult situation with two equal lines in the refrain followed by a hopeless lament in line 3.

Just as the introduction of the speaker's personal disadvantage changes the dynamics of the first three lines of the poem, it also leads to a different kind of conclusion in lines 5 and 6. Because the speaker lacks even the usual gift of speech that might be expected of a lover, Froissart identifies his worst fear as being banished from the lady's presence, an idea that did not even occur to the lover in the previous poem. Whereas the first lover was able to hold on to some hope of success which encouraged him to accept the inevitable risk, this lover's initial assumptions leave him a choice only between a bad situation-- remaining silent and getting nowhere--and one that is even worse-- speaking awkwardly and being sent away. By having this lover arrive at a firm conclusion and resign himself to a life of silent pain, Froissart demonstrates how deeply a difference in initial perspective can influence the outcome of two essentially similar dilemmas.

As a group, these four poems illustrate not only Froissart's skill at adapting the genre for expressing different meanings, but also his awareness of the limitations inherent in taking only a single point of view. Like four separate people locked within their own circumstances and personalities, these *rondeaux* each express valid sentiments which are, nonetheless, only a part of a much more complex total picture. Although the lovers' concerns over whether to speak or not are, on one level, merely another manifestation of the artificial system of refined love, Froissart's handling of different perspectives demonstrates his sure sense of the way numerous individual perceptions must come together if anyone is to form a real understanding of any aspect of human experience.

Froissart's recognition of the potential of the *rondeau* for presenting individualized perceptions in capsule form is, like his use of the same genre for expressing tensions and glossing proverbs, a reflection of the way he habitually sought out the subject matter and treatments that were most suitable for the various fixed form structures available to the poets of his day. Just as he found a variety of ways to create meaning out of the logical progressions and juxtaposed illustrations that were traditionally associated with the three stanzas of the *ballade*, he explored the compact two-voice interplay of the *rondeau* and the more limited pattern of amplification in the *virelay* with an eye to offering his audience different ways of thinking as well as different tones and rhythmic moods. In all three of the short lyric forms he applied specialized techniques to create a harmonious blend of sound, structure, and meaning, creating a collection of poems that is notable for the way each genre is used to its best advantage.

Notes: Chapter IV

1. For a full discussion of the origins and histories of these genres, see Poirion, 313-395. On the question of whether the audience ever actually joined in singing the refrains, Poirion quotes a passage from Froissart's *Prison Amoureuse* (1. 401) where the ladies joined hands and danced to a *virelay*; the singer "chantait" and the audience "repondait" (318). Given the complexity of both the music and the text of most fourteenth-century lyrics, this practice must have been extremely rare by Froissart's day, but, as Poirion points out, the fact that the refrain originally represented the "collective voice" of society explains the frequency of poems structured around a proverb or a piece of common wisdom.

2. Poirion, 320, 374. The difference between the genres is magnified in Froissart's poetry because his *rondeaux* are mostly of the eight-line variety. This very short form uses a two-line refrain; after its full and partial repetitions, there are only three lines available for new material.

3. Baudouin, li-lii. For a table showing Froissart's choice of stanza forms, lines, and rhyme schemes in all the *ballades*, see Baudouin, liii.

4. Poirion, 366-67.

5. For a table showing the frequency of the various stanza lengths used by major fourteenth-century lyric poets, see Poirion, 374-75. *Ballade* stanzas of more than twelve lines are very unusual; Froissart's never exceeded ten.

6. Whiting, "Froissart as Poet," 210. Whiting cites Froissart's poetic "skill," his "original" use of mythological examples, and his occasional choice of unconventional subjects to back up his statement.

7. Poirion, 367.

8. For an overview of the various occurrences of these and other rhetorical devices, see Baudouin, xli-xlviii.

9. Poirion, 361.

10. Poirion, 361. For a discussion of the rose window as a metaphor in medieval narrative, see John Leyerle, "The Rose-Wheel Design and Dante's *Paradiso*," *University of Toronto Quarterly* 46 (1977): 280-308.

11. To compare examples of Chaucer's skill with the catalogue style, see in particular *The Monk's Tale* and the Proem to Book III of *Troilus and Criseyde*.

12. This version of stanza three is taken from the collected lyrics. An alternate version, which appears in the *Paradys d'Amour* (ll. 1627-53), will be discussed below.

13. As Baudouin points out (108), these references are particularly reminiscent of lines 1615-16, where the roses "estoient en un destor, / D'une haie bien enclos entor" and lines 3592 ff., where Jealousy has a wall built around the roses, with a tower in the middle which encloses Fair Welcome (F. Lecoy, ed., CFMA).

14. The ease with which Froissart and his contemporaries blended traditions is shown here by the fact that this characterization of Love

seems to have more in common with the guiding figure in Dante's *Vita Nuova* than with the archer who pursues the Dreamer in the *Roman de la Rose*. As Huot points out, Froissart's *Paradis* "conflates the *Rose* and a principal set of responses to it" (*From Song to Book*, 304), creating a kind of composite which, like his characteristic reworkings of Ovidian narrative, has been consciously refocused to suit his thematic emphasis.

15. If Froissart is in fact using this stanza as a playful reminder to his audience of his own work, this passage is similar to his repeated references to the characters of Heros and Cephëus, as discussed in Chapter 3. See Dembowski, "Tradition, Dream Literature, and Poetic Craft in *Le Paradis d'Amour* de Jean Froissart," *Studies in the Literary Imagination* 20 (1987): 99-109, for a more complete discussion of how Froissart asserts his "strong professional personality" through his handling of lyrics in *Le Paradis*.

16. One simple indication of the number of *ballades* that are structured this way is the fact that the word "car" appears at or near the beginning of stanza two in at least sixteen poems.

17. Baudouin points out in her notes on this poem that the reference to languishing "in a faraway land" (27-28) is a commonplace in the rhetoric of refined love. She adds, however, that "on peut se demander s'il n'y a pas là une allusion au premier séjour de Froissart en Angleterre." The approximate date that she assigns to the poem would be consistent with this interpretation, though most biographical evidence indicates that Froissart enjoyed his visit to England, rather than "languishing" there.

18. The complete text and translation of Ballade 9 appear in Appendix A. McGregor identifies Tholomee as Ptolemaea, who "died for love of Nestor in India according to an unidentified incident" (371).

19. McGregor, 48, quotes a passage from Deschamps which had previously been cited by Scheler (II, 476-77).

20. Baudouin, lii.

21. This *ballade*, like Lay 13 (examined in Chapter 2), appears in the *Joli Buisson de Jonece* (3996-4013). Both are part of an overall pattern (including also Lai 11) in which the fire of love is a recurring motif.

22. The choice of a short stanza and short lines is typical of Froissart's *ballades équivoquées*. His other three poems of this type all have a six-line stanza with seven-syllable lines.

23. The only exception to Froissart's rule of preferring a personal tone when writing on a non-traditional subject is Ballade 31, in which he recounts the mythological story of how Brutus left Italy to establish a new race in Albion; this poem and its translation appear in Appendix A.

24. This speaker, with his lack of confidence, is reminiscent of Chaucer's narrator in *Troilus and Criseyde*, who complains of his "unliklynesse" (16). In both cases the effect is to emphasize the innocence of the speaker's enthusiasm as he waxes eloquent over the love affair he is describing. Although Froissart's poem probably precedes Chaucer's (see Baudouin, xiv-xvii), the similarity is too broad to lead to any conclusion about direct influence; rather, this example of Froissart's gentle humor in presenting himself as a character suggests that the two poets were sufficiently compatible in spirit to account for Chaucer's willingness to borrow lines, mythological references, and even an occasional suggestion of tone.
The complete text and translation of Ballade 33 appear in Appendix A.

25. As Baudouin points out in her note on this poem, Chaucer makes a similar reference to wines in the *Canterbury Tales*, v. 1470: "clare, pyment, and Rochele." The complete text and a translation of this poem appear in Appendix A.

26. Dembowski suggests that the reason this poem is omitted from manuscript B may be that it was too indelicate and "anti-courtoise" for French tastes (*Le Paradis*, 9).

27. Froissart uses a two-line refrain in only four poems, Ballades 1 and 2 in the collected lyrics and two *ballades* from a short narrative entitled the *Joli mois de may*. If the manuscript order is, as the critics generally agree, chronological, this means that Froissart used the longer refrain only very early in his career.

28. Poirion, 346.

29. Whiting, "Froissart as Poet," 210.

30. The two manuscripts each include a collection of thirteen *virelays*, only three of which are original poems not appearing elsewhere in a narrative context. Even more telling is the fact that the narratives include sixteen *virelays* which are not included in the collection, compared to only three uncollected *ballades* and seven uncollected *rondeaux*.

31. The term *stanza* is used here as a matter of convenience even though, as Wilkins points out, the *virelay* and *rondeau* "do not lend themselves to being discussed in terms of stanzas" in the ordinary sense of the word (339). My use of the word will refer to groups of lines which are separated from others by having a distinct pattern of rhyme and rhythm corresponding to the progression of musical sections.

32. I am following Poirion's use of the term *cauda* for this section (327); this term seems appropriate since by its modern definition a coda occurs at the end of a movement and brings it to a formal close (in this case the return of the refrain). For the preceding section, which I am referring to as a "rhythmic variation," Poirion uses the terms *ouvert* and *clos*. These terms are quite correct in describing the symmetrical pattern of rhyme and rhythm that occurs in this section, but they have the disadvantage of making two units out of a single pattern of thought.

33. According to Poirion, Machaut repeated the whole pattern twice, for a total of three sets of interior stanzas; Froissart, along with other poets of his day, usually included only two sets of interior stanzas; in Virelay 2 he includes only one. Poirion suggests that this movement towards the shorter form may have arisen from the poets'

desire to gather their thoughts into a form that was "plus dense, moins disloquée" (344).

34. Poirion, 332.

35. Poirion, 327.

36. I am following Wilkins in assuming that the refrains in Froissart's poems are to be fully expanded (346). McGregor's practice of printing the first line of the refrain at the end of each coda seems unsatisfactory since it distorts the rhyme pattern and also frequently leaves an incomplete grammatical unit standing alone.

37. Virelay 13 is unusual in adopting the cynical tone of an experienced lover who now recognizes the folly of his youth and will no longer search for happiness in love. As the last of the three independent *virelays*, it seems to be part of a series: in Virelay 11, a sorrowful lover begins his lament, "If I am dressed in black . . ."; in Virelay 12, a successful lover begins with the line, "If I am gay and joyful"; in Virelay 13, the refrain begins "Take the white, take the black" and concludes by saying that even after taking all the colors a person will "fail to obtain" what he wants. These *virelays* and their translations appear in Appendix A. Froissart's skill in handling a similar series of *rondeaux* will be discussed below.

38. Wilkins lists five possible variations in the length of the *rondeau*, having found examples with a total length of eight, eleven, thirteen, sixteen, and twenty-one lines. Froissart uses the thirteen-line form only once, in a *rondeau* found in *L'Espinette amoureuse* (Rondeau V in Baudouin's edition).

39. Baudouin, lvi. Figures on Machaut's choice of long and short lines come from Poirion, 325.

40. The distinction between the *rondeaux* which appear in narrative contexts and those which do not is quite striking, since all of the intercalated *rondeaux* have a seven-syllable line. It is possible that Froissart found the shorter line rhythmically pleasing as a variation from the eight-syllable lines of the narrative couplets.

41. I have expanded all of the *rondeaux* without indicating where lines were abbreviated in the manuscripts since there is no disagreement among editors with regard to the proper form for the eight-line *rondeau*.

42. Poirion discusses this type of *rondeau* at some length (320-25). My reference to the two "voices" of the *rondeau* in subsequent discussions will always refer to the interplay between the generalized idea as it is presented in the refrain and the personal response which appears in the remaining lines.

43. The use of a question in the opening line is especially common in those *rondeaux* which address the lady or express strong emotions.

44. Rondeau 43 is parallel in rhetorical structure, though not in tone, to Rondeau 44 (discussed below). These two poems could be read together as a pair, since 43 responds to its question in a conventional way, while 44 challenges the convention. Both Rondeaux 43 and 97 are translated in Appendix A.

45. For a similar problem with poetic authority in Chaucer, see the Prologue to the *Legend of Good Women*. For a discussion of Machaut's poems, see William Calin, *A Poet at the Fountain: Essays on the Narrative Verse of Guillaume de Machaut* (Lexington: UP of Kentucky, 1974).

46. Poirion mentions Froissart's treatment of proverbs with little interest, raising the question of whether the poet intended to reduce the role of poetry to "cette activité sérieuse et morose d'endoctrinement" (339). Baudouin, on the other hand, simply comments that, like interrogation, the proverb seems more suited to the "ton didactique" sometimes found in the *rondeaux* than to the tone of the "ballades amoureuses" (xliii-xliv).

47. Morawski, 23-25, 84-86.

48. Whiting, "Proverbs in the Writings of Jean Froissart," 294.

49. Randle Cotgrave, *A Dictionarie of the French and English Tongues* (1611); rpt. Menston, England: The Scolar Press, 1968.

50. See Baudouin's note, 135.

51. In her note on this poem (135), Baudouin glosses the difficult third line as "Il ne tient qu'à vous de le savoir."

52. In McGregor's edition, this poem is punctuated with a comma at the end of line 2 rather than a period. Following this suggestion, the translation would make line 2 part of the question: "And if I am not blessed with the gift of eloquence, / Then what shall I do?" I prefer Baudouin's punctuation since it makes it possible to maintain a consistent reading in the final line of the poem.

V
Conclusion

In his distinctive handling of five short lyric genres, Froissart demonstrates an artistic competence that makes his poetry a particularly valuable source of information about fourteenth-century literary tastes and practices. It is true that his reliance upon conventional subjects, forms, and images generally precluded the kind of innovation that made his prose *Chroniques* a landmark in literary history. Yet the range of poetic effects he achieved while working within these constraints is impressive, offering a convincing demonstration of how the consistent and familiar poetic elements of the fixed forms could serve as a framework for an entire fabric of subtle variations, which in turn allowed his poetry to represent the finely tuned spiritual ideals and complex thought processes valued in medieval courtly society. Understood in this context, his highly developed technical skills, strong sense of structural relationships, and imaginative grasp of narrative perspectives can be reinterpreted as evidence of a level of intellectual and aesthetic engagement worthy of far more critical appreciation than it has previously received.

It is indeed only by recognizing the subtle variations between and within genres that Froissart's achievements can be fully understood. In mastering a metrical system that included both the short, uneven lines of the *lay* and the stately decasyllables of the *chanson royale*, Froissart equipped himself to evoke everything from a sense of psychological turbulence to a mood of eloquent self-discipline. His choice of the comparatively short seven- or eight-syllable line to enhance the highly concentrated progressions of meaning in the *ballade à rime enchaînee* provides merely one example of the conscious artistry that lay behind his treatment of the various *formes fixes*. Clearly, he understood the difficulties of form not merely as a challenge for those who wished to display technical virtuosity, but as an opportunity to create an additional layer of meaning through development of the potential relationships between rhythms and patterns of thought.

For scholars interested in the history of English verse, Froissart's expertise with the ten-syllable line has special significance. In the *chansons royales*, numerous *ballades*, and nearly all the *rondeaux*, his use of this line demonstrates not only the unhurried grace characteristic of the comparatively long line, but also the potential for altering tone and emphasis through patterns of alliteration and changes in the position and intensity of the caesura. While Froissart himself preferred the eight-syllable line for narrative genres such as the *dittie* or *pastourelle*,[1] his imaginative handling of rhythm in the decasyllabic lyrics served, surely, as an important precedent for the versatile iambic pentameter which Chaucer introduced into Middle English.

Likewise, Froissart's experimentation with numerous stanzaic forms and arrangements can be appreciated both for its effectiveness in individual poems and, at times, for its potential influence. In the *virelays*, for example, Froissart often rises above the simple musicality of the genre by using the required alternating metrical patterns and repetitions to reflect the combination of unmovable resolve and emotional intensity expected of an ideal lover. In both this genre and in the *chanson royale*, Froissart exploits the relationship between a highly artificial, strictly controlled stanzaic form and the condition of the speaker of the poem, who must be both eloquent and ideologically strict at the same time. In contrast, he uses the three balanced stanzas of the *ballade* in a way that is less exclusively linked to a single courtly concept. In this case, the structure is made to serve various patterns of logic, with each stanza contributing to a progressive argument and leading towards an increased understanding or fresh insight at the end of the poem. His frequent practice of emphasizing a separate rhetorical device in each successive stanza reinforces the impression that every group of lines corresponds to a distinct and concise unit of thought. Like the ten-syllable line, the *ballade* stanza, in its various forms, appears only in Froissart's lyrics, not in his narrative frames. But the clarity and the emphasis that Froissart achieves with the seven-line *rime royale* or the traditional eight-line *ballade* stanza are qualities which could easily have inspired Chaucer's choice of these same forms for such poems as *Troilus and Criseyde* and the *Monk's Tale*.

Still, it would be a mistake to forget that Froissart's lyric achievements extend beyond aesthetic control to larger issues of theory and meaning. As Huot has pointed out, Froissart ended the "lyrico-narrative anthology" he had created in his manuscripts by taking leave of lyric poetry, preferring to dedicate himself instead to the *Chroniques* and other literary forms that could serve the public by offering insight into larger social and cultural concerns.[2] This impulse to move beyond the fantasies of *fin' amors* appears plainly in the broad patterns of development that Huot has identified in her analysis of the symbolism, thematic emphases, and evolving concepts of the writer-persona in the major *dits*. But it is also evident at times within the contents of the lyric collections themselves. In the *rondeaux* and *virelays*, Froissart's awareness of the problems of genre is most evident where he juxtaposes poems expressing conflicting sentiment on a single theme, drawing attention, especially through the addition of authorial commentary in a third poem, to the limitations of the traditional lyric point of view. Without the structure of a narrative frame to provide a context for the lover's changing moods, these juxtaposed lyrics unmask the conventional poet-persona, substituting instead a self-conscious author who is ironically aware of the narrowness and inconsistency of such an artificially predetermined range of sentiments. Froissart's desire to ground his poetry in reality is reflected even more clearly in the *pastourelles*, where very early in his career he decided to replace the traditional observer-narrator with one who existed in the specific times and places of history. With his facility for creating shifting perspectives and his persistent desire to promote and define chivalric values in the real world, Froissart invited his audience to consider the relationship between classes not just as an idealized lyric fantasy, but as a part of the cultural milieu that could, like *fin' amors* itself, be both appreciated and refined.

Thus, far from having created a uniform body of material distinguished only by conventional variations in matter and form, Froissart reveals in his lyric poems the vitality of an active mind. His strengths in technique, structure, and point of view combine to produce a body of poetry that is both pleasingly varied and intellectually challenging, both the reflection of an age and the achievement of a distinctive individual. For the scholar who wishes to understand the complexities of fourteenth-century literary theory and technique, there is much in the lyric poems to be learned, and for the reader who is willing to enter into the spirit of their artistry, there is much to be enjoyed.

Notes: Conclusion

1. The one exception to this rule is *L'Orloge amoureus* which, unlike all the other *dits*, is written in decasyllables. See Dembowski, "Metrics and Textual Criticism," for a more thorough discussion.

2. Huot, *From Song to Book*, 322-23.

Appendix A:
Poems and Translations

The poems I have chosen for the appendix provide, in combination with those poems discussed in each chapter, a representative overview of Froissart's short lyric works. I have selected some poems in each genre that are typical of the most conventional styles and subjects, as well as several that offer a fresh topic, an experimental tone, or an interesting interplay with other treatments of the same idea. In some cases, such as Chanson Royale I, I have already commented briefly on the poem's significance within my discussion of the genre and am including the text and translation for further reference. In other cases, I have provided notes to direct the reader towards significant features or possible difficulties of interpretation, with the overall intention of making the corpus of Froissart's lyric work more accessible for future research and study.

Chanson Royale 1

Tant sont d'amours li recort gratieus,
Et tant en est la poissance excellente,
Et tant en sont li douls biens plentiveus,
Et tant en est li ordenance gente,
Que coers humains penser ne le poroit,   5
Car s'uns amans ja jour ne possessoit
Dou don d'otroi de dame entirement,
Se dispense il son tamps si noblement
Que pour tous biens amoureus concevoir
Prendre ne puet, ne eslire autrement,   10
Vie qui puist le bien amer valoir.

[Remembrances of love are so pleasing,
And its power is so excellent,
And its sweet virtues are so abundant,
And its manner of conduct is so noble,
That the human heart could not imagine it,
For even if a lover never possessed his lady's
Permission to court her with confidence,
Yet he would spend his time so nobly
That for bringing forth all the goods of love
He could not assume, or otherwise hope to choose,
A life that can measure up to loving well.]

Et che appert par les vrais amoureus,
Aux quels Amours ses nobles biens presente,
Car de priier cascuns se tient songneus,
Quant Dous Regars par Plaisance en eulz ente   15
Les vrais pensers qu'uns amans avoir doit.
Or a Amours ordonné de son droit
Refus en dame, et on voit clerement
Que par detri recoevre amans souvent
Sens, temps, avis, parler, force et sçavoir   20
De ses secrés monstrer plus sagement,
Car par le coer apperent li voloir.

[And this is evident among those truly in love,
Those to whom Love presents his noble goods,
For each lover remains diligent in his pursuit,
Since, through Pleasure, Sweet Glances place in him
The true thoughts that a lover must have.
Now it is right that Love has ordained
Refusal in the lady, and it can be clearly seen
That through delay the lover often reestablishes
The good sense, timing, prudence, discourse,
            strength, and wisdom
To show his secrets with wiser discretion,
For feelings are made manifest by the heart.]

S'est li amans sages et euwireus
Qui corps et coer, sens, penser et entente
Met en amer et se tient curieus   25
De obeïr a si trés noble atente
Comme a Amours ou tous biens on conçoit.
Car quant uns vrais amans sa dame voit
Et il voelt priier trés sentanment,
Plaisance si habondamment l'esprent   30
Et vraie amour a sur lui tel pooir
Que, quant il voelt parler de sentement,
Bouce ne poet ne parolle mouvoir.

[Thus the lover is wise and fortunate
Who puts body and heart, intelligence, thought and
    intention
Into loving and remains eager
To be obedient to such a noble hope
As Love, in which all good things are perceived.
For when a true lover sees his lady
And wishes to beseech her with deep feeling,
Pleasure sets him on fire so forcefully
And true love has such power over him
That, when he wishes to express his feelings,
He cannot move his mouth or bring forth words.]

En cel estat vit amans cremeteus,
En soing d'avoir merci, qui li est lente,   35
Mais tous jours sert de dous regars piteus.
Car souvenirs enracine en soi l'ente
De vrai espoir; c'est li confors qu'il croit.
Or vient avis, qui de sens le pourvoit,
Et biaus parler ossi en lui descent.   40
Lors supplie il si amoureusement
Que, quant dame le poet ytel veoir,
Humilité juge en lui proprement
Que tenue est de faire ent son devoir.

[In this state the fearful lover lives,
Anxious to receive mercy, which is slow for him,
But always benefiting from sweet and pitying looks.
For the memory of pitying glances plants the
Seed of true hope in his heart; there is comfort in
    this thought.
Then wisdom comes, and provides him with good
    judgment,
And eloquence descends on him as well.
Then he supplicates her so passionately
That, when the lady can see him in such a state,
Her humility leads her to judge correctly
That she is obliged to devote herself to him.]

Dame qui j'aim, jou qui sui diseteus   45
D'avoir merci, més assés m'en contente,
Car en vos yeux douls, simples et joieus,
Preng reconfort quant dous espoirs me tempte,
Car autrement trop malement m'iroit,
Et vostre amour m'anonce et ramentoit   50
Joie et confort par un si douls present
Que, se jamais n'avoie aliegement,
Si bien me plaist le vivres en espoir
Que tousjours voel demorer liegement
En cel estat, car mieulz ne puis manoir.   55

[Lady whom I love, I, who am in need
Of receiving mercy, nevertheless content myself,
For in your gentle eyes, humble and full of joy,
I take comfort when sweet hope tempts me,
For otherwise my life would be too hard to bear,
And your love promises and brings to mind
Joy and consolation by such a sweet presence
That, even if I were never to receive comfort,
The life of hoping pleases me so well
That I wish always to live like a liege man
In this way, for I can do no better.]

Princes, pour ce ai mis trés mon jouvent
A dame amer sens et entendement,
Pour le haut don de sa merci avoir,
Car jones coers, selonc mon jugement,
Ne doit prisier au jour dui autre avoir.   60

> [Prince, for this reason I have since my youth
> Applied wit and understanding to loving a lady,
> In order to have the high gift of her mercy,
> For a young heart, in my opinion,
> Must not value acquiring anything else today.]

Pastourelle 2

[The earliest of the historical *pastourelles*, this poem was written in 1364 when King John returned voluntarily to captivity in London, after his son, who was a hostage under the Treaty of Bretigny, left without leave. The tone of the poem combines celebration of the king's arrival with light satire of the peasants.]

Entre Eltem et Westmoustier,
En une belle praerie
Cuesi pastouriaus avant ier;
La avoit en le compagnie
Mainte faitice pastourelle,   5
Dont au son d'une canemelle
Cascuns et cascune dansoit.
Dist uns bregiers qui la estoit:
"Efforçons nous, pour Saint Denis,
Car errant par chi passer doit   10
Chils qui porte les fleurs de lis."

> [Between Eltham and Wetminster
> In a beautiful meadowland
> I saw some shepherds days before yesterday;
> They had in their company

Many pretty shepherdesses,
And each of them, lads and lasses,
Danced to the sound of pipes.
Said one of the shepherds who was there:
"Let's do our best, by Saint Denis,
For passing by here will be
The one who bears the fleurs de lis. "]

Adont dist Marés dou Vivier:
"Or me dittes, je vous en prie,
Porte il ces fleurs en un panier,
Ou il les donne, ou il les crie?   15
Qu'en vent il plain une escuielle?
C'est une flourette moult bielle;
De le fleur de lis orendroit,
Qui un chapiel fet en aroit,
Il en seroit trop plus jolis;   20
Je croi que bien en fineroit
Chils qui porte les fleurs de lis.

[Then Marés dou Vivier said:
"Now tell me, I beg of you,
Does he carry these flowers in a basket,
To hawk them or give them away?
Does he sell a container full?
It's a beautiful little flower;
With fleurs de lis, immediately,
Whoever had a chaplet made of them
Would be filled with gaiety.
I believe business will be good for
The one who bears the fleurs de lis.]

"Pour ce me vorrai avancier
Et aler ent a chiere lie
Vers li, et li vorrai priier   25
Qu'i m'en doinst par sa courtoisie,
Et il ara me cornuelle,
Le musette et le flahutelle,
Dont mes freres m'esbanioit."

Dist Raouls qui oï l'avoit: 30
"Esce or a bon sense que tu dis?
Cuides tu c'uns bregiers ce soit
Chils qui porte les fleurs de lis?

> ["And so I would like to proceed
> And go towards him in good cheer
> And would like to ask of him
> That he graciously give me some.
> And he will have my small horn,
> The bagpipe and little flute
> That my brother used to enjoy."
> Raoul, who had heard him, said,:
> "Is this sensible now, what you say?
> Do you believe him to be a shepherd,
> *The one who bears the fleurs de lis?*]

"Nennil, point n'est de no mestier,
Ains est rois de noble lignie,   35
Si que, pour li mieuls festiier,
Il nous couvient a ceste fie
Mettre en ordenance nouvelle."
--"C'est voirs," ce respont Peronnelle,
Qui moult bien oïe l'avoit,   40
"Et si bien see desgiseroit,
Més qu'il euïst tous ses abis,
Que ja ne le congnisteroit
Chils qui porte les fleurs de lis."

> ["Not at all, he's not of our trade,
> But a king from a noble line,
> So that, to celebrate him better,
> We chould on this occasion
> Arrange ourselves in a new way."
> --"That's true," responded Peronnelle,
> Who had understood very well,
> "And he will disguise himself so well
> Provided he has all his clothes,

That he will never be known at all by
The one who bears the fleurs de lis. "]

Lors prisent a entrecangier   45
Leurs abis de le bregerie.
Gobins vesti un grand loudier
Et Guios une soukanie,
Sus se çaindi d'une cordelle;
Et Perrotins sus une asselle   50
D'un blanc bastonciel tamburoit,
Et Adains le danse menoit,
Qui souvent disoit par grans ris:
"Diex, pour quoi ores ne nous voit
Chils qui porte les fleurs de lis?"   55

[Then they began to interchange
The clothes they wore for shepherding.
Gobins put on a full overcoat
And Guy a hooded cowl,
Tied on with a little cord.
And Perrotins was beating on a wooden plank
With a little white stick of wood.
And the dance was led by Adains,
Who with a big smile often said:
"God, why can't we be seen at this moment by
The one who bears the fleurs de lis?"]

Princes, je les vi la endroit,
Ou cascune et cascuns chantoit
A l'usage de leur pays:
"Li trés bien venus ores soit
Chils qui porte les fleurs de lis!"   60

[Prince, I saw them in that spot,
Where each shepherd and shepherdess sang
In the style of their own homeland:
"Let there be a hearty welcome now to
The one who bears the fleurs de lis. "]

Pastourelle 5

[This poem appears only in manuscript B, the one apparently intended for a French audience. Although it incorporates many traditional features in its setting and characterizations, its theme—touching on the complexities of aristocratic alliances as well as the pleasures of drinking—cuts across social boundaries. The first shepherd adopts a complex ironic tone, and the audience's enjoyment depends in large part on their being able to participate vicariously in the shepherds' game of wits.]

Ens uns beaus prés vers et jolis,
Assés prés de Bonne Esperance,
Bregieres et bregiers assis
Vi l'autre ier en bonne ordenance,
Car il orent de pourveance   5
Oisons rostis et gros pastés,
Boef, mouton et gambons salés,
Bon frommage, puns de jouvent,
Mices tant en voes, tant en prent,
Vins en barils et en flacons.   10
Dist li uns, qui estoit de Mons:
"Beau seignour, c'est drois que je songne
Qu'un mariage ci faisons
De Poitevin et de Gascongne.

[In a beautiful green meadow,
Near the Abbey of Bonne Esperance,
The other day I saw shepherds and shepherdesses
Seated together in groups,
For they had there, at their disposal,
Roasted goslings and plump pasties,
Beef, mutton, and salted ham,
Good cheese, fresh apples, so many small
　　　　loaves of bread
That they could take as much as they wished,
Wine in barrels and wine in bottles.
And one of them, who was from Mons, said:
"Gentlemen, it is important to me, and rightly so,

That we are making a marriage here
Of Poitevin and Gasconne.]

"Car Poitevins est mes amis,   15
S'est moult bien raisons que l'avance,
Et s'ai esté en son paÿs,
Se sçai bien qu'il a grant puissance."
Dont dist uns qui ot barbe blanche:
"Cils Poitevins dont vous parlés,   20
Esce uns bregiers acoustumés?
Sauroit il faire un ongement,
Une houce ou un vestement,
Ou un jupel a alerons?
Cognoist il brebis et moutons,   25
Les scet il garir de la rongne?
Dittes le moi puisque parlons
De Poitevin et de Gascongne."

["For Poitevin is my friend,
So it is natural for me to favor him,
And since I have been in his country,
I know indeed that he has great power."
To this, a fellow with a white beard answered,
"This Poitevin you're talking about,
Is he a skillful shepherd?
Would he know how to make an ointment,
A long cloak or other garment,
Or a tunic with little wings?
Does he know ewes and rams,
Can he cure them from the mange?
Tell me this since we are speaking
Of Poitevin and Gasconne."]

Dont respondi Sohiers li gris,
Qui au prendre un hanap se lance: 30
"Par ma foi, tu es uns chetis
Et plains de trés grant ignorance,
Quant tu as tant esté en France,
Et se ne cognois ne ne scés

Encor ou Poitevins fu nés,   35
Qui sont si frere et si parent.
Il a des amis plus de cent;
Moult vault sa grasce et ses bons noms;
Amés est de tous compagnons,
Et pour tant, somme de besongne, 40
Le mariage ci ferons
De Poitevin et de Gascongne."

> [And then he was answered by gray-headed Sohiers,
> Who was starting on a new goblet of wine,
> "By my faith, you are a foolish man
> And full of the greatest ignorance,
> When you have been in France so long,
> And still don't know even yet
> Where Poitevin was born,
> And who his brothers and relatives are.
> He has hundreds of friends;
> His favor and reputation are highly esteemed;
> He is loved by all his comrades;
> And therefore, in short,
> We perform the marriage here
> *Of Poitevin and Gasconne.*"]

"C'est voirs," ce respondi Thieris,
Qui fu homs de grant cognissance,
Car il ot esté a Paris   45
Aux escoles trés son enfance,
S'ot moult tost conçut la substance
Dont Sohiers les ot enfourmés.
"Beau seignour," dist il, "or versés
De ce vin bien et largement   50
En ces beaus gobelés d'argent,
Et puisqu'assis en revel sons,
Jamés de ci ne partirons,
Et venist le duc de Bourgongne,
Tant que fait la droiture aurons, 55
De Poitevin et de Gascongne."

["This is true," answered Thieris,
Who was a man of great knowledge,
For he had been in Paris
At school throughout his youth,
And thus had immediately understood
What Sohiers was talking about.
"Gentlemen," he said, "Now pour
This wine generously into
These beautiful silver goblets,
And since we are sitting here revelling,
We will never leave this place,
And even if the Duke of Burgundy were to come,
We would have a suitable amount
Of Poitevin and Gasconne.]

Dont prisent flacons et barils
Et verserent sans detriance;
Le rouge avec le blanc ont mis
Pour faire ent certainne alliance   60
A euls oïr pris grant plaisance,
Car Sohiers, qui fu li ainsnés,
Lor dist: "Beau seignour, regardés
Comment Poitevins se desfent:
Il sault et trepe et frit et fent   65
Celle Gascongne; or en buvons,
Entroes que le goust en avons.
Il soit pendus qui le ressongne,
Car li mariages est bons
De Poitevin et de Gascongne."   70

[Then they took their bottles and casks
And poured the wine freely;
They put the red and white together
To create a permanent alliance;
I took great pleasure at hearing them,
For Sohiers, who was the eldest,
Then said: "Gentlemen, look at the way
Poitevin defends himself:
He leaps and jumps and strikes and cleaves

This Gasconne; now let us drink some
While we still have a taste for it.
May the man who is afraid be hanged,
For I declare that the marriage is good
Between Poitevin and Gasconne."]

Princes, il burent jusqu'au fons
De leur barils grans et parfons,
Telement que par yvretongne
Il ordenerent la chançons
De Poitevin et de Gascongne. 75

[Prince, they drank to the very bottom
Of their large and deep barrels,
So much so that in drunkenness
They composed the song
Of Poitevin and Gasconne.]

Pastourelle 13

[This rather odd and less effective poem seems to be satirizing the notion of
education in the lower class. McGregor suggests in his note that the refrain,
which makes little sense by itself, is probably the "title and first line of a
poem about the Golden Fleece." Froissart uses the story of the Golden
Fleece also in Ballade 36.]

L'autrier vi bregier et bregiere,
Qui bien avoient sis vins ans
Entre euls deus, garder a prangiere
Leurs brebisettes sus les camps.
La vint li uns de leurs enfans, 5
Qui voloit aler a l'escole,
Et demanda a dame Cole,
Sa mere: "Ça, mon avantage!"
--"Tu n'aras ne pain ne froumage,"
Respondi celle, "par ma foi, 10
S'aras a ton pere et a moi

Dit quelque voir ou quelque fable."
Et chil respondi: "Je l'otroi:
Dou mouton d'or est il notable."

[The other day I saw a shepherd and shepherdess
Who, between them, were six score years old
And in the noon hour they were watching
Their little lambs in the fields.
There came one of their children,
Who had been wanting to go to school,
And he demanded of the lady Cole,
His mother: "Now pack me my lunch!"
--"You will have neither bread nor cheese,"
She answered, "By my faith,
Until you have told your father and me
Some true story or some fable."
And he answered: "I agree:
Of the golden sheep it is worthy to tell."]

Pere et mere sont tret arriere,   15
Qui avoient des cheviaus blans
Bien pour emplir une aloiiere,
Et dient: "Tu ies ja tous grans,
Et si t'avons tenu long tamps
La ou les aultres on escole;   20
Onques més ne peuins parole
Avoir de toi en ton eage
Qui nous peüst donner corage
De doctrine ne de castoi,
Et puisque tu ies en bon ploi,   25
Di nous par voie raisonnable
Ou on troeve ne en quel loi
Dou mouton d'or est il notable."

[Father and mother, who had white hair,
Drew back away from the road
In order to fill a travelling pouch,
And said, "You are already all grown up,
And we have kept you here a long time

While others went to school;
Never yet have we heard a word from you
Since you have been of age
That would give us any encouragement
To send you on to school,
So since you are in a good disposition,
Tell us in a reasonable way
Where and in what religion one finds that
Of the golden sheep it is worthy to tell. "]

Dist chils, qui a la remontiere
Voet avoir ou tartes ou flans;   30
"Quant Diex ot fait ciel et lumiere,
Terre et mer et poissons noans,
Puis fu une beste apparans
En Colque en l'ile d'Astropole:
De mouton avoit fourme et mole,   35
Tonson d'or portoit cest ymage;
Serpent et troi toriel sauvage
Le gardoient de tout anoi,
Nuls n'osoit aler jusqu'a soi,
Tant iert la cose espoentable.   40
Quant j'ai parlé, aler m'en doi,
Dou mouton d'or est il notable. "

[Said the boy, who in the afternoon
Wished to have a tart or a flan,
"When God made the sky and light,
Earth and sea and fish that swim,
Then there appeared a creature
In Colchis on the isle of Astropole:
It had the shape and form of a sheep,
And this image wore a golden fleece;
A serpent and three ferocious bulls
Guarded it from any torment,
No one dared go near it,
As desirable as the thing might be.
Since I have spoken, I must go away now.
Of the golden sheep it is worthy to tell. "]

Lors dist sa mere a lie chiere:
"Tu ies uns clers moult souffissans.
J'ai des brebis sus la bruiere   45
Qui sont bonnes et bien mengans;
Tu en aras, je ne sçai quans,
Escript tout cela en ton role."
Dist ses maris: "Vous estes fole,
. . . .   50
. . . .
Encor n'a il dit ce ne quoi.
Ne nul sens en lui je ne voi
Qui me soit bon ne agreable.
Or me destintés mieuls, Joffroi,   55
Dou mouton d'or est il notable."

> [Then the mother said with a joyous countenance,
> "You are a most distinguished young scholar.
> I have some ewes in the heathland
> That are healthy and good to eat;
> You will have them, though I don't know when,
> But write that all down in your roll."
> Said her husband: "You are crazy,
> . . . .
> . . . .
> He still hasn't said anything.
> Nor do I see any sense in him
> That is good or pleasing to me.
> Now explain to me clearly, Jeffrey, why,
> *Of the golden sheep it is worthy to tell."]*

Respont chils: "Ceste beste fiere,
Avoecque ses crueuls servans
Qui li gardoient sa barriere,
Fu tant dedens Colque habitans   60
Q'uns chevaliers preus et vaillans
--Jasson ot nom chils parole--
Quant parler oÿ de l'ydole,
Pour conquerre enprist le voiage;

Et le conquist par vasselage   65
Avoecque l'aÿde et l'arroi
De Medee, la fille au roi,
C'est cose toute veritable.
Or dittes, se men temps j'emploi.
Dou mouton d'or est il notable. "   70

    [He answered: "This proud beast,
    Along with his cruel servants
    Who guarded his pen for him,
    Was living so long in Colchis
    That a hardy and valiant knight
    --Those who speak of him call him Jason--
    When he heard people speak of this idol,
    Undertook a voyage to conquer it;
    And he conquered it through vasselage,
    With the help and careful planning
    Of Medea, daughter of the king,
    And this is entirely true.
    Now say if I'm using my time well.
    Of the golden sheep it is worthy to tell. "]

Princes, pere et mere tout doi
Disent: "Biaus fils, par Saint Eloi,
Tu serras aumés a no table,
Car bien nous as monstré l'envoi.
Dou mouton d'or est il notable.   75

    [Prince, father and mother both
    Said: "Dear son, by Saint Eloi,
    You will be esteemed at our table,
    For well have you told us this tale.
    Of the golden sheep it is worthy to tell. "]

Pastourelle 14

[Among the historical *pastourelles* that could most accurately be called an occasional piece, this poem celebrates the marriage of Louis de Châtillon, the son of Guy de Blois, to Marie, the daughter of Jean, Duc de Berry, in August 1386. Froissart's interest in the relationship between the classes is reflected in stanza four, when the foolish shepherd fears the loss of his sheep but is then reassured that aristocrats who are truly noble behave in a way that enriches everyone. This poem is one of only three *pastourelles* with a two-line refrain, the others being similar historical poems, Pastourelle 15 describing wedding preparations "Pour le pastourel de Berri / Et la pastoure de Boulongne," and 16 describing "Comment la roÿne de France / Est premiers entree en Paris." All of these poems appear only in MS B.]

Assés prés de Roumorentin,
En l'ombre de deus arbrisseaus,
Vi l'autre jour en un gardin
Pastourelles et pastoureaus,
Et la ordonnoient entre eaus   5
Chapelés de belles flourettes,
Et la oÿ deus bregerettes
Dire tout hault a leurs amis:
"Se sus le chiés vous aviens mis
Ces chapiaus, en aroins gré?"   10
--"Oïl," ce respont Fouqueré,
"Donne moi ent un, je t'en pri,
Se m'en irai de coer joli
A Bourges veoir, car c'est drois,
La pastourelle de Berri   15
Avec le pastourel de Blois. "

[Rather near to Roumorantin,
In the shadow of two shrubby trees,
The other day in a garden I saw
Shepherdesses and shepherds,
And they were arranging amongst themselves
Crowns of beautiful little flowers,
And there I heard two shepherdesses
Say out loud to their shepherd friends:

"If we had put these garlands on your heads,
Would you be well pleased?"
--"Yes," answered Fouqueré,
"Give me one of them, I beg you now,
And I'll go away with a happy heart
To Bourges where I'll see, for it's true,
The shepherd girl of Berri
With the shepherd lad of Blois."]

Respont ceste: "Par Saint Martin,
Se tu voes qu'il soit bons et beaus
Et loiiés de fillet de lin
Qui fu pris ou marchié a Meaus,   20
Et qu'encor y ait trois houpeaus
De flour blanches et vermillettes,
Ou qu'il soit tous de violettes,
Ensi que je le t'ai prommis,
Tu me diras tou ton avis,   25
Pourquoi ores tu as parlé,
Ne qui te moet en volenté
De maintenant partir de ci
Et d'aler ent sans nul detri
Veoir a Bourghes ceste fois   30
La pastourelle de Berri
Avec le pastourel de Blois."

[The shepherdess answered, "By St. Martin,
If you want it to be well-made and beautiful
And tied with a fine linen thread
That was bought at the market in Meaux,
And that it also will have three little tufts
Of white and vermillion flowers,
Or that it will be made of violets,
Just as I promised you,
You will tell me your whole intention,
Why you've spoken as you have,
And what provokes in you the desire
To leave her at this time
And go away without delay

To see at Bourges right now
The shepherd girl of Berri
And the shepherd lad of Blois?"]

"Belle," dist cils, "par Saint Martin,
Point ne me sera li chapeaus
Retollus; pour dire ent la fin,   35
C'est uns mariages nouveaus,
Ou moult grans sera li reveaus
De bacelers et de filletes,
Et se sont les noces estrettes
De lyons et de flours de lys.   40
Li mariés a nom de Loÿs;
Il est de Haynau d'un costé,
Et de Flandres pour verité,
Et s'est fils au bon conte Gui
De Blois; siques pour bien te di   45
Veoir vendras, se tu m'en crois,
La pastourelle de Berri
Avec le pastourel de Blois."

["Pretty one," he said, "by Saint Martin,
The crown won't be held back from me
At all; to come to the point,
It's a wedding we're going to,
Where the revels of young men and women
Will be exceedingly grand,
And this is a marriage descended
From the lion and the fleur de lis.
The groom has the name of Louis,
And he's from Hainaut on one side,
And from Flanders actually,
And he's the son of the good count Guy
At Blois; and thus for your benefit I tell you,
You will come see, if you believe this is true,
The shepherd girl of Berri
And the shepherd lad of Blois."]

"On aura la et pain et vin,
Gras moutons, cabrils et agneaus;   50
Se nous y portons un cretin,
Nous aurons des bons glous morseaus."
--"Haro," ce respondi Anseaus,
"Reponre me fault mes germettes,
Mes moutons et mes brebisettes;   55
Se je les perc, je sui honnis."
--"Va, meschant," ce dist Aloris,
"Tu as trop simplement visé:
Ce sont seignour tant honnouré,
Si hault, si noble et si garni,   60
Que tout en serons enrichi:
Tous biens nous donront en ce mois
La pastourelle de Berri
Avec le pastourel de Blois. "

> ["They'll have both bread and wine there,
> Fat sheep, young kids and lambs;
> If we take along a basket,
> We'll have some good tasty morsels."
> --"Alas," ansered Ansel,
> "I'll have to hide away my young lambs,
> My sheep and my little ewes;
> If I lose them, I'll be ruined."
> --"Go on, you bad fellow," said Aloris,
> "You've looked at this half-wittedly:
> These are lords that are so honored,
> So high, so noble, and well furnished,
> That we will all be enriched by them;
> In this month we'll be given all sort of good
>   things by
> *The shepherd girl of Berri*
> *And the shepherd lad of Blois.* "]

"C'est voirs," dist la fille a Robin,   65
"Or vestons donques nos jupeaus
Et alons la le bon matin,
Et si emportons nos freteaus,

Nos muses et nos canimeaus,
Et pas n'oublions nos holettes,   70
Ne nos panetieres bien fettes,
Le signours en auront grant ris;
Car aussi ai je ja apris
Qu'a Cambrai se sont espousé
Frere et soer, soer et frere né   75
De Bourgongne et Haynau aussi,
Dont nous sommes tou resjoÿ;
Tout ce dirons a hautes vois:
La pastourelle de Berri
Avec le pastourel de Blois. "   80

    ["It's true," said the girl to Robin,
    "So let's put on our coats
    And go there while the morning is young,
    And also, let's take along our panpipes,
    Our bagpipes and reed instruments,
    And let's not forget our holettes
    And our bread-sacks that are made so well,
    At which the nobles will have a good laugh,
    For I also have just now learned
    That at Cambrai there have been married
    Brother and sister, sister and brother born
    In Burgundy and Hainaut as well,
    For which we are all very glad;
    All this we will say in loud voices to
    The shepherd girl of Berri
    And the shepherd lad of Blois. "]

Princes, quant de la me parti,
En ordenance je les vi
Pour venir veoir, trois et trois,
La pastourelle de Berri
Avec le pastourel de Blois. "   85

    [Prince, when I left that place,
    I saw them getting lined up in groups

To go see, three by three,
*The shepherd girl of Berri
And the shepherd lad of Blois.]*

Ballade 1

[This *ballade*, in its enumeration of the lady's physical and moral qualities, demonstrates Froissart's careful attention to the fine distinctions in courtly vocabulary. The movement from antithesis in stanza two to conventional images and allusions in stanza three provides a typical example of the way Froissart combines traditional elements. Like 22 of the 43 *ballades*, this one is decasyllabic; the two-line refrain, however, occurs in only two of the independent lyrics and two intercalated ones, all believed to have been written early in Froissart's career.]

Jone, joians, jolie et amoureuse,
Bonne, belle, bien faite et bien parlans,
Sage, soués, courtoise et gratieuse,
Lie, loyaus, legiere et avenans,
France, frice, faitice et tres plaisans,   5
Dame d'onneur, de bien enluminee,
Dame digne d'estre en tous lieus amee:
Tels est li corps feminins ou mis ai
*Corps, coer, avis, sens, entente et pensee,
Et au sourplus quanq que faire porai.*   10

[Young, joyous, merry and full of love,
Good, beautiful, well-formed, and pleasing in speech,
Wise, gentle, courteous and gracious,
Cheerful, loyal, dainty and well-mannered,
Noble, lively, elegant and very pleasant,
Lady of honor, made finer by her goodness,
Lady worthy of being loved everywhere:
Such is the feminine being in whom I have placed
*Body, heart, reason, sense, desire and thought,
And, in addition, everything I can do.]*

Mes de m'amour n'est mie convoiteuse.
Com plus le sieuch, et plus m'est eslongans,
Com plus li pri, et plus m'est desdagneuse,
Plus m'offre a li, et plus m'est refusans.
Dure est a mi, et as autres rians;   15
Plus le requier, plus est de moi tanee:
Ensi me het, et s'est de mi amee,
Car par desirs amoureeus li donnai
Corps, coer, avis, sens, entente et pensee,
Et au sourplus quanq que faire porai.   20

> [But she has no desire for my love.
> The more I follow, the more she moves away,
> The more I beg, the more she disdains me,
> The more I offer myself, the more she refuses.
> She is harsh to me, while she smiles at others;
> The more I seek her, the more she tires of me,
> Thus she hates me, and thus she is loved by me,
> For out of loving desire I have given her
> Body, heart, reason, sense, desire and thought,
> And, in addition, everything I can do.]

Ensement vifs en prison dolereuse,
Ne nuls confors ne m'est representans;
S'en ai souvent l'entente peu joieuse,
S'en affoiblist et muert en mi li sans.
Non ai Amans et en sournoms Tristrans;   25
Pour joie m'est dolours representee,
Pour bon eür pesande destinee;
Mais quoi au'aviegne, a ma dame lairai
Corps, coer, avis, sens, entente et pensee,
Et au sourplus quanq que faire porai.   30

> [And so I am living in a sorrowful prison,
> And no prospect of comfort presents itself to me;
> Thus am I often filled with joyless thoughts,
> And thus my blood grows weak and dies within me.
> My name is Lover, and my surname Tristan;
> Instead of joy, suffering comes to me,

Instead of luck, a heavy destiny;
But come what may, I will let my lady guide
Body, heart reason, sense, desire and thought,
And, in addition, everything I can do.]

Ballade 3

[This poem is one of eleven *ballades* with an octosyllabic line; the eight-line stanza is the most common in the collection, with fourteen occurrences. With its informal quotations and its insistence on a first-person point of view, this poem introduces a more personal tone to the traditional elements of the genre.

S'empereour, roy ou soudant,
Prince, duch, conte ou aultre gent,
Soient gentil homme ou marchant,
Seculer ou gens de couvent,
Avoient cascuns plainnement   5
Otant qu'a ou monde de biens,
Se vous ai je bien en convent:
Qui n'a se plaisance, il n'a riens.

[If emperors, kings or sultans,
Princes, dukes, counts or other men,
Whether they be gentlemen or merchants,
Men of the world or cloistered monks,
Had, each one of them, fully,
All the goods existing in the world,
Yet I can certainly assure you
Whoever lacks what delights him, he has nothing.]

Je le di pour moi; non pour quant
Li pluiseur m'en blament souvent,   10
Et me mettent ces poins devant:
"Prens que tu aies ton talent,
Aras te pour ce plus d'argent?"
Mes je leur di: "Avoir est fiens,
Ne je ne prise che noient;   15
Qui n'a se plaisance, il n'a riens."

[I say this for myself; but nonetheless
The majority often find fault with me for saying it,
And propose to me this argument:
"Assuming you get what you long for,
Will you, as a result, have more wealth?"
But I tell them: "Riches are a dung-hill,
And I do not value such worthless stuff at all;
Whoever lacks what delights him, he has nothing. "]

J'aroie plus chier maintenant,
De ma douce dame au corps gent,
Un tout seul amoureus samblant,
Ou un baisier secretement,   20
Que ne feroie en un moment
Estre sires des terriiens.
Pour quoi? Pour ce certainnement:
Qui n'a se plaisance, il n'a riens.

[I would now consider it more precious
To have, from my sweet and elegant lady,
A single amorous look,
Or one secret kiss,
Than I would to become in a single moment
Master of the land.
Why? Because of this, of course:
Whoever lacks what delights him, he has nothing. "]

Ballade 6

[This very conventional poem is comparable to Machaut's Ballade 38 and 39, Chaucer's Absalome Ballade, and Froissart's own Ballade 38. It is one of nine written in a seven-line stanza, all with the rhyme pattern *ababbcC*.]

Ne quier veoir Medee ne Jason,
Ne trop avant lire ens ou mapemonde,
Ne le musique Orpheüs ne le son,

Ne Hercules, qui cerqua tout le monde,
Ne Lucresse, qui tant fu bonne et monde,   5
Ne Penelope ossi, car, par Saint Jame,
Je voi assés, puis que je voi ma dame.

[I have no wish to see Medea or Jason,
To read further in the mysteries of the globe,
To know the music of Orpheus or its sound,
Or Hercules, who travelled all the world,
Or Lucretia, who was so good and pure,
Or even Penelope, for by Saint James above,
I see enough when I see my lady love.]

Ne quier veoir Vregile ne Platon,
Ne par quel art eurent si grant faconde,
Ne Leander qui tout sans naviron   10
Nooit en mer qui rade est et parfonde,
Tout pour l'amour de sa dame la blonde,
Ne nul rubis, saphir, perle ne jame:
Je voi assés, puis que je voi ma dame.

[I have no wish to see Virgil or Plato
To learn what art gave them such eloquence,
Nor Leander, who alone, without a ship,
Swam the sea, which was violent and deep,
All for the love of his lady fair and blonde,
Nor any ruby, sapphire, pearl, or stone,
I see enough when I see my lady love.]

Ne quier veoir le cheval Pegason   15
Qui plus tost ceurt en l'air ne vole aronde,
Ne l'ymage que fist Pymalion,
Qui n'eut parel premiere ne seconde,
Ne Oleüs qui en mer boute l'onde.
S'on voelt savoir pour quoi, pour ce, par m'ame: 20
Je voi assés, puis que je voi ma dame.

[I have no wish to see Pegasus the horse,
Who ran in the air more easily than the swallow flies,

Nor do I wish to see the image Pygmalion made,
Which was unsurpassed and matchless in its form.
Nor Aeolus whose billows swelled the sea;
If you wonder why? For this reason, by my soul:
I see enough when I see my lady love.]

Ballade 9

[This poem has a female speaker, as do Ballades 19 and 22. For a detailed discussion of how Froissart both follows and deviates from the mythology of love created in the *Roman de la Rose* and developed by Machaut, see Baudouin, pp. 109-11.]

Hé, Cupido, que tu m'as fet de painne,
Depuis le jour que Venus m'assalli!
Tu me monstras ja d'Eqo la fontainne
Ou en esbat les quatre dames vi.
Ens me mirai, che fu par leur merci,   5
Et si en buch, car je cuidai ce jour
De Cupido estaindre en moi l'ardour;
Mes depuis ai senti, pour mar fu nee,
Comment on poet veoir ne par quel tour
Candasse, Helainne, Yseut et Tholomee.   10

[Well, Cupid, how you have made me suffer,
Since the day when Venus first assailed me!
You showed me then the fountain of Echo
Where, in pleasure, I saw the four ladies.
I looked at my reflection, by their grace,
And also drank, for I intended on that day
To conquer the ardour of Cupid in myself.
But I was born in an evil hour and, since, have felt
How one can see, no matter where one looks,
Candace, Helen, Isolde, and Ptolomaea.]

Arcipoles tient un arc taint en grainne,
Dont si droit tret q'un coer perce parmi;

Et ce sont chiaus c'Uiseuse ou vregier mainne
Dont portier sont li fil Mercurii.
La vient Venus, qui amainne avoec li   15
Dan Vulcanus, son mestre et son signour.
La ont mestier d'Ovide li pluisour;
Mes Mars leur dist: "Poursieués le meslee
Et les tournois, ensement qu'on fist pour
Candasse, Helainne, Yseut et Tholomee".   20

> [Arcipoles has a bow dyed scarlet red
> Which he draws so straight that it goes right through
>   the heart,
> And those are the hearts that Leisure leads to the
>   garden
> Whose porters are the sons of Mercury.
> Venus comes there, and she brings with her
> Sir Vulcan, her master and her lord.
> There most would follow Ovid and live as lovers;
> But Mars says to them: You must pursue combat
> And tournaments, exactly as was done
> *For Candace, Helen, Isolde, and Ptolomaea.*]

Candasse fu en bien amer certainne
Le noble roi Alixandre, et ossi
Moult de grietés eut pour Paris Helainne,
Et pour Tristran Yseus maint mal souffri;
Et Tholomee ama tant son ami,   25
    Le preu Nestor, qui fu d'Inde Majour,
Qu'elle en morut a doel et a tristour,
Car Eneas l'ocist a sen espee.
Or vous ai dit verité de l'amour
Candasse, Helainne, Yseut et Tholomee.   30

> [Candace was sincere in her deep love
> For the noble king Alexander, and also
> Helen endured many pains for Paris,
> And for Tristan Isolde suffered much woe,
> And Ptolomaea loved her lover so much--
> The valiant Nestor, who was from India--

That she died in mourning and sadness,
Because Aeneas killed him with his sword.
Now I have told the truth about the love
Of Candace, Helen, Isolde and Ptolomaea.]

Ballade 13

[The opening line of this *ballade* is similar to the proverb recorded by Morawski (110) as ""Aprés grant guerre grant paix." Froissart used the shortened fifth line in thirteen of his *ballades*.]

En grant guerre ne gist que bonne pais,
Mes je me voi guerriiés asprement
D'Ardant Desir et de tous ses soubjés,
Qui nuit et jour m'assallent telement
    Que je ne puis nullement   5
Avoir arest, tant fors est leurs assaus;
Et si ne puis mie veoir comment
De ce peril je puisse escaper saus.

    [Out of a great war comes a good peace,
    But I see myself bitterly warred upon
    By Ardent Desire and all his subjects,
    Who night and day assail me to such extent
        That I cannot have any repite
    At all, so strong is their assault;
    And so I cannot see in any way how
    I might escape from this peril unharmed.]

Car Plaisance et Biauté me sieuent pres,
Qui ont pooir et droit commandement   10
De moi monstrer le douls viaire fres
De ma dame et son contenement.
    En ce regardant, souvent
Me faut avis, sens, pourpos et consaus.
Or me couvient viser que temprement   15
De ce peril je puisse escaper saus.

[For I am closely pursued by Pleasure and Beauty,
Who have the power and the just authority
To show me the gentle fresh face
Of my lady and her countenance.
In looking upon her, often
Prudence, good sense, purpose and reason fail me.
Therefore I must make it my aim that immediately
I might escape from this peril unharmed.]

Se Bonne Amour a cui je me sui tres,
Ne met en mon desir atemprement,
Par quoi il soit de ceste ardeur retrés
Et q'un petit aie d'aliegement,   20
    D'avis et de hardement
De remonstrer com griés est li travaus
Que je rechoi, je ne voi aultrement
De ce peril je puisse escaper saus.

[If Good Love, to whom I am attracted,
Does not put moderation in my desire,
Through which it may be withdrawn from this ardor,
And if I don't have a little alleviation,
    Some judgment and some courage
To point out how grievous is the torment
I receive, I see no other way that
I might escape from this peril unharmed.]

Ballade 15

[This octosyllabic *ballade* focuses on amorous doctrine, discussing the characteristics of the "vrais amans" in a didactic tone similar to that of the *chanson royale*. The poet assumes the role of authority in stanza two, and the refrain has a proverbial ring, resembling the common saying "A coeurs vaillant il n'est riens impossible" (Hassell C231)].

Sus racine de toute honneur
Se doit uns vrais amans fonder,

Et recongnoistre se si meur
Sont tel qu'il s'en puist aquiter.
Et chils qui cuide avant aler,   5
Qui se voit ou se sent meffés,
Si visce le font reculer,
Car tout vaint coers qui est parfés.

    [Upon the root of pure honor
    A true lover must establish himself,
    And recognize whether his behavior
    Is such that he can satisfy his obligation.
    And he who believes he will advance
    Yet sees or feels that he has done some wrong,
    His shortcomings make him recoil,
    For the heart that is perfect conquers all.]

Or me poroient li pluiseur
Raisonnablement demander   10
Comment on poroit toute erreur
Fuïr et vertus empetrer.
Et j'en responderoie au cler:
Par estre liés jolies et ges,
Et avoir grasce de donner,   15
Car tout vaint coers qui est parfés.

    [Now, many people could
    Reasonably ask me
    How a person could avoid all error
    And lay claim to all virtues,
    And I would respond with confidence:
    By being joyous, happy and gay
    And practicing gracious generosity,
    For the heart that is perfect conquers all.]

Ja villain ne aver dou leur
Ne se saront si bien rieuler
Qu'il recongnoissent le douceur
Des biens d'amours, qi sont sans per; 20
Car coers qui aimme ou voelt amer

Doit par raison estre moult nes,
Visces fuïr, vertus haper,
Car tout vaint coers qui est parfés.

[Never will thieves or misers
Have sufficient discipline in their behavior
To come to understand the sweetness
Of the goods of love, which are without equal;
For the heart that loves or wishes to love
Must, as reason dictates, be very pure,
Flee vices, seize virtues avidly,
For the heart that is perfect conquers all.]

Ballade 17

[This *ballade* appears in *La Prison amoureuse*, ll. 2090-2113, one of three
(with 14 and 18) that the narrator claims to have written at the same time. As
Baudouin points out, the opening line is highly conventional, almost identical
to one used by Machaut in his Ballade 35.]

Je puis moult bien comparer mon desir
Au Tantalus, et ma vie a sa painne,
Qui boire voelt et n'i poet avenir,
S'est il entrés en la douce fontainne
    Qui li ceurt tout environ   5
Et qui l'atouce au nes et au menton;
Mes, quant il voelt boire, l'aige le fuit.
En ce parti ne voi point de deduit.

[I can very aptly compare my desire
To that of Tantalus, and my life to the pain of him
Who wishes to drink and cannot succeed in doing it
Although he has entered into the sweet fountain,
    Which flows all around him,
And which touches him on the nose and chin,
But when he wishes to drink, the water runs away:
In this plight, I see no pleasure at all.]

Ensi Amours me fait moult a souffrir,
Car ardanment un tel desir m'amainne   10
Dont je ne puis ne partir ne joïr
Ne resjoïr, pour cose que g'i painne.
　　Si voi je assés le façon
De ma dame, mes ne sçai qu'on face on,
Car si atrait sont tout de dangiers duit.   15
En ce parti ne voi point de deduit.

> [In this same way, Love makes me suffer greatly,
> For I am ardently led by just such a desire
> Which I can neither part from nor enjoy
> Nor be glad of because I suffer pain;
> 　　Thus I see clearly enough
> My lady's behavior, but I don't know what to do,
> For her charms are all accompanied by resistance:
> *In this plight, I see no pleasure at all.*]

Se m'est moult dur quant je le voel servir:
Elle me fuit, et se m'est si prochainne
Que si regart me donnent a sentir
Toute douchour; mes elle m'est lontainne,   20
　　Car, quant je li donne en don
Mon coer, m'amour, n'en ai pour guerredon
Fors escondis et refus, jour et nuit.
En ce parti ne voi point de deduit.

> [Thus she is very hard on me when I wish to serve
> 　　her:
> She flees from me, and yet she is so near
> That her glances give me feelings of
> Total sweetness; but she is distant from me,
> 　　For when I give her, as a gift,
> My heart, my love, then I have no reward
> But refusal and denial day and night:
> *In this plight, I see no pleasure at all.*]

Ballade 21

[This *ballade* appears in *Le Joli Buisson de Jonece,* at line 2991. It is one of only two combining a seven-syllable line and a seven-line stanza.]

Maniere in plaisant arroi
Est forment recommendee
En fame, et fust fille de roi.
Car, quant ell en est paree,
Elle est de tous honneree,   5
Amee et prisie ossi,
Pour le bien qu'on voit en li.

[A pleasing orderliness of behavior
Is to be strongly recommended
In a woman, even if she is daughter to a king.
For, when she is adorned with it,
She is honored by all,
Loved and esteemed as well,
For the good that is seen in her.]

Et c'est raison, par me foi,
Car maniere a oint arree,
Soit a vue ou en requoi,   10
Est volentiers regardee.
C'est vertus moult renommee;
Onques coers ne le haï
Pour le bien qu'on voit en li.

[And it is right that this is so, by my faith,
For comportment that is perfectly arranged,
Either in public or in private,
Is regarded with pleasure.
It is a highly celebrated virtue;
No heart ever despises it
For the good that is seen in it.]

Et pour ce que je perchoi   15
Que ma dame en est armee,
Sui je hors de tout anoi;
Car elle est des biens doee,
De grasce et de renommee,
La parfaite au coer garni,   20
Pour le bien qu'on voit en li.

[And because I perceive
That my lady is armed with it,
I am exempt from all distress,
For she is endowed with virtues,
With favor and high repute,
Perfection in a well-bred heart,
For the good that is seen in it.]

Ballade 31

[One of only two *ballades* that do not treat a courtly love theme (see also 34), this poem is based on material from *Le Roman de Brut*, ll. 680-89. Since it appears only in Manuscript A, it appears to have been written especially for presentation to the royal family of England, either, as Baudouin speculates, upon the birth of the future Richard II in 1367 or upon his accession in 1377. If all the *ballades* are arranged chronologically, as most seem to be, the latter date seems more probable. For a detailed discussion of the relationship of this material to Wace, as well as similar treatments by Deschamps, see Baudouin, pp. 119-121.]

Trop ne se poet Calcas esmervillier
De ce qu'il voit la generation
Au roy Bructus ensi fructefiier
Et raemplir les sieges d'Albion
De la ligne au fort roi Pharamon.   5
Mais Helenus dist que Fortuen dort,
Et qu'averi sont maintenant li sort
Que Merlins a son mestre Blase dist.
Et s'a Dyane as habitans dou Nort
Moult bien tenu quanq qu'elle leur promist.   10

[The prophet Calchas could not cease to marvel
At seeing those descended from the race
Of King Brutus thus reach full fruition
And fill the seats of power in Albion
Through the lineage of the strong king Pharamond;
But the Trojan Helenus said that Fortune sleeps
And the destinies that were foretold by Merlin
To his master Blaise have now been realized,
And thus Diana has, for the Northern peoples,
Held fast to everything she promised them.]

Bructus couvint Ytalie vuidier,
Car il four fist toute sa region.
Lors en ala la deessee priier
Qu'en aucuns lieus euïst sa mansion,
Et respons ot a sa devision.   15
S'entra en mer o chiaus de son confort,
Et Zephirus venta pour euls si fort
Qu'en Albion les ariva et mist.
Depuis leur a Dyane en son deport
Moult bien tenu quanq qu'elle leur promist.   20

[Brutus had no choice but to leave Italy,
For he lost the rights to all his territory.
Then he went away to pray to the goddess
That he might have another home somewhere,
And he received an answer in accordance with his
   wish.
So he set out to sea with those who wished to aid
   him,
And Zephyr blew for them so mightily
That he brought them to shore and placed them in
   Albion.
Since then Diana has in her benevolence
Held fast to everything she promised them.]

Dyane dist a Bructus: "Moult t'ai chier.
Tu t'en iras dessus Septentrion,
La ou le plus veras Phebus baissier.

Toi et li tien en generation
Demorront la en leru possession;   25
Dencores plus, le dieu en sont d'acort,
Moult conquerront soit a droit, soit a tort."
Et Bructus fist ce que Dyane dist.
Depuis leur a, qui prent garde ou recort,
Moult bien tenu quanq qu'elle leur promist.   30

[Diana said to Brutus: "You are dear to me,
You will go away to the lands of the far North,
There where you will see Phebus at his lowest.
You and yours from generation to generation
Will live there with the land in their possession;
What's more, the gods are in agreement,
They will conquer much, whether it be right or
    wrong."
And Brutus did what Diana said.
Since then she has, as anyone can tell,
Held fast to everything she promised them.]

Ballade 33

[This poem, discussed briefly in Chapter 4, combines a conventional lover's
complaint with insistence on a personal point of view. It is here that Froissart
introduces the god Morpheus, later borrowed by Chaucer.]

On me dist, dont j'ai grant mervelle,
Que de dormir c'est temps perdus.
Tant qu'a moi, je m'en esmervelle,
Car li dormirs me vault trop plus
Que li veilliers. C'est mes argus: 5
Dormirs est grant aise de corps,
A desplaisance ne vit nuls;
Je n'ai nul bien se je ne dors.

[People tell me, to my great surprise,
That they consider sleep a waste of time;

As for me, I am amazed at that,
For sleeping is worth much more to me
Than being awake. This is my opinion:
That sleeping is a great comfort to the body,
Which no one finds displeasing;
I have nothing good if I do not sleep.]

Car en dormant je me conselle,
Ce m'est vis, au dieu Morpheüs   10
Qui mes besongnes, qu'on touelle,
Remet assés bellement sus,
Car avoir me fait ris et jus
De ma dame et pluiseurs depors,
Dont en veillant sui moult ensus;   15
Je n'ai nul bien se je ne dors.

[For while I sleep I take advice,
It seems to me, from the god Morpheus,
Who takes all my affairs, which are confused
And rather nicely sets them straight again,
For he makes me have laughter and amusements
From my lady, and many pleasures,
Which I certainly don't have when I'm awake;
I have nothing good if I do not sleep.]

Encor li boute il en l'orelle
Qu'a merci soie recheüs;
Et ceste qui est non parelle,
De donner dangiers et refus,   20
Les met a sa priiere jus,
Et me dist: "M'amour je t'acors."
Ensi en dormant voi vertus;
Je n'ai nul bien se je ne dors.

[Moreover he whispers in her ear
That I should be received into her mercy,
And this lady, who is like no other
At offering resistance and refusals,
Dismisses them at his request,

And says to me: "I grant you my love."
Thus in sleep I see a happy outcome;
I have nothing good if I do not sleep.]

Ballade 34

[Like Ballade 31, this poem from late in Froissart's lyric career introduces a
topic from outside the usual sphere of *fin' amors*; like Ballade 33, it has a
distinctly personal tone. It is one of only two *ballades* written in a ten-line
stanza with octosyllabic lines.]

Pluiseurs ymaginations
A uns homs: ce n'est pas mervelles,
Car il est de moult d'actions
Forgiés, qui ne sont pas parelles,
Mais diverses et desparelles,   5
Qui toutes les scet esclarcir.
Tant qu'a moi je voel revenir,
Car bien sçai, sans autrui querelle,
En quoi, de veoir et d'oïr,
Mes esperis se renouvelle.   10

[A man has many ideas:
This is not surprising,
For he is formed from many influences
Which are not alike,
But diverse and dissimilar,
And he is able to explain them all.
Therefore I wish to come back to myself,
For I know quite well, without worrying about what
        others think,
By what sights and sounds
My spirit is renewed.]

Quant je voi vallees et mons
Et vignes en kars et en trelles,
Je di que li pays est bons;
Et si destoupe mes orelles

Quant j'och vin verser de boutelles,   15
Car au boire preng grant plaisir;
Ossi fai je en biaus draps vestir;
En viande fresce et nouvelle,
Quant a table m'en voi servir,
Mes esperis se renouvelle.   20

> [When I see valleys and mountains
> And bunches of grapes on wagons and arbors,
> I say that the countryside is good;
> And so I listen attentively
> When I hear wine flowing from bottles,
> For I take great pleasure in drinking;
> Also I like to dress in fine clothes;
> When at the table I see that I'm served
> Food that is fresh and unusual,
> *My spirit is renewed.*]

Violettes en leurs saisons
Et roses blances et vermelles
Voi volentiers, car c'est raisons,
Et cambres plainnes de candelles,
Jeus et danses et longes velles,   25
Et biaus lis pour li rafresquir,
Et au couchier, pour mieuls dormir,
Espesces, claret et rocelle.
En toutes ces coses veïr
Mes esperis se renouvelle.   30

> [Violets in their season
> And roses white and red
> I gladly see, for this is natural,
> And rooms full of candles,
> Entertainment and dancing and staying up late,
> And beautiful beds for resting,
> And at bedtime, in order to sleep better,
> Spiced wine, claret and wine from La Rochelle
> At the sight of all these things
> *My spirit is renewed.*]

Ballade 38

[This conventional poem is comparable to Ballade 6, and to poems by Machaut and Chaucer, in its content. It is one of only three in which Froissart combines a seven-line stanza with decasyllables and a shorter (heptasyllabic) fifth line.]

J'ai tout veü quant j'ai veü ma dame;
Ne puis ne doi au veoir demander
Nulle autre riens: rubis, saphir ne jame,
Cache de chiens ne oisiaus pour voler,
    Jeuer, danser ne chanter.   5
J'ai tout veü, a parler par droiture,
Quant j'ai veü si gente creature.

[I've seen it all when I have seen my lady,
I cannot and I must not ask to see
Any other thing: ruby, sapphire or gemstone,
A pack of hunting dogs, or birds to fly,
    Playing, dancing or singing,
I've seen it all, to speak quite honestly,
When I've seen a creature of such nobility.]

Car sus lui n'a tache, visce ne blame,
Mais sens et bien et arroi de parler
Areement, mieuls que nulle aultre fame.   10
Nature l'a faite pour regarder,
    Ne riens ne me poet grever,
Ce m'est avis, le jour com lons qu'il dure,
Quant j'ai veü si gente creature.

[For in her there is no flaw, vice, or blame,
But wisdom and goodness and a becoming manner of
    speaking
Appropriately, better than any other woman.
She was made by nature to be looked upon,
    Nor is there anything that can do me harm,
In my opinion, as long as the day may be,
When I've seen a creature of such nobility.]

On poroit bien, soit escarboucle ou dragme   15
Ou aultre piere en or mettre et ouvrer;
Mais on ne puet, je le vous jur par m'ame,
Plus frisce corps veoir ne compasser.
  Pymalion, c'est tout cler,
Diroit ensi: "J'ai perdu ma mesure,   20
Quant j'ai veü si gente creature."

  [One could even set and work in gold
  A carbuncle, a gem, or any other stone,
  But one could not, I swear it by my soul,
  See or fashion a form more bright and gay.
    Pygmalion, it is entirely clear,
  Would say: "My standard of excellence was lost to
    me,
  When I saw a creature of such nobility."]

Virelay 1

[This *virelay* appears in the *Prison amoureuse* (l. 934) as well as the independent lyrics. In order to emphasize the musical structure of the poem, I am separating repetitions of the first lines of refrains as if they introduced complete and separate stanzas, rather than showing them attached to the end of each coda (the second interior stanza), as McGregor does. This poem is typical of Froissart's *virelays* in having two sets of interior stanzas for a total of seven musical units; Machaut more often included three sets.]

  Depuis ce jour en avant,   *[Refrain]*
  Ce que j'ai sans remanant,
    Jusques a l'ame
  Vous present, ma chiere dame,
  A faire vostre commant,

    [*From this day forward,*
    Whatever I have without exception,
      Even my soul
    I present to you, my dear lady,
    To do your commandment.]

Et certes moult bien l'emploi,   [Rhythmic
Car mieuls qui n'affiert a moi   Variation A]
  Estes vous digne;
Més bonne amour, par ma foi,
A cui bien obeïr doi,
  Et li douls signe

  [And certainly it will be put to good use,
  For you are worthy of better than
    What pertains to me;
  But good love, by my faith,
  Whom I must indeed obey,
  And the gentle appearance]

De vo grascieus samblant   [Coda A]
M'ont conquis. Or ne sçai quant
  De ceste flame
Garirai, car moult m'enflame
Vostre amour en desirant,

  [Of your gracious countenance
  Have conquered me. Now I do not know when
    I will be healed
  From this burning, for your love
  Inflames me greatly with desiring,]

Depuis ce jour en avant . . .   *[Refrain]*

  [*From this day forward . . .*]

Tant d'onneur en vous conchoi,   [Rhythmic
Bonté, biauté, maintien qoi,   Variation B]
  Sens et doctrine,
Que le grant bien que g'i voi
Et que recorder en oi,
  A vous m'encline.

  [I perceive so much honor in you,
  Goodness, beauty, tranquil conduct,

Wisdom and knowledge,
That the great goodness that I see
And that I hear reported about you,
Inclines me towards you.]

Et je pense a faire tant   [Coda B]
Que de mon petit le grant
Sans avoir blame,
Ou tost serai sous le lame,
Ou sont mis le vrai servant.

[And I aspire to act in such a way
That my small qualities will appear great
Without being worthy of blame,
Or soon I will be under the gravestone,
Where true servants are put.]

Depuis ce jour en avant . . .   *[Refrain]*

[From this day forward . . .]

Virelay 2

[This poem is the only one of Froissart's *virelays* to have just a single set of
interior stanzas. It appears in *Prison amoureuse*, at line 3842.]

Assis comme la piere en l'or
Ai je mon coer et mieuls encor;
Tous sui garis de ma dolour,
Puis que ma dame par douçour
Me daigne regarder dés or.

[My heart is set like a stone in gold
And even better still;
I am cured of all my sadness,
Since my lady through her kindness
Now deigns to acknowledge me.]

Je m'en tieng a bien euwireus,
Quant de ses douls yeux amoureus
    Ai les regars,
Car plus liés ne plus gratieus,
Mieuls attraians ne si joieus,
    Je ne regars.

    [I consider myself happy
    When her gentle loving eyes
        Send me a glance,
    For eyes more gay or gracious,
    More charming or more joyous,
        I see nowhere.]

Enrichis sui d'un grant tresor,
Car son gent corps, si cheviel sor,
Son sens, son bien et sa valour
Me representent toute honnour,
Et fuisse ossi vaillans qu'Ector.

    [I'm enriched by a great treasure,
    For her chestnut hair and graceful figure,
    Her wisdom and her goodness and her worth
    Show me all there is of honor,
    Were I as worthy as Hector,]

Assis comme la piere en l'or . . .

    [Set like a stone in gold . . .]

Virelay 11

[Virelays 11, 12, and 13 are the only ones in the collection that do not also appear as intercalated lyrics in a narrative poem. The three form a logical group, taking first one point of view on love, then an opposing position, and finally a new perspective that rises above questions of *fin' amors* with a consideration of fortune.]

Se je sui vestis de noir,
C'est drois pour mi,
Car j'ai le coer si marri,
Au dire voir,
Que sur moi ne doit avoir
Riens de joli.

[If I am dressed in black,
That's right for me,
For my heart's so full of sorrow,
Honestly,
That wearing something merry
Would be wrong.]

Parlés a ces amoureus,
Les jolis, les gratieus,
Les envoisiés,
Et laissiés les anoieus,
Les tristes et dolereus
Et les blechiés

[Speak to the joyous lovers,
Those who've found favor
And feel gay,
And let those who are thwarted,
The sad and grieving,
Wounded ones,]

Faire un peu de leur voloir,
Je vous em pri;

Car il sont en tel parti
  Que main ne soir
De resjoïr n'ont povoir.
  Pour moi le di:

  [Do as they please a while,
      I beg of you;
  For they are in such straits
      That night or day
  They have no power to rejoice.
      I say it for myself:]

Se je sui vestis de noir . . .

  [If I am dressed in black . . .]

Pensés vous que ce soit jeus
D'estre merancolieus
  Ne courouchiés?
Nennil, et je sui de cheus,
Qui ne puis estre joieus,
  Bien le sachiés,

  [Do you think it is amusing
  To be melancholy
      And vexed?
  Why, no! and I am among those
  Who cannot be joyful,
      As you well know,]

Car je n'ai sens ne espoir
  D'avoir merchi
Quanque soit jour ne demi,
  Que puet valoir?
Homs qui vit en desespoir
  C'est dur pour li.

  [For I have neither thought nor hope
      Of gaining favor

Whether it be bright or dark,
What can it matter?
For the man who lives in despair,
Life is hard.]

Se je sui vestis de noir . . .

[If I am dressed in black . . .]

Virelay 12

[Apparently in response to Virelay 11 and its sorrowful lover, this poem justifies a display of good humor.]

Se je sui gais et joieus
Et envoisiés,
Je vous pri, or assaiiés
Les envieus.
Dittes leur que c'est pour euls
Que je sui liés.

[If I am gay and joyful
And in good humor,
I beseech you, put those who envy me
To a test.
Tell them that it is for them
That I am joyous.]

Si les ferés tout quoi taire,
Ou plus haut criier et braire
Qu'il ne font presentement.
Envieus en son afaire
Ne scet ne dire ne faire
Nulle riens d'esbatement,

[Thus you will cause them to be completely silent,
Or make them cry out and bray more loudly

Than they already do.
The envious man who is in difficulty
Does not know how to say or do
Anything amusing,]

Mais est merancolieus
    Et courouchiés
Dou bien d'autrui. Or laissiés
    Les dolereus,
Car point ne voel de tels neus
    Estre loiiés.

[But rather is melancholy
    And vexed
At the well-being of others. Then forsake
    The sorrowing ones,
For in no way do I wish to be bound
    By such knots.]

Se je sui gais et joieus . . .

[If I am gay and joyful . . .]

Amours, a vous me voel traire
Pour la grant dolour retraire
Que j'ai porté longement.
Ordonnés pour mon solaire
Que la douce et debonnaire,
Ou gist mon aliegement,

[Love, I wish to draw myself to you
In order to shake off the great sorrow
That I have long endured.
Ordain for my reward
That the sweet good-natured lady,
In whom lies my comfort,]

De ses douls yeux amoureus,
Dont sui blechiés,
Soie un peu assouagiés,
Et euwireus
Me tenrai et pour trés preus,
Bien le sachiés.

[Might with her gentle loving eyes,
Which wounded me,
Grant me a little relief,
And I will consider myself
Fortunate and very happy,
As you well know.]

Se je sui gais et joieus . . .

[If I am gay and joyful . . .]

Virelay 13

[This poem reaches its conclusion by referring to a proverb, "Tels pleure au main qui rit au soir." In Cotgrave's dictionary, this saying is quoted in the opposite sense as "Tel au matin rit qui au soir pleure," and it is translated as "No glad man knows how soone he may be sorie." As the final *virelay* in the collection, this poem is notable for its directness of tone and its thoughtful, almost anti-courtly, ending.]

Prendés le blanc, prendés le noir,
Prendés selon vostre estavoir,
Prendés toutes couleurs aussi,
Mais je vous di
Que dou dimenche au samedi
Vous faurrés bien a vo voloir.

[Take the white, take the black,
Take whatever suits your need,
Take all of the colors too,

But I tell you
That from Sunday to Saturday
You'll fall far short of your desire.]

Pour moi le di certainnement,
Car j'ai pensé en mon jouvent
    Si hautement,
Que ma folie me reprent
Et en voel faire amendement
    Trés grandement.

    [For myself I can speak with certainty,
    For in my youth I aspired
        So loftily,
    That now my folly chides me
    And I wish to make amendment
        On a grand scale.]

Peu de cose est de fol espoir,
Et s'est assés, au dire voir;
Car le couart il fait hardi,
    Et le joli.
Selonc les meurs qui sont en li,
Il li fait ordenance avoir.

    [Foolish hope is a small thing,
    But it's enough, to tell the truth;
    For it makes both the coward and the lover
        Bold.
    According to his talents, it gives him
    Command and order in his life.]

Prendés le blanc, prendés le noir . . .

    [Take the white, take the black . . .]

Or vorrai vivre liement
En joie et en esbatement.
    Vechi comment:

Je passerai legierement
Le temps a venir et present;
    Parellement

> [Now I will choose to live happily
> In joy and in amusement.
>   This is how:
> I will pass my time light-heartedly
> In the future and in the present;
>   And likewise]

Tout meterai en noncaloir.
Tels pleure au main qui rit au soir;
Amours ont maint homme enrichi
    Et resjoï
Dou bien d'autrui par leur merchi;
Encontre eür n'a nuls povoir.

> [I will have little care for anything.
> Those who cry in the morning laugh at night;
> Loves have enriched many men
>   And gladdened them
> By giving them what rightfully is another's;
> Against fortune no one has any power.]

Prendés le blanc, prendés le noir.

[Take the black, take the white . . .]

Rondeau 5

[Entirely conventional in its imagery and language, this poem is typical of the earliest *rondeaux* in the collection.]

> *Je voel morir poursieuans ma querelle*
> *Comme loyaus servans au dieu d'Amours;*
> Tout pour l'amour de ma dame la belle,
> *Je voel morir poursieuans ma querelle.*
> Quant mors serai, quoi que soit dira elle,
> Mes esperis le servira tous jours.
> *Je voel morir poursieuans ma querelle*
> *Comme loyaus servans au dieu d'amours.*

> *[I wish to die in the pursuit of my cause*
> *As a loyal servant to the god of Love;*
> All for the love of my most beautiful lady,
> *I wish to die in the pursuit of my cause.*
> When I am dead, whatever she may say,
> My spirit will serve her eternally.
> *I wish to die in the pursuit of my cause*
> *As a loyal servant to the god of Love.]*

Rondeau 7

[Less polished in its logic than some of the later poems, this *rondeaux* shows Froissart moving away from straight-forward glosses of doctrine as he introduces one source of tension in line 3 and another in lines 5 and 6, without drawing a clear connection between the two.]

> *J'ai plus perdu assés que gaegnié*
> *Au bien amer, che la puis je veoir,*
> Si ai je alé, venu et langagié.
> *J'ai plus perdu assés que gaegnié,*
> Et telement tout mon coer engagié
> Que ne l'en sçai ne ne l'en puis ravoir.
> *J'ai plus perdu assés que gaegnié*
> *Au bien amer, che la puis je veoir.*

[I've lost a great deal more than I have gained
In pursuit of love, that I can clearly see,
And yet I've continued to go and come and speak;
I've lost a great deal more than I have gained,
And I've pledged my whole heart with such intensity
That I don't understand and can't get it back again.
I've lost a great deal more than I have gained
In pursuit of love, that I can clearly see.]

Rondeau 9

[The use of an opening apostrophe to address the lady, Love, other lovers, or allegorical characters is typical of Froissart's *rondeaux*, occurring in twenty-two of the collected poems. Like the proverb, the apostrophe creates an easily identifiable voice that can alternate with commentary.]

Ma dame, a cui je prie de confort,
Regardés moi en quel point m'avés mis.
On dist que j'ai samblance d'omme mort,
Ma dame, a cui je prie de confort;
Et se tels sui, certes je n'ai pas tort,
Car m ieuls me plaist a estre mors que vis.
Ma dame, a cui je prie de confort,
Regardés moi en quel point m'avés mis.

[My lady, to whom I humbly beg for comfort,
Look at me and the state you've put me in.
People say that I look like a dead man,
My lady, to whom I humbly beg for comfort;
And if that is how I look, I am not mistaken,
For I would rather be dead than be alive.
My lady, to whom I humbly beg for comfort,
Look at me and the state you've put me in.]

Rondeau 14

[As Baudouin points out, the opening line of this poem is phrased as if it were
proverbial, though no analogous expression exists in Morawski. It is, in any
case, the earliest of the thirteen *rondeaux* to be built upon such a piece of
generalized wisdom.]

> *Le tamps perdu ne poet on recouvrer,*
> *Avoec le honte y a damage au perdre:*
> Legierement le puis dire et prouver,
> *Le tamps perdu ne poet on recouvrer.*
> Dont qui en voelt tres sagement ouvrer,
> Jones se doit au bien amer aherdre.
> *Le tamps perdu ne poet on recourvrer,*
> *Avoec le honte y a damage au perdre.*

> > *[Time that is lost can never be regained,*
> > *In such a loss there is harm as well as shame:*
> > I can say this and prove it easily,
> > *Time that is lost can never be regained.*
> > Therefore the man who wishes to act wisely,
> > Must devote himself in youth to loving well.
> > *Time that is lost can never be regained,*
> > *In such a loss there is harm as well as shame.]*

Rondeau 17

[This poem illustrates the alternation between a statement of doctrine in the
refrain lines and the voice of the individual poet/lover in the commentary. As
short as the poem is, Froissart has created a sense of movement from the first
half, where the speaker states his commitment to Espoir, and the second half,
where he considers the implications of this commitment.]

> *Onques Espoirs, qui bien y eut fiance,*
> *Ne peut fallir a loyal compagnon,*
> Et j'ai a li fait certainne aliance.
> *--Onques Espoirs, qui bien y eut fiance--*
> Or me soit pres, car, voir, je li fiance

Que j'amerai, ja soie amés ou non.
Onques Espoirs, qui bien y eut fiance,
Ne peut fallir a loyal compagnon.

> *[Hope, for the one who has fully trusted in her,*
> *Can never fail to serve a loyal friend,*
> And I have made a solid alliance with her.
> *--Hope, for the one who has fully trusted in her--*
> Now let her stay near me, for I truly promise
> That I will love, whether I be loved or not.
> *Hope, for the one who has fully trusted in her*
> *Can never fail to serve a loyal friend.]*

Rondeau 18

[This poem is typical of the way Froissart starts with a broad statement of conviction (lines 1 and 2), suggests one possible direction of development (3), and then chooses an antithetical interpretation (5 and 6), causing the original statement to expand in meaning rather than narrow to a single thought.]

Uns vrais amans, par loyaument amer,
Deveroit bien estre oïs de sa dame.
Lors se poroit pour euwireus clamer
Uns vrais amans, par loyaument amer;
Mes li pluiseur aimment jusqu'au flamer,
Et ja n'aront garison de le flame.
Uns vrais amans, par loyaument amer,
Deveroit bien estre oïs de sa dame.

> *[A true lover, through loving faithfully,*
> *Should certainly be acknowledged by his lady.*
> And then he could declare himself content
> *A true lover, through loving faithfully;*
> But most men love until they are on fire,
> And never will recover from the flame.
> *A true lover, through loving faithfully,*
> *Should certainly be acknowledged by his lady.]*

Rondeau 21

[This is the only independent *rondeau* written in the eleven-line form, though Froissart used this longer form in four of his intercalated lyrics, and it was common among other poets. McGregor expands it into twelve lines, perhaps to complete the idea of the comparison, but there is no precedent for a twelve-line form.]

Amours se met de trop plus liet corage
Avoec les coers humles, dous et piteus,
Qu'elle ne fait entre les hayneus:
Les coers divers crient trop plus que l'orage.
--Amours se met de trop plus liet corage--
Et chiaus qui sont discré, courtois et sage,
Obeissant, secré et amoureus,
Elle les aimme et s'abandonne a euls.
Amours se met de trop plus liet corage
Avoec les coers humles, dous et piteus,
Qu'elle ne fait entre les hayneus.

> *[Love takes on a much merrier disposition*
> *Towards hearts that are humble, gentle and full of*
> *pity,*
> *Than she does towards those whose hearts are full of*
> *hate:*
> Wicked hearts rage mightier than the storm.
> *--Love takes on a much merrier disposition--*
> And those who are discreet, courteous and wise,
> Obedient, well-guarded and affectionate,
> She loves them and puts herself at their command.
> *Love takes on a much merrier disposition*
> *Towards hearts that are humble, gentle and full of*
> *pity,*
> *Than she does towards those whose hearts are full of*
> *hate.]*

Rondeau 43

[This poem, along with Rondeaux 44 and 45, appears to form part of a group in which the opening line asks a conventional question about the nature of love. See Chapter 4 for a discussion of this series.]

Dont muet amours et de quel part vient elle?
Par pluiseurs fois en ai fait argument,
Mais on n'en scet respondre a ma querelle.
Dont muet amours et de quel part vient elle?
Je di ensi que bonne amour loiielle
Part d'un desir quant dous regars l'esprent.
Dont muet amours et de quel part vient elle?
Par pluiseurs fois en ai fait argument.

> *[Where does love come from and what is its source?*
> *I have proposed an answer many a time,*
> But no one knows how to respond to my argument.
> *Where does love come from and what is its source?*
> I say that a good and loyal love
> Comes from desire enflamed by a sweet look.
> *Where does love come from and what is its source?*
> *I have proposed an answer many a time.]*

Rondeau 45

[As the last in a series of three poems based on conventional questions, this *rondeau* leaves behind the ironic tone of Rondeau 44 and returns to a highly conventional point of view. See discussion in Chapter 4.]

Ou quel des mois doit on priier sa dame
Pour le plus tost venir a sen amour?
Dites le moi, je vous pri, par vostre ame:
Ou quel des mois doit on priier sa dame?
Car je ne puis garir de l'ardant flame
S'elle n'i met atemprance et douçour.

Ou quel des mois doit on priier sa dame
Pour le plus tost venir a sen amour?

> *[In which month must a man beseech his lady*
> *To achieve success most quickly in his love?*
> Tell me this, I beg you, by your soul:
> *In which month must a man beseech his lady?*
> For I cannot be cured from the burning flame
> Unless she acts more temperate and sweet;
> *In which month must a man beseech his lady*
> *To achieve success most quickly in his love?]*

Rondeau 48

[The word "fortune" has been glossed by Scheler to mean "tempête," while Baudouin prefers "chance, hasard." These two interpretations reflect the metaphorical ambiguity of this poem, which is perhaps more "lyrical," in the modern sense of focusing on the feelings of an individual, than most of the fixed form lyrics.]

> *En un isle de mer, ensus de gens,*
> *Ou on ne poet entrer fors par fortune,*
> Sont mes amours, ce n'est mie grans sens.
> *--En un isle de mer, ensus de gens--*
> Je waucre autour, mes je ne puis dedens,
> Pour ariver n'i voi voie nesune;
> *En un isle de mer, ensus de gens,*
> *Ou on ne poet entrer fors par fortune.*

> > *[On an island in the sea, far from people,*
> > *Where no one can get in except by chance,*
> > My passions dwell, which makes no sense at all.
> > *--On an island in the sea, far from people--*
> > I wander around, but I cannot get in;
> > I see no path by which I can arrive.
> > *On an island in the sea, far from people,*
> > *Where no one can get in except by chance.]*

Rondeau 50

[This poem is spoken from the lady's point of view. It could be seen as forming a pair with Rondeau 52, which is also in the lady's voice but less sympathetic to the lover's entreaties.]

> *Se mon ami pooie plus souvent*
> *Reconforter, je le conforteroie,*
> Mais je ne puis veoir voie comment;
> *--Se mon ami pooie plus souvent--*
> Or li suppli qu'il prende en paiement
> Aucuns regars quant mon coer li envoie.
> *Se mon ami pooie plus souvent*
> *Reconforter, je le conforteroie.*

> > *[If I were able to console my suitor*
> > *More often, I would surely comfort him.*
> > But I cannot see any way to do it.
> > *--If I were able to console my suitor--*
> > So I beg him now to accept as compensation
> > Whatever glances my heart might send to him.
> > *If I were able to console my suitor*
> > *More often, I would surely comfort him.]*

Rondeau 52

[This poem, like Rondeau 50, takes the lady's point of view. The expression "au chief dou samedi" is glossed by Baudouin as "le samedi soir."]

> *Se mon ami avoit otant de painne*
> *Pour men amour que j'endure pour li,*
> Et de pensers au long de la semainne,
> *--Se mon ami avoit otant de painne--*
> Il me diroit, c'est bien cose certainne,
> Pluiseurs pourpos au chief dou samedi;
> *Se mon ami avoit otant de painne*
> *Pour men amour que j'endure pour li.*

[If my sweetheart were having as much pain
For my love as I endure for him,
And thinking as many thoughts the whole week long,
If my sweetheart were having as much pain,
He would tell me, this I know for certain,
A number of things when the week came to an end;
If my sweetheart were having as much pain
For my love as I endure for him.]

Rondeau 56

[As Baudouin points out, the refrain of this poem is based on a traditional topos used by Machaut and others. It can be seen as corresponding to Rondeau 59, where the lady expresses her feelings at being left behind.]

Li corps s'en va, mais li coers vous demeure:
Treschiere dame, a Dieu jusqu'au retour.
Trop me sera lontainne la demeure,
Li corps s'en va, mais li coers vous demeure;
Mais douls pensers, que j'arai a toute heure,
Adouchera grant part de ma dolour,
Li corps s'en va, mais le coers vous demeure:
Treschiere dame, a Dieu jusqu'au retour.

[The body leaves, but the heart remains with you:
Dearest lady, good-by 'til my return.
My sojourn will take me much too far away,
The body leaves, but the heart remains with you.
Yet sweet thoughts, which I'll have continually,
Will help to ease a great part of my woe.
The body leaves, but the heart remains with you:
Dearest lady, good-by 'til my return.]

Rondeau 59

[One of five *rondeaux* taking the lady's point of view, this poem seems to correspond to the lover's farewell in Rondeau 56.]

> *Mon douls ami, a Dieu jusqu'au revoir*
> *Qui bien briefment deviers moi vous remainne;*
> De vous ferai loyaument mon devoir.
> *Mon douls ami, a Dieu jusqu'au revoir.*
> Se souhedier pooient estre voir,
> Vous me veriés trente fois la sepmainne.
> *Mon douls ami, a Dieu jusqu'au revoir*
> *Qui bien briefment deviers moi vous remainne.*

> > *[My gentle love, good-by 'til our next meeting*
> > *Which very shortly brings you back to me;*
> > I will do my duty towards you loyally.
> > *My gentle love, good-by 'til our next meeting.*
> > If only wishing were the same as seeing,
> > You would see me thirty times a week.
> > *My gentle love, good-by 'til our next meeting*
> > *Which very shortly brings you back to me.]*

Rondeau 63

[This poem is based on a proverb quoted in Morawski (1587) as "Par le petit vient len au grant." The repetition of the first line in the middle of the poem is less well integrated than some others, serving a more musical than logical purpose.]

> *Dou petit grant et dou grant le petit*
> *Font li pluiseur souvent, c'est vraie cose.*
> Je l'ai bien fait, mais Fortune s'en rit;
> *--Dou petit grant et dou grant le petit--*
> Mes quoi qu'en voie, ou damage ou pourfit,

Je l'en grasci, car courouchier ne l'ose.
Dou petit grant et dou grant le petit
Font li pluiseur souvent, c'est vraie cose.

> *[Great things from small beginnings and small*
> *   from big*
> *Are accomplished by many people, it is true.*
> I've done the same myself, but Fortune mocks me;
> *--Great things from small beginnings and small*
> *   from   big--*
> Yet whatever results I see, either loss or gain,
> I thank her, for I dare not anger her.
> *Big things from small beginnings and small from big*
> *Are accomplished by many people, it is true.]*

Rondeau 64

[The philosophical tone of this *rondeau* is unusual in that it includes no explicit reference to *fin' amors*.]

> *Oultre mau temps que vault doel et soussi?*
> *De riens qu'aviegne on ne doit faire compte,*
> Mais tous jours vivre en un estat onni.
> *Oultre mau temps que vault doel et soussi]?*
> Nous ne savons, quant nous partons de chi,
> Quel part alons: j'ai au penser grant honte.
> *Oultre mau temps que vault doel et soussi?*
> *De riens qu'aviegne on ne doit faire compte.*

> > *[Except in bad times, what good are sorrow and care?*
> > *One must not attach importance to chance events,*
> > But always live in a simple, modest way.
> > *Except in bad times, what good are sorrow and care?*
> > We do not know, when we depart from here,
> > Where we will go: I feel shame at the thought.
> > *Except in bad times, what good are sorrow and care?*
> > *One must not attach importance to chance events.]*

Rondeau 66

[This poem is one of two (along with Rondeau 86) that is addressed to Espoir as an allegorical figure. As Baudouin points out, the apostrophe is an especially common device in the *rondeaux*, with the lady herself being addressed most often.]

Haro, Espoir, qu'estes vous devenus?
Vous me soliés faire grant compagnie,
Mais bien perchoi que ne me dagniés plus.
Haro, Espoir, qu'estes vous devenus?
Revenés tost, ou estes vous repus?
Sans vous ne puis ne heure ne demie.
Haro, Espoir, qu'estes vous devenus?
Vous me soliés faire grant compagnie.

[Alas, Hope, what has become of you?
You used to keep me company faithfully,
But I see you don't find me worthy anymore.
Alas, Hope, what has become of you?
Come back to me soon, where are you hiding?
Without you I can't go on another hour.
Alas, Hope, what has become of you?
You used to keep me company faithfully.]

Rondeau 69

[Like Rondeau 66, this poem opens with an apostrophe. The word "coer" shifts in meaning, first referring metonymically to the rival lover who is addressed, then to the emotional state of the female speaker, and then to the lover who is accepted, thus conflating people and moods into a single construct.]

Ensus de moi, coer merancolieus!
Vous ne m'avés que faire d'aprochier,
Car j'ai le mien joli et amoureus.
Ensus de moi, coer merancolieus!
Et ossi a chils qui se tient joieus,

Quant je le voel d'un de mes yeux gignier.
Ensus de moi, coer merancolieus!
Vous ne m'avés que faire d'aprochier.

    [Get away from me, dejected heart!
    You have no business drawing near to me,
    For my own heart is amorous and gay.
    Get away from me, dejected heart!
    And also I have a heart who fills with joy
    When I deign to give him a glance out of one eye.
    Get away from me, dejected heart!
    You have no business drawing near to me.]

Rondeau 92

[In making a reference to the *margerite* in this poem, Froissart adds his trademark to the collection of *rondeaux*.]

    On escript bien tel lettre a le candelle,
    Qui plaist moult bien quant on le list au jour.
    Amours, je sui en le cause parelle;
    --On escript bien tel lettre a le candelle--
    J'ai en mon coer escript la non parelle
    Qui nommee est la margerite flour.
    On escript bien tel lettre a le candelle
    Qui plaist moult bien quant on le list au jour.

    [By candlelight one writes the kind of letter,
    That is pleasing indeed when it is read by day.
    Love, I am in a similar situation;
    --By candlelight one writes the kind of letter--
    I've written in my heart the one who is matchless,
    The one whose name is "margerite" flower.
    By candlelight one writes the kind of letter
    That is pleasing indeed when it is read by day.]

Rondeau 96

[This *rondeau*, probably written near the end of Froissart's lyric career, takes a retrospective stance and expresses a desire to abandon the pursuit of *fin' amors*. This attitude is consistent with the tone of Virelay 13, as well as with the shift away from love at the end of the *Joli Buisson de jonece*.]

J'ai bien veü le temps que je soloie
Estre amoureus, mes plus ne le serai;
A perdu tieng ce que mis y avoie.
--J'ai bien veü le temps que je soloie--
Mais mieulz me vault rescourre un peu de joie
Que tout parperdre, et pour ce je dirai:
J'ai bien veü le temps que je soloie
Estre amoureus, mes plus ne le serai.

> [*I've certainly seen the time when it was my habit*
> *To be in love, but I will not be again;*
> I consider whatever I put into it lost,
> *--I've certainly seen the time when it was my habit--*
> But it's better for me to save a little joy
> Than to lose it all completely, and so I'll say:
> *I've certainly seen the time when it was my habit*
> *To be in love, but I will not be again.*]

Rondeau 97

[This *rondeau* addresses the conflicting traditions of the nightingale as bird of joy and the nightingale as harbinger of violence, playing on the double meaning of the word "occi," which is both a representation of the cry of the nightingale and the imperative of the Old French verb *occir*, "to kill." For a detailed discussion of these and other interpretations of the nightingale in medieval literature, see Joseph L. Baird, "Introductory Essay on the Nightingale Tradition" in *Rossignol: An Edition and Translation*, ed. Joseph L. Baird and John R. Kane (Kent OH: Kent State UP, 1978), pp.1-58.]

Pour quoi tient on le chant a grascieus
D'un oisellon qu'on claimme rosegnol?

Pour ce qu'il est jolis et amoureus,
--*Pour quoi tient on le chant a grascieus?*--
Et dist: "Oci! Oci! joieus! joieus!
Fui de chi, fui!" Tout m'est bon, dur et mol.
Pour quoi tient on le chant a grascieus
D'un oisellon qu'on claimme rosegnol?

> [*Why do people find the song of the bird*
> *Called nightingale to be so full of grace?*
> Because it is happy and it is amorous,
> --*Why do people think it is full of grace?*--
> And it says: "Oci! Oci! Joyful! Joyful!
> Away, away!" Harsh words and gentle seem equally
>   good to me.
> *Why do people find the song of the bird*
> *Called nightingale to be so full of grace?]*

Rondeau 99

[This poem is composed almost entirely of proverbial-sounding statements. Line one corresponds to Hassell 724 ("Il faut prendre le temps comme il vient") or Morawski 1463 ("Len doit prendre le temps comme Dieu l'envoye"), while, as Baudouin has indicated, line 3 is similar to "Ne veit jour més que ne reviegne" (Morawski 1390). The words "toutdis" in line 2 and "tous les mois" in line 6 reinforce the emphasis on common wisdom.]

On doit le temps ensi prendre qu'il vient;
Toutdis ne poet durer une fortune,
Un temps se piert et puis l'autre revient.
On doit le temps ensi prendre qu'il vient.
Je me conforte a che qu'il me souvient
Que tous les mois avons nouvelle lune.
On doit le temps ensi prendre qu'il vient;
Toutdis ne poet durer une fortune.

> [*One must accept each season as it comes;*
> *A single fortune can't endure forever,*

One season is lost and then the other returns.
One must accept each season as it comes.
I take comfort in the fact that I remember
That every month we have a new moon.
One must accept each season as it comes;
A single fortune can't endure forever.]

Rondeau 107

[In this *rondeau*, the tight rhyme pattern, strict adherence to conventional imagery, and demanding word play are reminiscent of the style of the *ballade équivoquée*.]

Vous me tenés, ma dame, en vo prison,
Vostre vair oel m'i ont emprisonné.
Las, en quel lieu tele prise prise on,
Vous me tenés, ma dame, en vo prison.
Faire n'en puis ne sçai comparison,
Mais tout bien sont pour moi en prison né.
Vous me tenés, ma dame, en vo prison,
Vostre vair oel m'i ont emprisonneé.

> *[You hold me captive, my lady, in your prison,*
> *Your gray eyes have made me a prisoner there.*
> Alas, what is the value of such captivity?
> *You hold me captive, my lady, in your prison.*
> I cannot make nor do I know of any comparison,
> But all good things for me begin right there.
> *You hold me captive, my lady, in your prison,*
> *Your gray eyes have made me a prisoner there.]*

Appendix B:
Dates, Locales, and Subjects of Pastourelles

Poem[1]	Date	Locale	Subject
1	----	Near Valenciennes	"houppelande"
2	1364	Near London	arrival of Jean le Bon in England
3 *MS. B*	1364	Near Paris	new coin
4	----	In Hainaut	shepherd'sdecision to marry
5 *MS. B*	----	In Hainaut	mixing of wines
6	1372	In Hainaut	freeing of Duke Wenceslas
7	----	In Hainaut	rustic festivity
8	1388[2]	In the Pyrenees	gift of four dogs to Gaston de Foix
9	1388	In the Pyrenees	coats of arms, Gaston de Foix
10	----	(unspecified)	rustic beauty contest

Poem	Date	Locale	Subject
11	----	Near Paris	visit to fountain of love
12 *MS. B*	1382	Flanders	Charles VI's march against the Flemish
13	1382(?)	Near Blois	shepherd boy's lesson on Golden Fleece[3]
14 *MS. B*	1386	Bourges	marriage of son of Guy de Blois and daughter of Jean de Berry
15 *MS. B*	1389	Auvergne	marriage of Duke of Berry to Jeanne de Boulogne
16 *MS. B*	1389	Near Paris	Entry into Paris by Isabella of Bavaria
17	----	(unspecified)	the *margherite*
18 *MS. A*	----	(unspecified)	birthday of John the Baptist
19	----	(unspecified)	shepherd girl chooses who will get garland
20	----	Northern France	rustic beauty contest

Notes: Appendix B

1. All poems are in both manuscripts unless otherwise indicated. Numbering follows McGregor's edition.

2. Froissart's two *pastourelles* which are set in the South of France (8 and 9) are clearly intended to honor Gaston de Foix, whom Froissart visited in 1388. Hoepffner speculates that they may appear out of chronological order in the manuscripts in order to avoid separation of the two wedding poems (1386 and 1389), but he can offer no explanation for their actual placement so much before their correct chronological position.

3. The poem on the Golden Fleece and the poem on the birthday of John the Baptist are among the most unusual of Froissart's *pastourelles*. In 13 a shepherd boy convinces his aging parents that his schooling is worthwhile when he repeats the story of Jason (see Appendix A for text and translation); in 18 a group of very knowledgeable shepherds retell the story of John the Baptist and discuss the various observances connected with his birthday. Both poems have sections in which the meaning is obscure; 18 appears only in manuscript A.

Bibliography

Arnaud, Leonard E. "The *Sottes Chansons* in *Ms. Douce 308* of the Bodleian Library at Oxford." *Speculum* 19 (1944): 68-88.

Baird, Joseph L. "Introductory Essay on the Nightingale Tradition." In *Rossignol: An Edition and Translation*, ed. Joseph L. Baird and John R. Kane, 1-58. Kent: Kent State University Press, 1978.

Barber, Richard. "Jean Froissart and Edward the Black Prince." In *Froissart: Historian*, ed. J.J.N. Palmer, 25-35. Suffolk: Boydell, 1981.

Bastin, Julia. *Froissart: Chroniqueur, romancier et poète.* 2nd ed. Brussels: Office de Publicité, 1948.

Baudouin, Rae S., ed. *Ballades et Rondeaux.* See Froissart, Jean.

Baum, Paull F. *Chaucer's Verse.* Durham: Duke University Press, 1961.

Bennett, Philip E. "The Mirage of Fiction: Narration, Narrator, and Narratee in Froissart's Lyrico-Narrative *Dits.*" *Modern Language Review* 86 (1991): 285-97.

Bossuat, Robert. *Le Moyen Age.* Paris: Gigord, 1931.

Bradley-Cromey, Nancy. "Mythological Typology in Froissart's *Espinette amoureuse.*" *Res Publica Litterarum* 3 (1980): 207-21.

Brewer, Derek S. "The Ideal of Feminine Beauty in Medieval Literature, Especially 'Harley Lyrics,' Chaucer, and Some Elizabethans." *Modern Language Review* 50 (1955): 257-69.

Brownlee, Kevin. *Poetic Identity in Guillaume de Machaut.* Madison: University of Wisconsin Press, 1984.

Burke, Mary Ann. "A Medieval Experiment in Adaptation: Typology and Courtly Love. Poetry in the Second Rhetoric." *Res Publica Litterarum* 3 (1980): 165-75.

Burnley, J.D. *Chaucer's Language and the Philosophers' Tradition.* Cambridge: Brewer, 1979.

Calin, William. *A Poet at the Fountain: Essays on the Narrative Verse Of Guillaume de Machaut.* Lexington: University Press of Kentucky, 1974.

Cartier, Normand R. "Froissart, Chaucer, and Enclimpostair." *Revue de Littérature Comparée* 38 (1964): 18-34.

Cerquiglini, Jacqueline. *"Un Engin Si Soutil": Guillaume de Machaut et l'écriture au XIVe siècle.* Geneva: Slatkine, 1985.

Chaucer, Geoffrey. *The Riverside Chaucer.* Ed. Larry D. Benson. Boston: Houghton Mifflin, 1987.

Clemen, Wolfgang. *Chaucer's Early Poetry.* Trans. C.A.M. Sym. London: Methuen, 1963.

Cohen, Gustave. *Anthologie de la littérature française du moyen-âge.* Paris: Delagrave, 1946.

Cotgrave, Randle. *A Dictionarie of the French and English Tongues.* London, 1611; rpt. Columbia: University of South Carolina Press, 1950.

Darmesteter, Mary. *Froissart.* Paris: Hachette, 1894.

Davidson, F.J.A. "Froissart's Pastourelles." *Modern Language Notes,* 8 (1898): 229-31.

Dembowski, Peter F. "Chivalry, Ideal and Real, in the Narrative Poetry of Jean Froissart." *Medievalia et Humanistica* ns. 14 (1986): 1-15.

------. *Froissart and His Meliador: Context, Craft, and Sense.* Lexington: French Forum, 1983.

------. "Metrics and Textual Criticism." *L'Esprit Créateur* 27 (1987): 90-100.

------. *"Li Orloge amoureus* de Froissart." *L'Esprit Créateur* 18 (1978): 19-31.

------. Ed. *Le Paradis d'amour; Li Orloge amoureus.* See Froissart, Jean.

------. "La Position de Froissart-poète dans l'histoire littéraire: bilan provisoire." *Travaux de linguistique et de littérature* 16 (1979): 131-47.

------. "Tradition, Dream Literature, and Poetic Craft in *Le Paradis d'Amour* of Jean Froissart." *Studies in the Literary Imagination* 20 (1987): 99-109.

Diller, George T. *Attitudes Chevaleresques et Réalités Politiques Chez Froissart.* Geneva: Droz, 1984.

Dronke, Peter. *The Medieval Lyric.* London: Hutchinson University Library, 1968.

Faral, Edmond. *Les Arts poétiques du XIIe et du XIIIe siècle.* Paris: Champion, 1924.

------. "La Pastourelle." *Romania* 49 (1923): 204-259.

Figg, Kristen M. "Jean Froissart's *Lay de la Mort la Royne d'Engleterre.*" *Allegorica* 14 (1993): 61-76.

Fisher, John. "Chaucer and the French Influence." In *New Perspectives in Chaucer Criticism*, ed. Donald M. Rose, 177-91. Norman: Pilgrim Books, 1981.

------. *John Gower.* London: Methuen, 1965.

Freeman, Michelle A. "Froissart's *Le Joli Buisson de Jeunesse*: A Farewell to Poetry?" In *Machaut's World: Science and Art in the Fourteenth Century*, ed. Madeleine P. Cosman and Bruce Chandler, 235-47. Annals of the New York Academy of Sciences 314. New York: New York Academy of Sciences, 1978.

Froissart, Jean. *Ballades et rondeaux.* Ed. Rae S. Baudouin. Geneva: Droz, 1978.

------. *Chronicles of England, France, Spain, and Adjoining Countries.* Trans. Thomas Johnes. 2 vols. London: Henry C. Bohn, 1852.

------. *Chroniques.* Ed. S. Luce, et al. Société de l'Histoire de France. 15 vols. Paris: Librairie Renouard, 1869- (in progress).

------. *Dits et Debats.* Ed. Anthime Fourrier. Geneva: Droz, 1979.

------. *L'Espinette amoureuse.* 2nd ed. Ed. Anthime Fourrier. Paris: Klincksieck, 1972.

------. *Le Joli Buisson de Jonece.* Ed. Anthime Fourrier. Geneva: Droz, 1975.

------. *The Lyric Poems of Jehan Froissart: A Critical Edition.* Ed. Rob Roy McGregor, Jr. North Carolina Studies in the Romance Languages and Literatures, 143. Chapel Hill: University of North Carolina Press, 1975.

------. *Œuvres de Froissart.* Ed. Kervyn de Lettenhove. Brussels: Devaux, 1867-77.

------. *Le Paradis d'amour; L'Orloge amoureus.* Ed. Peter Dembowski. Geneva: Droz, 1986.

------. *La Prison amoureuse.* Ed. Anthime Fourrier. Paris: Klincksieck, 1974.

Graham, Audrey. "Froissart's Use of Classical Allusion in His Poems." *Medium Ævum*, 32 (1963): 24-33.

Gray, Douglas. *Themes and Images in the Medieval English Religious Lyric.* London: Routledge & Kegan Paul, 1972.

Hassell, James Woodrow, Jr. *Middle French Proverbs, Sentences, and Proverbial Phrases.* Toronto: Pontifical Institute of Mediaeval Studies, 1982.

Hoepffner, Ernest. "La Chronologie des *Pastourelles* de Froissart." *Mélanges offerts à M. Emile Picot.* 2 vols. Paris, 1913: 27-42.

Huot, Sylvia. "The Daisy and the Laurel: Myths of Desire and Creativity in the Poetry of Jean Froissart." *Yale French Studies* (1991): 240-51.

------. *From Song to Book: The Poetics of Writing in Old French Lyric and Lyrical Narrative Poetry.* Ithaca: Cornell University Press, 1987.

Jackson, W.T.H., ed. *The Interpretation of Medieval Lyric Poetry.* New York: Columbia University Press, 1980.

Johnston, O.M. "Froissart's *Le Dittié de la Flour de la Margherite.*" *Modern Language Notes* 33 (1918): 122.

Jones, William Powell. *The Pastourelle: A Study of the Origins and Traditions of a Lyric Type.* Cambridge: Harvard University Press, 1931.

Kelly, Douglas. "The Genius of the Patron: The Prince, the Poet, and Fourteenth-Century Invention." *Studies in the Literary Imagination* 20 (1987): 77-97.

------. "Les Inventions ovidiennes de Froissart." *Littérature* 41 (1981): 82-92.

------. *Medieval Imagination: Rhetoric and the Poetry of Courtly Love.* Madison: University of Wisconsin Press, 1978.

Kervyn de Lettenhove, J.M.B.C. *Froissart: Etude littéraire sur le XIVme siècle.* 2 vols. Paris: Durand, 1857.

Kibler, William W. "Poet and Patron: Froissart's *Prison amoureuse.*" *L'Esprit Créateur* 18 (1978): 32-46.

------. "Self-Delusion in Froissart's *Espinette amoureuse.*" *Romania* 97 (1976): 77-98.

Kittredge, George L. "Chaucer and Froissart." *Englische Studien* 26 (1899): 321-36.

La Curne de Ste. Palaye, Jean-Baptiste de. *Memoirs of the Life of Froissart*. Trans. Thomas Johnes. London: Nichols and Sons, 1801.

Leleu, Maurice Alexis. "Les Poésies de Froissart." *Mémoires de l'Académie des Sciences, de Lettres et des Arts d'Amiens* 36 (1889): 31-131.

Leyerle, John. "The Rose-Wheel Design and Dante's *Paradiso.*" *University of Toronto Quarterly* 46 (1977): 280-308.

Maillard, Jean. *Evolution et esthétique du lai lyrique des origines à la fin du XIVème siècle*. Paris: Université de Paris, 1961.

McGregor, Rob Roy, ed. *The Lyric Poems of Jehan Froissart: A Critical Edition*. See Froissart, Jean.

Madeiros, M.T. de. "Le Pacte encomiastique: Froissart, ses *Chroniques* et ses Mécènes." *Le Moyen Age: Revue Historique* 94 (1988): 237-55.

Moore, Arthur K. "Chaucer's Use of Lyric as an Ornament of Style." *Comparative Literature* 3 (1951): 32-46.

Morawski, J., ed. *Proverbes français antérieures au XVe siècle*. Paris: Champion, 1925.

Morris, Rosemary. "Machaut, Froissart, and the Fictionalization of the Self." *The Modern Language Review* 83 (1988): 545-55.

Mullaly, Robert. "Dance Terminology in the Works of Machaut and Froissart." *Medium Ævum* 59 (1990): 248-59.

Musa, Mark, trans. *Dante's Vita Nuova*. Bloomington: Indiana University Press, 1973.

Nolan, Barbara. "The Art of Expropriation: Chaucer's Narrator in *The Book of the Duchess.*" In *New Perspectives in Chaucer Criticism*, ed. Donald M. Rose, 203-222. Norman: Pilgrim, 1981.

Nouvet, Claire. "Pour une économie de la délimitation: La *Prison amoureuse* de Jean Froissart." *Neophilologus* 70 (1986): 341-56.

Paden, William D., ed. *The Medieval Pastourelle*. 2 vols. New York: Garland, 1987.

Palmer, J.J.N., ed. *Froissart: Historian*. Suffolk: Boydell, 1981.

Picherit, Jean-Louis. "Le Rôle des éléments mythologique dans le *Joli Buisson de jonece* de Jean Froissart." *Neophilologus* 63 (1979): 498-508.

Planche, Alice. "Du *Joli Buisson de Jonece* au *Buisson ardent*: Le Lai de Notre-Dame dans le *Dit* de Froissart." In *La Prière au moyen-*

âge: Littérature et civilisation, Sénéfiance 10: 395-413. Aix-en-Provence: Université de Provence, 1981.

Poirion, Daniel. *Le Poète et le prince: L'Evolution du lyrisme courtois de Guillaume de Machaut à Charles d'Orléans.* 1965; rpt. Geneva: Slatkine Reprints, 1978.

Ribemont, Bernard. "Froissart, le mythe, et la marguerite." *Revue de Langues Romanes* 94 (1990): 129-137.

Robbins, Rossell Hope. "*Geoffroi Chaucier, poète français,* Father of English Poetry." *Chaucer Review* 13 (1978): 93-115.

Sage, Elizabeth. *A Study of Costume.* New York: Scribners, 1926.

Salter, Elizabeth. *Fourteenth-Century English Poetry: Contexts and Readings.* Oxford: Clarendon Press, 1983.

Scheler, Auguste. *Œuvres de Froissart. Poésies.* 3 vols. Brussels: Devaux, 1870-72.

Shears, F.S. *Froissart: Chronicler and Poet.* London: George Rutledge & Sons, 1930.

Smith, Roland M. "Five Notes on Chaucer and Froissart." *Modern Language Notes* 46 (1951): 27-32.

Taylor, Jane H.M. "The Lyric Insertion: Towards a Functional Model." In *Courtly Literature: Culture and Context,* ed. Keith Busby and Erik Kooper. Amsterdam: Benjamins, 1990.

Thiry, Claude. "Allégorie et histoire dans la *Prison amoureuse* de Froissart." *Studi Francesi* 61-62 (1977): 15-29.

Whiting, B.J. "Froissart as Poet." *Mediaeval Studies* 8 (1946): 189-216.

------. "Proverbs in the Writings of Jean Froissart." *Speculum* 10 (1935): 291-321.

Wilkins, Nigel. "A Pattern of Patronage: Machaut, Froissart and the Houses of Luxembourg and Bohemia in the Fourteenth Century." *French Studies* 37 (1983): 257-81.

------. "The Structure of Ballades, Rondeaux and Virelais in Froissart and in Christine de Pisan." *French Studies* 23 (1969): 337-98.

Wilmotte, Maurice. *Froissart.* Brussels: Renaissance du Livre, 1944.

Wimsatt, James I. *Chaucer and the French Love Poets: The Literary Background of the Book of the Duchess.* Chapel Hill: University of North Carolina Press, 1968.

------. "Chaucer and French Poetry." In *Writers and Their Background: Geoffrey Chaucer,* ed. Derek Brewer, 109-136. Athens: Ohio University Press, 1975.

------. "The *Dit dou Bleu Chevalier*: Froissart's Imitation of Chaucer."
Mediaeval Studies 34 (1972): 388-400.

------. *The Marguerite Poetry of Guillaume de Machaut*. Studies in the
Romance Languages and Literatures, 87. Chapel Hill: University
of North Carolina Press, 1970.

Ziolkowski, Jan. "Avatars of Ugliness in Medieval Literature." *Modern
Language Review* 79 (1984): 1-20.

Index of Poems

[Poems are listed by *incipit* in order of appearance in the manuscripts, except for *pastourelles*, which are listed by refrain.]

I. Lays

II. Chansons Royales

III. Pastourelles

IV. Ballades

V. Virelays

VI. Rondeaux